THINKING WITH HEIDE

Studies in Continental Thought

John Sallis, GENERAL EDITOR

Thinking with Heidegger

Displacements

Miguel de Beistegui

INDIANA University Press

Bloomington & Indianapolis

Publication of this book is made possible in part with the assistance of
a Challenge Grant from the National Endowment for the Humanities,
a federal agency that supports research, education, and
public programming in the humanities.

This book is a publication of

Indiana University Press
601 North Morton Street
Bloomington, IN 47404-3797 USA

http://iupress.indiana.edu

Telephone orders   800-842-6796
Fax orders   812-855-7931
Orders by e-mail   iuporder@indiana.edu

© 2003 by Miguel de Beistegui

The paper used in this publication meets the minimum requirements of American
National Standard for Information Sciences—Permanence of Paper for Printed
Library Materials, ANSI Z39.48-1984.

Manufactured in the United States of America

Library of Congress Cataloging-in-Publication Data

Beistegui, Miguel de, date
Thinking with Heidegger : displacements / Miguel de Beistegui.
p. cm. — (Studies in Continental thought)
Includes bibliographical references and index.
ISBN 0-253-34230-9 (alk. paper) — ISBN 0-253-21596-X (pbk. :
alk. paper)
1. Heidegger, Martin, 1889–1976. I. Title. II. Series.
B3279.H49 B435 2003
193—dc21

2002014990

1 2 3 4 5 08 07 06 05 04 03

Contents

Preface

This is a book that is clearly thematic. It is concerned with exploring not so much a single aspect of Martin Heidegger's thought, or his relation to central figures in the history of philosophy, as a number of themes or topics central to the philosophical tradition, all of which serve in their own right as points of entry into the essence of that thought, all of them resonating from within the same origin. Yet there would seem to be something out of place, if not altogether provocative, in a volume dedicated to various aspects of Heidegger's thought set out along the very lines of areas and categories that this thought precisely tries to avoid. For, in thinking the nature of humanity, of its *ethos* and its *polis*, of science, of art, poetry, and architecture, does Heidegger not want to overcome the very categories and disciplines in which these areas are traditionally thought, namely, "anthropology," "history" and "politics," "science," and "aesthetics," in an attempt, to use his own words, to think more "originarily"? Does Heidegger not place thought under the demand that it overcome metaphysics, to which all the previously mentioned areas remain indebted? And so, in reinscribing these categories as headings under which to think Heidegger's contribution to the history of philosophy, do we not simply run the risk of erasing from the start the very task he ascribes to thought, in its essential difference from metaphysics? Do we not in effect annul the operation whereby he tries to wrest such categories from the grip of metaphysical thought? This is a risk, and indeed a danger, of which this book is very much aware. Here, however, it is precisely a question of insisting and dwelling on that very operation, of witnessing, up close as it were, the very way in which these traditional themes, so central to philosophy, are revisited, at once reinscribed and displaced—in short, thought afresh, in the light of the one and only question Heidegger will have ever claimed to have thought, and thought *from*, to wit, the question concerning the meaning or the truth of being. It is precisely with a view to investigating the radical nature of Heidegger's move in thought that I insist on anchoring it, as a point of departure and for essentially strategic reasons, in the very vocabulary and metaphysical constructions it finds itself negotiating with. For it is not as if those very sites, or problems, which the classical categories of anthropology, aesthetics, history and politics, etc., had served to define up until now, were simply abandoned, in order to direct thought towards a new, hitherto ignored or neglected object. Rather, in turning to that "object," it is also and simultaneously a question of re-turning to the very sites or problems traditionally thematized under the classical categories and areas of metaphysics: to the problem concerning the meaning of being human, of art and architecture, of ethics and politics, of science and philosophy itself.

This is the point at which the title of this book needs to be clarified. *Thinking with Heidegger*: if anything like this is going to take place, if one can ever claim to be thinking *with* Heidegger, then the nature of thought, in its very attempt and ambition to raise questions and articulate problems in a way that is simply otherwise than metaphysical, in its ambition to turn to some of the most traditional *topoi* of philosophical thought by returning them to their forgotten yet still decisive ground, must itself be in question, and become an explicit question. And so, naturally as it were, this book begins by raising the question of the origin or the provenance of thought, the place from which it receives its own direction, which we cannot assume to be there from the start, readily available. How, under what circumstances, is thought set underway? And what exactly provokes such a movement? It is only in the light of this initial question, briefly dealt with in the Introduction, that we shall be in a position to turn to the more specific questions and sites this book is concerned to analyze. Needless to say, this opening question will remain operative throughout the entire book and the various itineraries sketched out therein. Thinking with Heidegger means, first and foremost, allowing oneself to be drawn into the general movement of thought as envisaged by him, and to question and analyze from within that space. It will mean, at times, to extend some of Heidegger's analyses in directions not provided by his own text, to question beyond Heidegger. But if the determination of thought operative throughout this book, the meaning of thought, is provided by Heidegger himself, if there is a genuine attempt to follow Heidegger in his own journey, and sometimes even to extend and broaden it in the light of developments or areas with which he was not familiar, or could not have anticipated, there is also a no less genuine attempt to take him to task wherever and whenever it is felt that his own analyses preclude certain questions and considerations. Most significant, in that respect, is his relation to science, and to the natural sciences in particular, which so radically differs from his relation to art, and to poetry in particular. In the chapter entitled "Science, 'Servant of Philosophy'?" I shall be asking whether, in order to develop a freer and more productive relation to science, a more nuanced and less traumatic account of science and of its relation to nature need not be articulated. Similarly, in the chapter entitled "Art, 'Sister of Philosophy'?" I shall need to ask whether philosophy's "special relationship" with art need not be addressed anew, and whether the centrality of language for art need not be called into question. Still by way of example, our exploration of Heidegger's relation to architecture (Chapter 6), while finding its initial impetus in his thought, will raise the question of how compatible it is with the current age of tele-techno-communications and globalized economy, and, in addition, will wonder whether the Heideggerian account does not remain blind to a central dimension of architecture, whether ancient or contemporary.

As for the subtitle, *Displacements,* it is there to qualify further the operation characteristic of Heidegger's thought when turning to those classical domains addressed in the course of this book. This is an operation I exposed in a fair amount of detail in relation to politics in my *Heidegger and the Political: Dystopias.* The Afterword to this current book, to which the reader may want to turn right away, develops further and justifies again the use of this somewhat inhabitual term as designating a singularly Heideggerian gesture, in which the movement of essence or truth itself is implicated. In the Afterword this operation is revealed most closely in connection with the question of translation, but in such a way as to illuminate retrospectively all the previous chapters and highlight the singular nature of that question for the very meaning of what it means to think from a Heideggerian perspective.

Acknowledgments

Two of the chapters in this volume have already appeared elsewhere. "The Politics of Repetition" was originally published under the title "The Time of Repetition" in D. Pellauer (ed.), *Philosophy Today* 43, no. 3 (fall 1999). "Boredom: Between Existence and History" was originally published in W. Mays (ed.), *The Journal of the British Society for Phenomenology* 32, no. 2 (May 2000). I am grateful to the editors of these journals for permission to reprint work which first saw the light of day under their auspices.

A first version of "Art, 'Sister of Philosophy'?" was written as a lecture delivered at the *Collegium Phaenomenologicum*, Perugia, in the summer of 1997. Many thanks to the director, James Risser, for his kind invitation.

Special thanks to Simon Sparks, who made many helpful suggestions during the revision of the manuscript and whose editorial skills I have benefited from once again.

List of Abbreviations

Works are cited in the original German pagination and followed by pagination in translation, where there is one. Translations often have been modified.

A   *Aufenthalte*. Frankfurt am Main: Vittorio Klostermann, 1989.

BDT   "Building Dwelling Thinking." Translated by Albert Hofstadter. In *Poetry, Language, Thought*. New York: Harper & Row, 1971.

Briefe   Hannah Arendt/Martin Heidegger: *Briefe (1925–1975)*. Edited by Ursula Ludz. Frankfurt am Main: Vittorio Klostermann, 1998.

DF   *Die Frage nach dem Ding*. Tübingen: Max Niemeyer Verlag, 1962.

EHD   *Erlaüterungen zu Hölderlins Dichtung*. Frankfurt am Main: Vittorio Klostermann, 1971.

GA 3   *Kant und das Problem der Metaphysik*. Gesamtausgabe Band 3. Frankfurt am Main: Vittorio Klostermann, 1991. Translated by Richard Taft as *Kant and the Problem of Metaphysics*. Bloomington: Indiana University Press, 1990.

GA 6.2   *Nietzsche II*. Gesamtausgabe Band 6.2. Frankfurt am Main: Vittorio Klostermann, 1997. Edited and translated by David Farrell Krell as *Nietzsche. Volume IV: Nihilism*. San Francisco: Harper & Row, 1979–87.

GA 19   *Platon: Sophistes*. Gesamtausgabe Band 19. Frankfurt am Main: Vittorio Klostermann, 1992. Translated by Richard Rojcewicz and André Schuwer as *Plato's Sophist*. Bloomington: Indiana University Press, 1997.

GA 20   *Prolegomena zur Geschichte des Zeitbegriffs*. Gesamtausgabe Band 20. Frankfurt am Main: Vittorio Klostermann, 1979. Translated by Theodore Kisiel as *History of the Concept of Time*. Bloomington: Indiana University Press, 1985.

Abbreviations

GA 24   *Die Grundprobleme der Phänomenologie.* Gesamtausgabe Band 24. Frankfurt am Main: Vittorio Klostermann, 1975. Translated by Albert Hofstadter as *The Basic Problems of Phenomenology.* Bloomington: Indiana University Press, 1982.

GA 26   *Metaphysische Anfangsgründe der Logik im Ausgang von Leibniz.* Gesamtausgabe Band 26. Frankfurt am Main: Vittorio Klostermann, 1978. Translated by Michael Heim as *The Metaphysical Foundations of Logic.* Bloomington: Indiana University Press, 1984.

GA 29/30 *Die Grundbegriffe der Metaphysik. Welt—Endlichkeit—Einsamkeit.* Gesamtausgabe Band 29/30. Frankfurt am Main: Vittorio Klostermann, 1983. Translated by William McNeill and Nicholas Walker as *The Fundamental Concepts of Metaphysics: World, Finitude, Solitude.* Bloomington: Indiana University Press, 1995.

GA 32   *Hegel's Phänomenologie des Geistes.* Gesamtausgabe Band 32. Frankfurt am Main: Vittorio Klostermann, 1980. Translated by Parvis Emad and Kenneth Maly as *Hegel's Phenomenology of Spirit.* Bloomington: Indiana University Press, 1988.

GA 45   *Grundfragen der Philosophie: Ausgewählte "Probleme" der Logik.* Gesamtausgabe Band 45. Frankfurt am Main: Vittorio Klostermann, 1984. Translated by Richard Rojcewicz and André Schuwer as *Basic Questions of Philosophy: Selected "Problems" of Logic.* Bloomington: Indiana University Press, 1994.

GA 53   *Hölderlin's Hymne "Der Ister."* Gesamtausgabe Band 53. Frankfurt am Main: Vittorio Klostermann, 1984. Translated by William McNeill and Julia Davis as *Hölderlin's Hymn "The Ister."* Bloomington: Indiana University Press, 1996.

GA 54   *Parmenides.* Gesamtausgabe Band 54. Frankfurt am Main: Vittorio Klostermann, 1982. Translated by André Schuwer and Richard Rojcewicz as *Parmenides.* Bloomington: Indiana University Press, 1992.

GA 55   *Heraklit. Der Anfang des abendländischen Denkens Logik. Heraklits Lehre vom Logos.* Gesamtausgabe Band 55. Frankfurt am Main: Vittorio Klostermann, 1979.

GA 56/57 *Zur Bestimmung der Philosophie.* Gesamtausgabe Band 56/57. Frankfurt am Main: Vittorio Klostermann, 1987. Translated by Ted Sadler as *Towards the Definition of Philosophy.* London: Athlone, 2000.

GA 65   *Beiträge zur Philosophie (Vom Ereignis).* Gesamtausgabe Band 65. Frankfurt am Main: Vittorio Klostermann, 1989. Translated by Parvis Emad and Kenneth Maly as *Contributions to Philosophy (From Enowning).* Bloomington: Indiana University Press, 1999.

Hw   *Holzwege.* Frankfurt am Main: Vittorio Klostermann, 1950/1980.

KR   *Kunst und Raum.* St. Gallen: Erker-Verlag, 1969.

OA   *De l'origine de l'œuvre d'art. Première version (1935).* Edited and translated by Emmanuel Martineau. Paris: Authentica, 1987.

Abbreviations

OWA   "The Origin of the Work of Art." Translated by Albert Hofstadter. In *Poetry, Language, Thought*. New York: Harper & Row, 1971.

SU   *Die Selbstbehauptung der deutschen Universität*. Frankfurt am Main: Vittorio Klostermann, 1983. Translated by Lisa Harries as "The Self-assertion of the German University." In *Martin Heidegger and National Socialism*, edited by Karsten Harries. New York: Paragon House, 1990.

SZ   *Sein und Zeit*. Tübingen: Max Niemeyer, 1927. Translated by John Macquarrie and Edward Robinson as *Being and Time*. New York: Harper & Row, 1962.

T   "The Thing." Translated by Albert Hofstadter. In *Poetry, Language, Thought*. New York: Harper & Row, 1971.

UK   "Vom Ursprung des Kunstwerkes. Erste Ausarbeitung." *Heidegger Studies* 5 (1989): 5–22.

US   *Unterwegs zur Sprache*. Pfullingen: Günther Neske Verlag, 1959. Translated by Peter D. Hertz as *On the Way to Language*. New York: Harper and Row, 1971.

VA   *Vorträge und Aufsätze*. Pfullingen: Günther Neske, 1954.

WhD   *Was heißt Denken?* Tübingen: Max Niemeyer Verlag, 1954. Translated by Fred D. Wieck and J. Glenn Gray as *What Is Called Thinking?* New York: Harper & Row, 1968.

Wm   *Wegmarken*. Frankfurt am Main: Vittorio Klostermann, 1967/1976. Translated by William McNeill et al. as *Pathmarks*, edited by William McNeill. Cambridge: Cambridge University Press, 1998.

THINKING WITH HEIDEGGER

Introduction

The Provenance of Thought

Philosophy has always been concerned with the question of its origin, its provenance. And while this question has often turned into an historical quest—where, and at what time, was philosophy actually born? Was it actually a Greek phenomenon, or was philosophy also born in India, in China?—it has also always exceeded such a quest. Far more intriguing and mysterious, perhaps, is the question regarding the transhistorical nature of thought, the fact that thought takes place, or, one could say, the event of thought. Whence thinking? Such is the question philosophy has always felt compelled to ask. For it seems that, at times, if not always, even when thought claims to be its very own foundation, as it once did, in a gesture constitutive of its own modernity, absolutely self-positing and self-grounding, it takes place as a response or a reaction—a response to something like a call, a reaction to something like a rapture. Thought, it seems, is always born of a shock, always set underway by something that blows from the outside, from elsewhere, the force of which captivates and enraptures. It is this force, this draught that we *feel* in reading great philosophical texts, and it is to this very force that those texts themselves respond. If reading those texts is like breathing fresh, new air, it is because they themselves have been carried away at high sea, leaving behind them, as Leibniz once noted, the safe shore of common knowledge and familiar markers. It is because they themselves have experienced something colossal. But what is this something that provokes or forces us to think? Whence does thought reach us? How exactly is it set underway?

In what can be described as the last stage of his life, at a time when philosophers ask themselves, "What exactly is this activity I have been

1

engaged in all my life? What was this force driving me all this time? Where did it all come from?" — in a text retrospectively illuminating his entire path of thought, Heidegger provides a remarkable and intriguing answer to the question regarding the origin of thought. At first, this answer may look like an evasive reply, as if, in the end, the question remained unanswerable, too mysterious to be addressed adequately. In what is in effect an introduction to two lecture courses, delivered in the winter semester of 1951–52 and the summer semester of 1952, and published together in 1954 under the title *Was heißt Denken?* Heidegger writes the following: "What most calls for thinking [*das Bedenklichste*], in our time that calls for thinking [*in unsere bedenklichen Zeit*], is that we are not yet thinking."[1] In other words, what is most worthy of being thought, what above all else gives food for thought, in a time such as ours, which calls for thinking, is that we are not yet thinking. How are we to understand such a claim? And to what extent does it address the question regarding the provenance of thought, that *whence* we think? How could the fact that we are not yet thinking be the very thing that sets thought underway, that provokes it? How could what seems to be the very lack or absence of thought, the fact that it is not taking place today, be precisely the very possibility, still more, the very necessity of thought itself? And in describing our time, and what in this time most calls for thinking, as the time in which we are not yet thinking, is Heidegger singling out "our" time — whatever this time may be, and however it may be defined — as the least philosophical time, as time spent in the wilderness? In short, is it a question of recognizing that philosophy has dried up, and of hoping for better days, or is it a question of something altogether different?

Let me begin, as a way into our initial question regarding the origin or the very event of thought itself, with what is perhaps the least complex of the questions I have just raised. Let me begin with the question regarding the current status of philosophical thought, and with what Heidegger may mean when referring to "our time" as a time that calls for thinking. First of all, we cannot stress enough the sense of urgency, the extreme demand that is displayed in the claim that our time calls for thinking, a demand which the lecture course as a whole tries to address. Our time, Heidegger emphasizes, demands to be thought; it calls for thinking and calls thinking forth. Yet how does Heidegger define this time, "our" time? As the time in which we are *not yet* thinking. "Not yet" is not the same as "not at all." Heidegger is not suggesting that we are simply cut off from thought, that thought is simply behind us, but that, somehow, it lies ahead of us, as a sort of future that is already orienting our present, already opening it up, albeit ever so imperceptibly. Now, this present, our present, it would seem, is defined purely negatively, as the time in which thought has not yet taken place, as the time that is waiting for thought to take place. What sort of claim is this? Is it a historical claim, such as the one we were referring to a few moments ago when asking about the current situation of philosophy, in comparison with other moments in the history of philosophy? This is an entirely legitimate question. For how can we not help noticing that philosophy does indeed take place, at various times and in various places, and often does so, it seems, rather mysteriously? Why in Athens, in 500–400 B.C., why in Germany in the late eighteenth and nineteenth centuries, why in France after World War II? There are elements of answers to these questions, and they are interesting ones to pursue. Yet they are not what is at issue here. The issue, in Heidegger's claim, does not concern the current situation of philosophy, as opposed to its past situation, its many phases and many developments throughout the Western world and its history. The issue does not concern the history of philosophy, and Heidegger's point is not that of a historian of philosophy and of ideas. At least not primarily. Yet the issue is historical in a more fundamental sense. It does go straight to the heart of what we need to understand by history, straight to the heart of the question regarding the origin of "our" history, the history of the Western world. "Our" time, then, as the time that demands to be thought and that calls for thinking, is not to be understood as the time that comes after, say, modernity, which itself came after the Middle Ages, a time characterized by the omnipresence of the Christian god in every aspect of human life and of nature. It is not to be understood as the present time, often referred to as postmodernity, which would itself come before this time intimated in Heidegger's sentence, a time that we could hope for, a better time, as it would mark the very advent and presence of thought itself. No, the time that is at issue here is not historical, chronological time. It is not the time of the history of philosophy. It is not even the time born of a philosophy of history, such as the one we find in Hegel or Marx, for example. It is not even the time of philosophy. By this, we need to understand that the time in question, the time that Heidegger has in mind when claiming that it calls for thinking, remains closed off to philosophy. It is precisely the time that philosophy cannot think, and this, precisely to the extent that "our" time is that of philosophy, the time that sees the unrestrained unfolding of the destiny of Western philosophical thought in what seems—but this is only an appearance, a historical illusion—to have no longer anything to do with philosophy, and to have left it behind: in contemporary science and technology, cybernetics and the social sciences.

But did we not begin by saying, did Heidegger himself not actually say, that our time, which indeed calls for thinking, does so precisely to the extent that it is not yet thinking? How can we reconcile the "not yet" of thinking with the consummation of metaphysical thought in the contemporary world? How can our time be seen as a time saturated with the effects of our metaphysical destiny, and as the time in which thought has not yet taken place? How, if not by drawing the sharpest and most decisive of distinctions between philosophy, or metaphysics, and thought? And, in fact, Heidegger is not asking about the general state of health of philosophy in the second half of the twentieth century. He is not asking whether philosophy is more alive today than it was yesterday. Such questions are for him only marginally interesting because they are superficial. They fail to get to the heart of the matter. They fail to recognize the community of destiny uniting the various moments in the history of philosophy. They fail to raise the question regarding the very origin and source of that history. This is the other question, other than the questions of philosophy itself, and the other sense of history, other than the chronological sense of history presupposed in and by philosophy itself. The question regarding "our" time, then, is no longer raised with a view to separating it from previous, and possibly subsequent, times and to delineating them chronologically. Rather, it is raised with a view to identifying its essence, to grasping it as such, in its unity, albeit one that unfolds historically and, yes, chronologically. "Our" time is, at the most fundamental level, time as such: not objective, measurable time, but the time that marks the unfolding unity and the continuity of a common destiny, that of the Western world. Philosophy thinks from within that history, it intervenes from within that time. But it does not think it as such, that is, it does not relate to that time in such a way as to experience its essence or provenance. It is in that respect, and in that respect alone, that it does not think. Our time, then, is the whole of time, the time of our metaphysical destiny, which is today perhaps reaching a point of absolute consummation, insofar as philosophy has, in a sort of *Aufhebung,* passed into something else, something that it itself generated, and that it cannot recognize as such but only as an "other" that it often attempts to think as one of its objects, thus becoming philosophy *of* science, *of* the *socius, of* technics, without realizing that what it is actually contemplating is nothing other than itself, its own becoming as it were, and not this other, autonomous object. Saturated with metaphysics and with its own supersession in contemporary techno-culture, our time does not think.

Yet, in claiming that our time does not *yet* think, and that this "not yet" of thinking is precisely what calls for thinking, Heidegger is not simply saying that we cannot think, that the contemporary historical space is saturated to the point of excluding the very possibility of thought. On the contrary: it is our very time, the time of our own historical and destinal essence, that calls for thinking. The call for thought does not come from elsewhere, from another place and an altogether different time (what would such a time be, if "our" time is indeed all the time there is?). Nor does it open onto another time, in the sense of another epoch, a post-metaphysical era as it were. The place from which thinking is called upon and the time onto which it opens is not awaiting us somewhere in the near or far future, doing so in such a way that we could hope that, although we are not yet thinking, thinking will take place one day. The call for thought resonates from within our time, yet it is not exhausted in this time, in the way in which, to a certain extent, this call is taken up in the metaphysical configuration of our history. For our time, this time that continues to unfold, and in thus unfolding, unfolds its own destiny and essence, unfolds *from* that very call, even if this call is such as to remain implicit in that history, even if it is never brought forth as such. Our time, this time that envelops us and traverses us, is a time born of an origin that it cannot think, the very origin that calls for thinking. Thus, even though philosophy and thought are to be absolutely distinguished, insofar as their relation to time is incommensurable, they share a common origin, they are born of the same event. Both are situated and find their place from within the same initial blow; both take place from within the sending of being. For this is what Heidegger has in mind when suggesting that our time at once lacks thought and calls for thinking: a community of destiny between philosophy and thought, a common origin to which one and the other turn differently, the first by turning away from it, the second by turning towards it. And this difference is, in turn, precisely what broaches a turning within history itself: while metaphysics and its techno-scientific *Aufhebung* move ever deeper into their own direction, away from the originary event or opening up of their own history, allowing this history to delve further into a forgottenness of that singular, yet always unfolding event, thought operates a sharp turning within that very history, a turning back to its very origin. In other words, thought turns towards that from which, from the start, philosophy has turned away. And in thus turning back, in swimming upstream, back towards the source, thought initiates a new sense of and for history. Not a new epoch, then, not a post-metaphysical era, nor indeed a return to a past era (since "our" time will have always already slipped into a forgottenness of its own origin), but a circling back into the origin from within "our" time, from within metaphysics. In no way, then, should the "not yet" of thought be understood as marking the site and the promise of a secure future, as indicating a moment of liberation from the hold of metaphysics that will actually take place. It cannot be a question, here, of opposing an ontology of liberation to one of alienation. If the advent of thought does indeed constitute a form of liberation, a form of disengagement from the metaphysical grip that has from the start begun to take hold of the world and of things within it, it is only in and through a confrontation with its history, and this means, ultimately, with an ability to return it, and itself with it, to its long since forgotten and abandoned origin. The counter-history that is being sketched here is not the negation and the leaving behind of that other, metaphysical history, but the returning of that very history to that which, from the very start, has always begun to unfold within it, the opening up of that history to that which, from the very start, has always opened up within it. It is, therefore, a way, and possibly the only way, of reconciling oneself with our time.

What, then, is this origin that is common to both metaphysics and thought, this very origin to which thought would turn and, in doing so, return metaphysics to its own essence? It is the origin which, from the very start, has turned away from us, has withdrawn, yet in such a way as to draw us into its very withdrawing. We think under the blow or the shock of a withdrawal, under the grip of what withdraws:

> That we are not yet thinking stems from the fact that the thing itself that must be thought about turns away from man.[2]

Furthermore,

> That which properly gives us to think [*was uns eigentlich zu denken gibt*] did not turn away from man at some time or other that can be fixed in history —no, what really must be thought has kept itself turned away from man since the beginning.[3]

The gift or the event of thought proper is paradoxical in that it stems from something which, by its very nature, turns itself away from man. What demands to be thought, what gives itself as the ownmost of thought, is precisely that which, of itself, turns away from thought and, in the very withdrawing of which thought is itself drawn, comes into being. That which gives itself to thought as to the ownmost of thought gives itself by pulling itself back, by withdrawing. It is only in being thus drawn into the withdrawal that thought is being born. This withdrawing is nothing other than the withdrawing of being itself, nothing other than the event of presence (*Anwesenheit*), which, in clearing a space for things, in broaching a world, withdraws in beings themselves. The withdrawing of being is the drawing forth of beings, their unfolding within presence. But beyond presence, in excess of things themselves, there is the event of presence, to which metaphysical remains structurally blind. Such is the reason why Heidegger can write,

> In fact, what withdraws may even concern and claim man more essentially than anything present that strikes and touches him [*alles Anwesende, das ihn trifft und betrifft*]. . . . The event of withdrawal [*das Ereignis des Entzugs*] could be what is most present in all things currently present [*in allem jetzt Gegenwärtigen*], and so infinitely exceed the actuality of everything actual.[4]

It is precisely in the withdrawing *from* and *in* the actuality that it opens up, in the turn away from those very things it brings into presence, that the event of being happens. Thought is brought into its own when drawn into this excess, when, turning away from things as essentially there, already present in the world, it turns towards the turning away of being. The origin of thought is thus distinct in that, in a sense, it can be seen as never having taken place, as having never coincided with an actual event. Yet, in a different sense, this is an origin that is taking place, an origin that has always already taken place, thus signaling a distinct temporality, irreducible to the present of anything actual. It signals something like a pure past, a past that never was present, but that nonetheless clears the very space of the present itself. This is a distinct origin, and indeed a distinct event, in that, while the "oldest" and most originary event, it never takes place as such, never coincides with a specific moment in time. Rather, it is the event that opens onto, and opens up, the world and all things within it, but that, in doing so, withdraws in those very things, and in the very sphere of presence it opens up. In a way, then, this is an event that always takes place as something other than itself, an origin that withdraws from the very world it discloses and effaces itself in the beings it brings to presence. Disclosing a world, it gives way to the disclosed, effacing itself behind the traces of its own event. Withdrawing from the world, the event presiding over the clearing of world abandons the world to itself, to presence and actuality, which becomes the very sense of being itself. This, then, is where metaphysical thought begins: at the point where the twofold event of being and time arrives, at the point where it has become something actual: a thing, a being, a state of affairs. Metaphysical thought does not begin at the source, with the very event of being and time, but at the end, with the very sphere of actuality onto which this twofold event opens. But the source itself remains in excess of the word it clears, and in which it withdraws. It continues to signal that which, in the actuality of things, remains in excess of them. Such will have been Heidegger's only concern: to reawaken thought to the very origin of the world, to the very event whereby "there is." In all given things, there is the thing that is actually given, the thing given in actuality. And the destiny as well as the force of metaphysical thought will have been relentlessly to raise the question of the sense of such an actuality, to think the essence of the actual. Yet in all given things there is also the giving in and through which such things and the world that harbors them are given. In excess of the thing in its actuality, there is the gift at the origin of this actuality, the virtual horizon whence it unfolds. This is a gift—a movement and an event—the sense of which can thus not be exhausted in the actuality it opens onto. This is an event irreducible to a sense of being as presence and of time as present. And yet it coincides with the very event, the very happening of being and time. "There is/it gives being" (*es gibt Sein*), "there is/it gives time" (*es gibt Zeit*), Heidegger writes, in an attempt to desubstantialize and desubjectivize the operation whereby "there is," in an effort to wrest the co-originary event of time and being from the metaphysics of substance, and to return it to its purely eventful nature. All things, and the world in which they are encountered, unfold from this singular horizon, all worldly events and states of affairs are born of this always already unfolding event. They are all the expression of the same event, each of them the object, whether direct or indirect, of the same verb.

And so, in a way, thought is itself also already underway. It has already begun to take place. For that towards which thought directs itself has always and already begun to turn itself towards thought. It has begun to turn itself towards thought as towards the possibility of its own memory and preservation. Thinking, insofar as it concerned with what, in excess of all existing things, beyond presence itself—classically considered to be the very sense and measure of all things—designates the horizon from which presence unfolds, cannot align itself with the image of thought as present and as directed at present, actual objects. Thinking is not representation. Rather, thinking unfolds only as the "safeguarding" (*Verwahrnis*) of this dimension in excess of world and things within it, as this dimension or horizon whence world and things themselves unfold. Thinking thinks and thinks from the most ancient of events, from what since time immemorial has begun to unfold, and it is to that extent that it is "memory." Not memory as this faculty through which we retain the past in the present, or allow it to return to the present—not as a faculty of re-presentation, then, but as the ancient Μνημοσύνη, daughter of Sky and Earth, mother of all Muses. Not *das Gedächtnis*, therefore, its late, psychological and subjective interpretation, but *die Gedächtnis*, the primitive, originary form of fidelity to the most originary event, the intimation and the recollection (the gathering) of what has always and already begun to take place:

> Memory is the gathering [*Versammlung*] of thought upon what everywhere wants to be thought in advance. Memory is the gathering proper to recollective thought [*Andenken*].[5]

Something has always set itself already underway to thought, thus setting thought itself underway to it. We ourselves have already begun to be drawn into the event of being, and into its own withdrawal. From the very start, we find ourselves under the power of this withdrawal, exposed to its force. We find ourselves, always and already, on the way to thought, since what calls for thinking, the very origin of thought, is what from the very start has been happening to us, has been coming towards us. That we are not yet thinking is in no way incompatible with the fact that we have always already been on the way to thought, not, of course, as something constituted given in advance, but as what takes place, in the form of a preserving and a harboring, in the very withdrawing of being:

> The assertion says, what most gives to think is that we are not yet thinking. The assertion says neither that we are no longer thinking, nor does it say roundly that we are not thinking at all. The words "not yet," spoken thoughtfully, suggest that we are already on our way toward thinking, presumably from afar, not only on our way toward thinking as a conduct some day to be practiced, but on our way *within* thinking, on the path of thinking.[6]

Thought unfolds between the memory of a pure past, of an event that has always and already begun to take place, and the openness to what, in excess of any present, constitutes the very future of thought, the horizon approaching us from afar. Such is the essence of thought, that it belongs to the very movement of essence. Consequently, the fact that we are not yet thinking is not just an avowal of impotence. And to have associated the very task of thinking with the impossibility of thought *actually* taking place amounts to nothing like a minimal ambition for thought. On the contrary. It amounts to the greatest ambition for thought, for it forces it out of the territory of philosophy, out of the mere actuality of the actual, and into the virtual, never present horizon whence this territory arises. It opens thought onto the abyssal space of virtual being, and its clearing of the space of actuality in which beings tower up. Heidegger will have had no concern other than to open thought onto the difference between beings in their presence and the event of being, between things as they are given, and the gift whereby they are given. Thought, for Heidegger, thinks only from within that difference, for this is where we dwell, in the space and the time opened up by it. Philosophy too thinks from within that difference, but it does not think it as such. Only thought does. But whence does thought arise? When does it take place? The question can no longer be asked in that way, since thought has proven to be already underway, already approaching. What remains to be done is to render ourselves worthy of what is coming towards us, of what, from the start and always, is happening to us. Could thought have aspired to a greater destiny?

PART I. ANTHROPOLOGY

1

Homo Heideggerians

Somewhat provocatively, I would like to suggest that Heidegger's thought was concerned with the fate of the human from the very start. And yet in no way and at no stage can Heidegger's thought be mistaken for a straightforward anthropology, even if, beginning with Husserl himself, there has been a long history of anthropological (mis)interpretations of Heidegger's early thought.[1] What renders this straightforwardly anthropological reading of Heidegger impossible is Heidegger's fundamental intuition according to which what constitutes the human as such, its essence if you will, is itself nothing human. This, however, does not take the question concerning the essence of man in the direction of either the infrahuman (*animalitas*) or the superhuman (*divinitas*). For the *essence* of man is indeed the essence of *man,* that which belongs to man most intimately, but in such a way that, through it, man is, from the very start, something more than just man. As soon as it is a matter of man, it is a matter of something other than man. And it is precisely through this excess, through an originary openness to a constitutive and non-human otherness, that man as such emerges. So the history that Heidegger recounts, the genesis that he sketches, is not that of the species "man" in its slow and progressive differentiation from other species. Nor is it, for that matter, the story of the creation of man by a supersensible being whose powers far exceed those of man himself. Heidegger's discourse concerning man must be rigorously distinguished from that of anthropology, biology, and theology.[2] Rather, the history that Heidegger recounts is that of man's relation to his essence, the history of the *essence* of man, in which the concepts of "man," "essence," and "history" come to be reformulated radically. How exactly? In such a way, first of all, that the concepts of essence and of history are no longer simply opposed to one another, but implicate one another: the concept of essence mobilized here does not refer to an extra-temporal and a-historical realm, one that would define man in its necessary and permanent being, independently of the vicissitudes and contingencies of its becoming, but to time itself, understood as the ecstatic-horizonal temporalizing whence history itself unfolds. This, in turn, allows one to identify a history of man as the history of man's relation to his own essence. Also, and by the same token, it is vital to note that even if man is what and who he is on the basis of an essence that exceeds him, he also *becomes* who he is through the repetition of this essence. It is in the very movement of returning to his essence, in the opening to the opening of being that he himself is, or exists, that man becomes man. And this particular repetition of his essence, this particular opening to that which always and from the very start has begun to open itself in him, has a history, is historical in the strongest sense of the term, that is, in the sense of an origin, or an epoch-making principle. It corresponds to the birth of the West in ancient Greece. And if we, today, are still Greek, it is as the inheritors of this repetition, and of the history which it opened up, but also and above all in that we too have to repeat or actualize this repetition and, in this very gesture, become men. We can only *become* men and, in this becoming, comport ourselves as Greeks. Therefore, one needs to acknowledge a double discourse and a double gesture on Heidegger's part. On the one hand, to the question concerning the essence or the origin of man, Heidegger will have always provided the same answer, revealed through an essentially onto-phenomenological analysis: man begins with the openness to the world or the Open as such. Man is essentially ek-sistence, openness to the truth of being. And yet Heidegger will have claimed throughout that the actual disclosedness to this disclosure, in other words, the peculiar repetition of this disclosure, in which the disclosure is held into view, thus becoming an explicit and thematic issue for man, is itself a historical event, in the twofold following sense. First, it is an event that actually took place, in ancient Greece. As we shall try to indicate, Heidegger goes to great trouble to show how, in Aristotle, for example, the very question of ethics, and of philosophy itself, revolves around the possibility for man of holding in view and of enacting that which man always and already is, in other words, his essence, understood as his ability to stand in the midst of things as in the midst of a unified *world*, and to find his abode therein. But second—and this amounts to a radical transformation of the concepts of event and of history—this repetition is historical in a more profound sense. For the event that is in question here is not an event that took place in history, once and for all, alongside other events, such as the Peloponnesian war or the battle of Marathon. Rather, it is the event in and through which Greece as such came to be constituted, the originary or founding event from out of which an entire epoch came to unfold, and in the sending of which we, today, are still situated. Much is at stake, then, in the possibility of this circling back or this repetition: nothing less than a new beginning, or beginning as such, an origin in the sense of an *Ur-sprung*, of something that surges forth and, in so doing, leaps ahead, thus clearing a space for a virtual set of events, opening up an epoch and a world. And while this origin unfolds temporally, it is itself not *in* time, but withdrawn from time, withdrawn from time in the very moment in which it makes history. What I wish to suggest, then, at the most general level, is that history in the Heideggerian sense is played out in the possibility of this repetition, in which man establishes with the world, with his own being and with the being of others, a relation of ap-propriation. Under what conditions is such a relation possible? Under what conditions can man be in the world so as to recognize this world as the site of his abode, as his *ethos?* How are ethics and philosophy possible — if ethics is indeed the operation whereby man relates to his own being as to the place of his abode, and if philosophy is indeed this attitude of wonder and questioning before the event of being, this stance and this comportment towards the truth of being?

The essence of man, then, is existence or, as Heidegger often prefers to spell it, so as to distinguish it from the medieval *existentia*, which refers to the mere *actualitas* of a thing (by contrast with its *essentia*): ek-sistence. What does this mean? It means that

> Man occurs essentially in such a way that he is the 'there' [*das 'Da'*], that is, the clearing of being. The 'being' of the *Da*, and only it, has the fundamental character of ek-sistence, that is, of an ecstatic inherence [*Innestehens*] in the truth of being.[3]

Man is man, then, insofar as he stands *ecstatically* in the midst of things. But insofar as man stands in the world ecstatically, that is, in such a way that his stance is itself a clearing, the configuring of a world, he stands open to more than just those things that surround and affect him: to the world as such and as whole, to the Open or the truth of being. It is this very connection to truth as disclosedness, this specific mode of standing in the world, that characterizes the essence of man. This is what *Being and Time* attempted to establish. In his letter from 1946 to Jean Beaufret, looking back on this attempt, Heidegger writes the following:

> What does existence mean in *Being and Time?* The word names a way of *being* [*eine Weise des Seins*], the being of that being which stands [*steht*] open for the openness [*Offenheit*] in which it stands in withstanding [*aussteht*] it. This withstanding [*dieses Ausstehen*] is experienced under the name of "care." The ecstatic essence of Dasein is thought in terms of care, and, conversely,

care is experienced adequately only in its ecstatic essence. Withstanding, experienced in this manner, is the essence of the ecstasis that is to be thought here. The ecstatic essence of existence is therefore still understood inadequately as long as one thinks of it as merely a "standing out" ["*Hin-ausstehen*"], while interpreting the "out" as meaning "away from" the interior of an immanence of consciousness or spirit. . . . The *stasis* of the ecstatic consists—strange as it may sound—in standing in the "out" and "there" of unconcealedness, as which being itself unfolds. What is meant by "existence" in the context of a thinking that is prompted by, and directed toward, the truth of being, could be most felicitously designated by the word "in-stance" [or in-sistence: *Inständigkeit*]. . . .

The proposition "the human being exists" means: the human being is that being whose being is distinguished by an open standing that stands in the unconcealedness of being.[4]

Thus, the being human of the human as ex-sistence refers primarily to a way of relating to the world, and to a stance within this world. Man stands in the world ecstatically, which means that he does not stand in the world in the mode of a thing, which is simply there, immanent to the world, its spatiality reduced to its very physical contours. Man is not an ob-ject, a thing thrown into the world in such a way that it stands opposite or before—an obstance. Nor does man stand within the world as a subject, as a being thrown under the world, sustaining it, underlying it. The stance of man is not that of a substance. Rather, if man is indeed thrown into the world, if it is indeed a throw, it is in the twofold sense of being thrown into the world, located and situated within it, in such a way that the world of existence is always a specific and concrete world, a context, and also, at the same time, throwing itself beyond itself, pro-jecting itself into a realm of possibilities and projects, in such a way that he is not simply here, but always out there, ahead of itself— not in a different world, in the world of ideas or in the after-world, but at the horizon, where a world begins to take shape and a destiny to unfold. Thus, at once absolutely immanent to the world, utterly unable to turn away from it or abstract itself from it, and constantly transcending the world, pro-jecting himself against a horizon of pure possibility. Neither ob-ject nor sub-ject, neither ob-stance nor sub-stance, but pro- and retro-ject, ek-sistence stands "in" the world insofar as it stands outside of itself, disclosing the world, clearing things within it, understanding it, inhabiting it.[5] If man is in the world not as an inert thing or as a mere instrument, nor even as a substance, it is not because he "lives" in it in an organic sense, but precisely to the extent that he dwells within it, that is, comports himself to it, relates himself to it in such a way that he under-stands it. "It," that is to say: the world as such and as a whole, and not just this or that thing within the world. And so, Heidegger insists, this understanding has nothing to do with a theoretical activity, with a λόγος in the sense of a rationality, or an understanding under-stood as faculty. These are metaphysical representations that need to be overcome in order for the true essence of man to come to the fore:

> Due to the manner in which it thinks of beings, metaphysics almost seems to be, without knowing it, the barrier that refuses human beings the pri-mordial relation of being to the human essence.[6]

Man is man not insofar as he can "think" and represent the world theoretically, but insofar as he under-stands it from out of his very tran-scendence, by virtue of his meta-physical nature. To exist is to under-stand. But to understand is not to represent, or to make use of a faculty. On the contrary: Heidegger goes as far as to state that understanding is "the genuine sense of acting" (*der eigentliche Sinn des Handelns*).[7] If man understands, it is precisely and only to the extent that he is open to the openness within which things come to matter for him. More even: understanding is the very mode of Dasein's openness to truth, the very way in which, for man, truth unfolds.

Thus, man is the being who stands in the truth (of being). This is his share and his destiny, his μοῖρα and his *fatum,* as well as it is his essence. In other words, this essence has a history, and the history of man is the history of his essence. The philosophical concept of history must therefore be distinguished from the scientific concept of history, regardless of the field to which it is applied.[8] It is the specificity of human history, or, rather, of the history of the essence of man, that Heidegger wishes to recognize and thematize:

> Ek-sistence can be said only of the essence of man, that is, only of the human way 'to be.' For as far as our experience shows, only man is admitted to the destiny [*Geschick*] of ek-sistence. Therefore ek-sistence can also never be thought of as a specific kind of living creature among others — granted that man is destined to think the essence of his being and not merely to give accounts of the nature and history of his constitution and activities.[9]

Now, this is not to deny the fact that man belongs to that history in a way that is quite definite and decisive. To deny the relevance and the importance of the many fields (anthropology, ethnology, history, biol-ogy, geography, physiology, psychology, etc.), which, in one way or another, take "man" as their object of scientific investigation would amount to nothing more than a dangerous kind of obscurantism and negationism. Rather, it is to acknowledge the possibility, and indeed the necessity, of questioning in the direction of that aspect of man to which the sciences remain necessarily blind, an aspect which, according to Heidegger, defines the stage on which the *destiny* of man is played out. It is thus a matter of envisaging man solely from the perspective of his essence, that is, from the perspective of his capacity for unconcealedness and manifestness—from the perspective of his unique and singular relation to truth.

In time, then, the question of history itself would need to be taken up in light of the essence of man. Prior to any such enterprise, however, it is necessary to articulate, as synthetically and precisely as possible, what could be called the structure of ek-sistence as man's relation to the truth of being. In the following pages, I shall therefore limit myself to the way in which this connection is described in Heidegger's early work, and particularly in the years around the publication of *Being and Time* (1927). Specifically, I shall bring out the various levels at which this connection takes place, and which can be grouped under the following headings: manipulation and production, prudence or resoluteness, speculation or philosophy—or, to put it economically and somewhat bluntly: technics, ethics, and theory. From the outset, I also want to emphasize the fact that none of these modes or operations of truth can be said to be more "practical" than the other. The operation of truth, Heidegger claims, exceeds all *theoria* and *praxis,* all contemplation and action,[10] because it is situated before such metaphysical distinctions can begin to intervene. It is a matter of understanding the extent to which all such modes of being are modes of a single and absolutely concrete operation, namely, truth, and that truth itself, far from being a state of affairs, or a static entity, is an event, a becoming or a verb—an ἀληθεύειν. In the 1924–25 lectures on Plato's *Sophist,* for example, Heidegger makes it quite explicit that ἀλήθεια is first and foremost the result of an operation, of an ἀληθεύειν that is characteristic of the human Dasein as a whole, which Aristotle designated as ψυχή. As such, ἀλήθεια is not the result of an operation of only the highest part of the soul, the νοῦς, or the intellect, but of the soul as a whole: it is existence as such that discloses and constitutes the very operation of truth, the disclosing within which things become manifest, the event or the advent of truth. Not only λόγος, then, traditionally thought to be the locus of truth, not just the intellect, but every part of the soul—intellect, heart, guts, hands, sexual organs—takes part in the operation of truth. The human body itself comes to be rethought on the basis of man's originary and constitutive relation to truth, on the basis of his essence, and not of physiology:

> The human body is essentially [i.e., from the point of view of its essence] something other than an animal organism. . . . The fact that physiology and physiological chemistry can scientifically investigate the human being as an organism is no proof that in this 'organic' thing, that is, in the body scientifically explained, the essence of the human being consists.[11]

The body itself, then, is not left out of the operation of truth. It is entirely implicated in it. How could it not, when who we are, our very essence, is no longer characterized in terms of an ability to think (*res cogitans*), or as a transcendental consciousness, but as a concrete and singular event that involves the whole of our being? Every operation or mode of truth implicates and configures the body in a specific and concrete way. Now, this is not to say that the body is the driving and unifying force behind the various modes of truth. Throughout, or at least in the context of fundamental ontology, Heidegger will have insisted that time, and specifically the temporalizing of temporality, is the force with which the phenomenon of truth coincides. It is the temporalizing of temporality that clears a space for beings. However, there is little doubt that that very mode or operation of truth orients and directs, affects and shapes the body in a certain way. If man indeed radiates, if its world is indeed a constellation and not a series of points, then the human body is not limited to its physical contours: it is itself a ray, or a sheaf of rays of truth shot across the world. It, too, is ecstatic. And truth is itself carnal and incarnate as well as temporal. The body of this being whom Heidegger calls Dasein is the expression of its power and of its facticity, of its ability to clear and disclose. Specifically, we shall have to see how every operation of truth, truth as such, is guided in advance, opened up as such by a certain seeing, a gaze which, above and beyond the mere sight of the living thing, always coincides with the event of disclosure. It is always a matter of a certain gaze, be it the peripheral look that embraces a practical situation (*Umsicht*), the eye that blinks, ever so briefly, in the moment of recognition of one's essence (*Augenblick*), or the eyes that remain wide open before the spectacle of raw being. More than something that one sees, truth is actual and proper seeing.

At a most general level, and in the context of *Being and Time,* the connection between ek-sistence and truth begins to unfold long before it is made explicit in §44, entitled "Dasein, disclosedness and truth." To the extent that, at least in the context of the analysis of Dasein, truth coincides with existence as such, it is even operative from the very start of the analysis. Yet it is perhaps in the sections devoted to Dasein's spatiality that the connection becomes clear. As *Ent-fernung* and *Ausrichtung,* that is, as the ability to bring things close by from out of their originary distance and to orient itself in the world on the basis of its needs, necessities, and possibilities, Dasein "frees" beings or "lets them be" for a totality of involvements. It frees their own spatiality and their function, it opens up the context or the world whence they appear as such or such a thing: as a thing of use, or as a thing for contemplation, as familiar or unfamiliar, as threatening or reassuring, etc. In other words, it makes room for them, provides them with their space. Dasein is essentially space-giving (*Raum-gebend*), or room-making (*Einräumend*). As existence, it gives or clears a space, it opens up a world inhabited by things, it discloses beings in their being. The "Da" of Da-sein captures this originary spatiality, that is, this clearing or this space-giving, this disclosure (*Erschlossenheit*) that is the very operation of ecstatic time. This is what existence is and does: it opens up, it clears and reveals, it wrests from unconcealment and brings into the open; it is itself a stretch, an ongoing process, an event: a world that comes alive as it is populated by things, men, animals, memories, gods, places, etc. Thus, it is not a point inscribed within a pre-given space, but a self-configuring force; it does not move as if along a pre-determined line, but radiates and reso-nates from the corners of its ecstases; it is not so much rooted as it is cosmic and stellar, not so much a tree as a spider, or a star. Yet existence exists its own disclosedness: it is not on the basis of something other than Dasein that Dasein is there: "Dasein is its disclosedness."[12] Dasein "is" its own clearing, it exists it, and only insofar as it "is" is it *there*. Dasein "is" being. It coincides with the operation whereby there is, whereby things come to populate the Open and find their place within it. Were it not for existence, and this means, ultimately, for the opera-tion of time or the temporalizing that Dasein is, there would be no-thing. Time is the meaning or the origin of being, the horizon of its pre-theoretical intelligibility. Being unfolds as time, yet time is the ecstatic time of existence. Existence is not constituted by hypostases, but by ecstases. Only thus is it true, true in the most genuine and primordial sense. *Erschlossenheit*, then, is the original phenomenon of truth, truth proper. Insofar as Dasein uncovers beings within-the-world, Dasein is true in the most primordial sense. The beings thus disclosed are them-selves true, yet they always presuppose the more originary operation of truth that existence is: "only with Dasein's disclosedness is the most pri-mordial phenomenon of truth attained."[13] Such is the reason why, somewhat provocatively, Heidegger claims that "'there is' truth only insofar as Dasein is and so long as Dasein is."[14] In the end, then, exist-ence is said to have an intimate connection with truth to the extent that existence itself is the very operation of truth, the clearing or disclosing without which nothing could ever be said to be true, for it would never be encountered, present in any way. Only that which can be disclosed can be true. Only that which ex-ists or is there can disclose. Truth and being are equiprimordial insofar as being, for Heidegger, means the Open as such, that is, the openness or the unconcealment whence everything takes place. To say that the essence of man, or Dasein, is truth proper does not contradict our opening statement according to which the essence of man is his openness to something that exceeds him: for it is precisely, according to Heidegger's own formulation, "the Dasein in man" that exceeds man. The "Dasein in man" is precisely to be under-stood as this excess or this transcendence to which man is from the start subjected.

Homo Faber

It is not surprising, then, that in the analysis of Dasein's everyday way of being, in the most originary and primitive analysis of truth, the body of Dasein, primarily through its hands, is granted a specific role. Everything happens as if truth needed the hand, as if the very operation of truth required certain bodily functions and postures, as if truth itself were a matter for the body.

In the analysis of Dasein developed in Division One of *Being and Time*, the operation of truth is analyzed in the way in which it occurs "proximally and for the most part," that is, in everyday existence, in the most mundane and habitual activities of Dasein. Heidegger turns the question of truth, of being as disclosedness, into a matter of everyday comportment, wresting it from its privileged locus (the human λόγος) and its traditional definition (*adequatio rei et intellectus*). With Heidegger, the question of truth is no longer *primarily* a matter of propositions, or judgment. It is primarily a matter of and for everyday practical existence. Nowhere is this more visible than in those sections of *Being and Time* devoted to the analysis of the everyday world of Dasein.[15] What do we find there?

Unlike the concept of "nature," which is a representation—a metaphysical construction, or an abstraction—and thus only a secondary and derivative phenomenon, the concept of "world," and the definition of "man" as being-in-the-world, aims to capture the essence of what it means to be human. It is an originary phenomenon, the human in its primordial phenomenality, or in its being. As such, it is more concrete, "truer" than any metaphysical "definition" of man, which always presupposes the being-in-the-world of Dasein, and yet fails to grasp it as a positive phenomenon. The primary task of the analysis of Dasein is thus to bring the human back to its originary and concrete soil, back to existence, from out of the metaphysical constructions that have been grafted onto it.

And so the task of the analysis of Dasein is to show how, at the most concrete, mundane, seemingly inconspicuous level, a certain operation of truth is already at play. It is to show the extent to which everyday practical existence is itself a happening of truth, an ἀληθεύειν in the sense developed by Aristotle in Book VI of the *Nicomachean Ethics,* and analyzed in detail by Heidegger in his lectures on Plato's *Sophist,* which in many respects constitute a preparatory analysis to *Being and Time.*[16] It is to demonstrate that man "understands" his being, what it "means" to be prior to any conceptualization or any representation of this being, at the pre-theoretical level of everyday existence. This first level Heidegger thus characterizes as "everydayness." The world it discloses is an

Umwelt, an environment, or a world that is not so much opposite as it is all around. It is this world to which there corresponds a peculiar kind of seeing, a seeing that Heidegger defines as an *Umsicht:* the concerned, absorbed, practical gaze that characterizes our everyday dealings with the world: the circumspect gaze that is on the look out for things. But the truth is that this gaze, this peculiar mode of envisaging the world as the world which is not there before me in the mode of an object, or of nature, in other words as a reality that is simply present, awaiting to be represented, but as this world which is all around me, surrounding me, and in which I am concretely situated, always "in position," this gaze, then, is immediately translated and actualized as handling: our everyday relation to the world, our way of being in the world "proximally and for the most" is "handy." Thus, the gaze that is at stake here is not that of the spectator or the observer, the gaze that holds things at a distance. It is precisely the gaze by which distance is abolished, and things brought into nearness:

> If we envisage things simply by way of a 'theoretical' look [*Blick*], we fail to understand them as readiness-to-hand. But when we deal with them by using them and manipulating them, this activity is not a blind one; it has its own kind of sight [*Sichtart*], by which our manipulation is guided and from which it acquires its specific thingly character.[17]

Thus, to the "practical" there corresponds a specific kind of seeing (*Umsicht,* or circumspection) which is quite distinct from the purely contemplative kind (traditionally referred to as "theory"), much in the same way that "theory" itself is not simply devoid of a specific mode of concern. And so, with respect to the body, if the hands are the primary instruments of this everyday relation to the world, they are at the same time the very extension of my "concerned" or practical gaze, of this gaze that envisages things with a *view* to accomplishing this or that practical task. The gaze that I throw onto the world and that guides me through it is first and foremost a practical gaze, the kind of seeing that results from my living in a world of practical necessities. It is the gaze that orients my body according to the many needs and obstacles that it encounters, and that converge in my hands as in the tip of my being. Thus, my primary relation to the world is one of *Handeln,* of action in the sense of handling, and the things which I encounter within the world are, for the most part and primarily, things to be handled, *manipulata,* πράγματα, *Zeuge* or *Zuhandene:* Such beings are not "objects for knowing the world 'theoretically'; they are simply what gets used, what gets produced, and so forth."[18] Thus, man is first and foremost *manipulans* and *faber,* and the hands of Dasein are the instrument of this specific kind of ἀληθεύειν, which Aristotle designated as τέχνη and which Heidegger translates back into the vocabulary of onto-phenomenology as *Sich-Auskennen*,[19] as finding one's way in the realm of practical concern (*Besorgen*), of manipulation (*Hantieren*), of production (*Herstellen*). In each case, the hands of Dasein disclose a world, reveal something about the concrete situation of Dasein; they are co-extensive with the practical operation of truth in which Dasein is involved.

At the most basic level, then, existence is an operation of disclosure or clearing whereby something ready-to-hand is freed for its use and function; in the realm of the practical, we let something ready-to-hand be so and so as it is already and in order that it be such. The operation of truth is a letting-be: a letting something be *for* what it is, the dis-covering of something in its readiness-to-hand within the world of practical concern. And co-extensive with this discovering is the "understanding" of the world on the part of Dasein. Dasein's relation to the world, as this practical, primarily "handy" disclosure of things within the world, reveals a world of "meaning," where meaning is not to be understood primarily in terms of an operation of signification which takes place at the level of a faculty of understanding or reasoning: we do not inject meaning into the world "intellectually" and *a posteriori;* rather, the world itself is meaningful by virtue of its very practicality: the chair is "meaningful" by virtue of the fact that I can sit on it, as this chair on which I can—or cannot, in which case it is negatively meaningful—sit. I "understand" the chair not by way of representation but by way of sitting; only as this chair on which I am sitting, or on which I would like to sit, can the chair be said to be understood "properly." It is not the I of the *cogito* that understands here, but the body itself, whose knowledge is constituted by habits contracted over the years. At stake, then, is a certain intelligence of the body, or at least a becoming-intelligent of the body: if the *intelligere* is itself indeed ecstatic, and this means temporal, it is nonetheless inseparable from this body which is the instrument, the vehicle, or the vector of my power—not of my might (*Macht*), but of my ability (*Können*), which is always the ability or the power to be (being): my body is the power or the ability to be, to act my being; it is that which has the power to be my being, that which "is" it, transitively and immediately.[20] For my ability to *be* is my *ability* to be, this power which "can be" my being. The *Seinkönnen* is nothing other than this capacity to "be" or to exist being, this power of being or this capacity to be. And if Dasein is indeed a power, a *potentialitas,* it is first and foremost as this ontological power, as this power of truth understood as disclosure. In other words, the intelligibility of the world has nothing to do with our ability to represent it; on the other hand, it has everything to do with our ability to *be* it (*Seinkönnen*)—to comport ourselves towards or exist it. Of course, I can still comport myself to the chair theoretically and raise questions such as "What is a chair?" "What is it for?" "Of what is it made?" etc., but these are abstract questions, questions that carry the world onto a different plane, the plane of representation, on which the chair, from its original status as a practical thing (a *Zuhandene*), is being turned or modified into an object of questioning (into a *Vorhandene*). But the point is that the primordial and meaningfully originary relation or comportment to the chair is the one where the chair appears as the "that-on-which-I-can-sit." This is the level at which meaning first emerges. If meaning as such cannot indeed be dissociated from a general structure of signification, such a structure does not refer so much to a capacity for abstraction and formalization as to existence itself, to the very existing of existence that *is* language. Dasein, and this means the assemblage Dasein-world, is itself a language, a structured totality of signs or references, a totality of referrals which constitute a world and which point inward to Dasein itself as the ultimate horizon, the for-the-sake of which or the ultimate signified of the referential totality. Dasein coincides with the whole of its world, future, past, and present: everything caught up in it is part of this world, an expression of it and an extension of Dasein, meaningful to the extent that it has a place within it, that it is inscribed as an instance and a moment of the general structure of referral. What the analysis of Dasein reveals, then, at its most concrete and mundane level is a world or a plane of meaning and signification and so of understanding, in which a faculty of representation plays absolutely no part, a mode of being populated with significations, references, connections which reveal a complex understanding of the world, albeit an understanding that is wholly devoid of any abstract mediation. Existence is itself a world, a web, or a totality of involvements populated with needs, necessities, and desires of the most practical kind and in which things are revealed as subordinated to or in reference with such goals and imperatives.

This, then, is what Heidegger means when he says that Dasein "understands" its world: it does not understand it in the way it understands a mathematical problem, that is, abstractly, but precisely to the extent that it has a world, or rather, that it *is* that world. It is only when we sever man from the world to which he necessarily belongs and wrest him from the soil whence he emerges that the question concerning the world can take the abstract and naïve form of exteriority and transcendence. It is only when he is cut off from his essence, and this means from his power or ability to be (being), that man begins to pose the question of understanding and of signification, of truth and of presence, in epistemological and metaphysical terms. This was clear to Heidegger as early as 1919, when he wrote the following:

> When the sense of existence is investigated in terms of its origin and our genuine basic experience of it, we see that it is precisely *that* sense of being that cannot be obtained from the "is" we use to explicate and objectify our experience in one way or another when we acquire knowledge about it. The sense of human existence is to be obtained rather from its own basic experience of having [later on, and specifically in *Being and Time*, Heidegger

will say: understanding] itself in a *concerned* manner [*aus der Grunderfahrung des* bekümmerten *Habens seiner selbst*]. This having [or understanding] is enacted prior to whatever knowledge about it we might later acquire by objectifying it with the "is," and such knowledge is in fact inconsequential for this enactment. If I seek this objectifying knowledge, the attitude of observation will become central for me. All my explications will then have an objectifying nature, *but they will put me at a remove from existence and from a genuine having* [or understanding] *of it* (concern [*Bekümmerung*]).[21]

It is there, then, in the operation whereby the sense of being is severed from the *Grunderfahrung* within which it is rooted that the scientific and metaphysical attitude becomes possible. But insofar as this attitude presupposes an essential modification of the sense of being in the way of reification, it remains abstract. Following Husserl's footsteps, the task of thinking for Heidegger will have consisted in an attempt to bring philosophy back to its concrete soil, to make philosophy concrete again. And because philosophy was to be returned to the concreteness of the question concerning the sense or the origin of being, it itself came to be viewed as the most concrete, and indeed vital, of all activities. I shall come back to this in the last part of this chapter.

Homo Prudens

The point here, however, is to know whether manipulation, as an instance of truth, constitutes the ultimate mode in which Dasein is disclosed to its own being. Is the disclosedness of existence visible as such in everydayness? Is Dasein disclosed to its own disclosedness in its familiar comportment towards the world? In a way, yes. But is disclosedness the very end or goal of the operation of truth that takes place at that level, or is there a way for to Dasein to be in which the essence of Dasein—that is, existence as disclosedness—becomes the very object or the very stake of the comportment? Can Dasein *be* in such a way that it becomes transparent to itself *as* disclosedness? Can it be in such a way that its very truthing comes to be the sole goal of its activity or truthing? Now, if the mode of being that governs man's relation to his everyday world as exposed in Division One of *Being and Time* can be seen as an onto-phenomenological "translation" of the Aristotelian concept of τέχνη, understood as the human "know-how" in the realm of concern, handling, and production (*Sich-Auskennen—im Besorgen, Hantieren, Herstellen*), Heidegger's concept of *Entschlossenheit* is in turn explicitly introduced as a translation of Aristotle's concepts of φρόνησις and βουλή in the first part of the *Sophist* lectures.[22] In other words, if Division One of *Being and Time* coincided with the realm of the technical, Division Two, insofar as it introduces *Entschlossenheit* as the phenomenon in which Dasein becomes transparent to itself in its essence through a repetition

of itself, coincides with the realm of the practical understood in its traditional Aristotelian sense. But Heidegger's entire struggle with respect
to what is normally referred to as the "practical" consists in wresting it
from the moral (from the practical in a modern, i.e., Kantian sense: from
the problematic of yet another faculty, the will, and its determination in
terms of freedom—which does not mean that the thematic of freedom
is simply abandoned: rather, it is reinterpreted along the lines of the
ability to relate to Dasein's power of being or ability to *be* its being
[*Seinkönnen*]) so as to return it to the ethical in the originary sense of
the term, that is, as an activity or a comportment in which what it
means to be human (to be open to the Open or truth as such, open to
the ontological difference), in which the Dasein as such and as a
whole becomes the sole concern and object of the activity itself. In such
an activity, the disclosedness or truth-character of Dasein is most
revealed, and thus elevated to another power. In *Entschlossenheit*, nothing "more" is added or revealed. It is only a matter of intensification, a
matter of letting Dasein's own power of disclosedness bear on itself as
disclosedness. It is, therefore, a matter of repeating that which already
is, of circling back onto that which is from the very start and necessarily,
but in such a way that the "thing" in question (i.e., Dasein) *is* more
intensely, in such a way that its very being is now brought to its full disclosure:

> The phenomenon of resolute disclosedness has brought us before the pri-
> mordial *truth* of existence. As resolute, Dasein is unveiled [*enthüllt*] to itself
> in its current factical ability and power to be [*in seinem . . . Seinkönnen*], and
> in such a way that Dasein itself *is* this unveiling and being-unveiled. To truth
> belongs a corresponding holding-for-true [*Für-wahr-halten*]. What corre-
> sponds explicitly to the disclosed or the discovered is the *being*-certain. The
> primordial truth of existence demands an equiprimordial being-certain, in
> which one maintains oneself in what resoluteness discloses. . . . Such cer-
> tainty must maintain itself in what is disclosed by the resolution. But this
> means that it simply cannot become rigid as regards the situation, but must
> understand that the resolution, in accordance with its own meaning as a
> disclosure, must be held open and free for the current factical possibility.
> The certainty of the resolution signifies that one holds oneself free for the
> possibility of bringing it back—a possibility which is factically necessary. . . .
> this holding-for-true, as a resolute holding-oneself-free for bringing back, *is*
> *the authentic resoluteness for the repetition of itself.*[23]

Thus, it is not a question of claiming that this mode of truth is more
or less practical than the previous mode; it is practical not in the prag-
matic sense of τέχνη, but in the ethical sense of πρᾶξις. It deals not with
things (*Zu-* and *Vorhandene*) but with Dasein as such. In it, its own being,
its own existence is at issue for it. It is concerned with the living well or
according to one's essence (εὖ), with the happy life (εὐδαιμονία).

Death

We have already seen how Dasein is essentially defined as this capacity to be (being), that is, as a power of being: Dasein *can* be, and this *Können* is what distinguishes it from other beings. In other words, Dasein can be said not simply to be, in the way in which a thing is, but to ex-ist; to ex-ist means precisely that: to be in the mode of power, of potentiality, of possibility. Dasein is essentially a pro-ject, throwing itself ahead of itself. As long as it is, Heidegger emphasizes, "right to its end," it comports itself towards its *Seinkönnen,* that is, towards itself as this ability to be its own being, or to ek-sist. This means that the being of Dasein is measured in terms of possibility more than actuality, that Dasein is somehow in reserve, that there is more to come, that Dasein as such, that is, as Da-sein, is precisely always "to come":

> The 'ahead-of-itself,' as an item in the structure of care, tells unambiguously that in Dasein there is always something *still outstanding* [*im Dasein noch immer etwas* aussteht], which, as a potentiality-for-being for Dasein itself, has not yet become 'actual.' It is essential to the basic constitution of Dasein that there is a continual incompleteness [*eine ständige Unabgeschlossenheit*].[24]

So the way in which, for Dasein, there is something outstanding differs from the way in which something belonging to a being is still missing, in the way in which, for example, the debt that is still outstanding is eventually liquidated, or the unripe fruit eventually ripens. In this case what is outstanding is awaiting to be "realized." In other words, it will eventually become actual, and this actualization signifies its fulfillment. Not so with the excess or the debt that characterizes Dasein, distinct in that it is "always" and irreducibly outstanding: "The 'not-yet' which belongs to Dasein, however, is not just something which is provisionally and occasionally inaccessible to one's own experience or even to that of a stranger; it 'is' not yet 'actual' *at all.*"[25] Yet, Heidegger insists, Dasein *is* its not-yet, that is, relates to it, not as something that it will eventually be, but as something *towards* which it is turned, always and from the very start. In other words, Dasein unfolds or deploys its being on the basis of a possibility in excess of actuality, in excess of the traditional inscription of the category of possibility within the logic of *dynamis-energeia* or *potentialitas-actualitas.* As Heidegger himself puts it: "Higher than actuality is possibility." This possibility, which is irreducibly possible, and yet the reality of which is felt at every moment, this possibility which, while purely virtual, nonetheless presides over the being of Dasein as such, and thus over the very possibility of the disclosedness of things within a world, of truth, then, Heidegger calls *death*. As being towards its death, Dasein *is* indeed its death, yet in such a way that it never coincides with it. For the death of Dasein is always and irreducibly "to come" (*zu-künftig*):

> By the term 'futural,' we do not here have in view a "now" which has *not yet* become actual and which sometime *will be* for the first time. We have in view the coming [*Kunft*] in which Dasein, in its ownmost *Seinkönnen*, comes towards itself [but it comes towards itself from afar, from a distance, from ahead of itself, not towards itself as towards a goal lying ahead of itself]. Anticipation makes Dasein *authentically* futural, and in such a way that the anticipation itself is possible only insofar as Dasein, *insofar as it is*, is always coming towards itself—that is, insofar as it is futural in its being in general.[26]

Death is the future, the pure form of the future, for it is this future that will never be present. As such, however, that is, insofar as it is not a future present, it is already coming, approaching. It is the very figure of the approach, that which comes or which never ceases to arrive—the pure form of the event, not as an actuality, but as the happening of what approaches, that which comes forth from its standing before me and ahead of me; it is insofar as it thus stands before (*bevor steht*), and arrives from a distance, that it is always there, impending (*bevorstehend*). And it is in the very approaching of death that existence comes to be, that a world is opened up. The death that is to come is not something other than me, something external that happens to me; rather, it is the very happening of existence as such, the very limit from out of which existence unfolds as disclosedness, the very horizon, therefore, from out of which the world worlds. To grasp existence as this unfolding that happens from ahead, or from death itself, is to grasp the phenomenon of the world *as such and as a whole,* and not just innerworldy things (we shall see how this grasping takes place for Heidegger). Death is thus not just a peripheral event, an accident, something external that befalls Dasein; rather, death, as the end *towards* which existence ex-ists, is at once the very closure of existence (for it is "the possibility of the impossibility of existence") and the very beginning of existence, the key to the opening of existence as such, that is, to existence as opening or disclosure: disclosedness *to* being, to the world as a whole and as such, and *of* being, for it is through the ek-sisting of existence that "there is." Death, insofar as it reveals a pure possibility, and thus the realm of the future as the pure form of time (which Heidegger qualifies as ecstatic) in excess of the present, also bears witness to the ontological characterization of existence as *Seinkönnen*, that is, as this being whose being is primarily a power, a virtuality which is the very condition of possibility of its freedom. Paradoxically, then, Heidegger claims that man "can" be being, that it *is* in the mode of the can-be precisely and exclusively to the extent that he is mortal. It is the very finitude of time that is the condition of its power. If there is freedom, it is to the extent that existence exists towards death; freedom is primarily of and for being, a power to be (being).

This possibility is further defined in the following two ways. First, insofar as death is this pure possibility and the end or the ultimate possibility, it is also the uttermost possibility. As the ultimate and the most extreme possibility, it is the first possibility, the possibility of all possibilities, the unactualizable on the basis of which everything that is possible first becomes possible, on the basis of which the field of the possible as such — of the *Seinkönnen* — is first opened up. It is that through the unfolding of which the possible is first disclosed as such, and the future as the to come initially made possible; if man has a future, if there is the form of the future for man, if he is open to time and if time is open to him, if he coincides with the event of temporality, it is precisely insofar as his being is entirely turned towards death.

But — and this is the second characterization — this holds only insofar as death is not death *in abstracto* (the death which one can represent: the phenomenon of death for the biologist, the theologian or the anthropologist), or even death as the death of the Other, which can affect me more profoundly and painfully than anything else, but my own death — this possibility which is mine, irreducibly, and which cannot be passed on to anyone else, exchanged, negotiated, delayed. Because death is this possibility which is absolutely and irreducibly mine, because it is my ownmost possibility, it is the possibility in which ownness (*Eigentlichkeit*) as such is inscribed and at stake: what, for Heidegger, an "authentic" existence may be, what a "genuine" mode of being may look like is entirely based on the possibility of appropriating oneself as this being whose being consists in being towards its own end, that is, on the basis of itself, of that which individualizes or singularizes it absolutely. "Authenticity," for Heidegger, means nothing outside the possibility of appropriating what is most proper to oneself, of being or existing this possibility to the full. And resoluteness, as we shall see later on, is the phenomenon in which such a possibility is revealed. Death, then, is a power of singularization, a source of individuation. It is on the basis of death and as mortal that the "I" becomes meaningful and possible, that "I" make sense. If, in the context of *Being and Time*, a kind of subjectivity remains operative, it is on the basis of the thinking of death as this possibility that is ownmost. The "I" does not precede death; rather, the "I," as this singular "I," emerges from out of the individuating power of death. As we suggested earlier, the Heideggerian subjectivity is not so much a subjectivity of the "I think" as a subjectivity of the "I can"; yet this "can" has its source in the impending, ownmost, and uttermost end towards which existing constantly throws itself.

Anticipation

The question then becomes one of knowing just what sort of relation Dasein might establish with death thus understood. We must distinguish here the everyday and improper relation from the singular and proper relation that Dasein might establish with itself as with he/she who must die his/her own death, and from which the possibility of a singular self unfolds. Dasein *is* towards death. But it can be this being-towards-death either properly, in which case Dasein exists or is in such a way that this possibility explicitly comes to bear on the existence of Dasein, or improperly, in which case death is operative only implicitly, and Dasein does not hold it into view. This is where—if anywhere—ethics is first played out. Heidegger formulates it quite clearly in the lectures on Plato's *Sophist:*

> Insofar as man himself is the object of the ἀληθεύειν of φρόνησις, it must be characteristic of man that he is covered up to himself, does not see himself, such that he needs an explicit ἀ-ληθεύειν in order to become transparent to himself. . . . A person can be concerned with things of minor significance; he can be so wrapped up in himself that he does not genuinely see himself. Therefore he is ever in need of the salvation of φρόνησις.[27]

In *Being and Time* this phenomenon comes to be described as "fleeing":

> Proximally and for the most part, Dasein covers up its ownmost being-towards-death, *fleeing* in the face of it. Factically, Dasein is dying as long as it exists, but proximally and for the most part, it does so by way of falling.[28]

And so φρόνησις, or the proper way to be Dasein, that is, the mode of comportment in which ex-istence is made transparent to itself as such, will be a matter for Dasein of uncovering itself, of twisting free from its average coveredness. Because Dasein is always in the world, it tends to be absorbed in this world which, by and large, is the world of its concern. So, far from constituting a direct face-to-face relation with its own finitude, and with the operation of owning which follows from such an encounter, the average life of Dasein is a fleeing in the face of its ownmost being-towards-death into the familiar world of concern, the world in which existences are not envisaged and behave not as singularities but as interchangeable instances of a universal structure. I feel at home in that world, unaware of the fact that underlying this familiar relation to the world lurks the primordial uncanniness of the fact that there is a world as such and as a whole for Dasein, the primordial event of truth. This factical tendency to cover itself up testifies to the fact that Dasein is in untruth: its relation to truth, that is, to itself as disclosure, is itself untrue or covered up. In other words, Dasein does not exist on the basis of itself as disclosure, or, rather, does not exist itself as the originary operation of truth.

Of course, this does not mean that death plays no role whatsoever in the average, "fallen" life of Dasein. But there, death is precisely never mine. It is always the death of another. Not even that; it is the anonymous death of the One: "one dies," as if death were primarily this event that can be witnessed and verified empirically. Instead of embracing death as one's ownmost, as that which concerns me from the very start, instead of allowing one's mortality to come to the fore and to greet the anxiety which such welcoming provokes, average existence transforms "this anxiety into fear of an oncoming event" and then proceeds to tranquilize itself by way of narratives, myths, or simply by way of a prompt return to the life of concern.[29] Death, as the ownmost possibility towards which *I* am, is simply thus bypassed altogether.

But can Dasein understand its death authentically as well as inauthentically? Can it develop a proper relation to that which is most proper, to its ownmost possibility and mode of being? "Anticipation" (*Vorlaufen*) is the word that, according to Heidegger, captures this genuine relation. In anticipating death, it is neither a matter of running ahead towards one's death, of actualizing it (for, as pure possibility, it can never be actualized); nor is it a matter of thinking about death, of "brooding over it," or of developing a morbid relation to one's life in the expectancy of one's demise.[30] It has little to do, then, with a death drive, or with the demand to die the right death. Indeed, I would like to suggest that it is quite the opposite, that the holding in view of one's mortality amounts to an increase in one's life potential, in one's ability to open oneself to life, or to one's being as potentiality (*Seinkönnen*). To envisage oneself as mortal, to see oneself as this being whose being is essentially finite, is to learn not to die, but to live; it amounts to an intensification of life. To allow death to come to bear on life itself is not conducive to a morbid or a somber mood, it entails neither resignation nor passivity—in other words, it does not lead to a "sad" passion in Spinoza's sense of the term; rather, it is joyful and sober: "Along with the sober anxiety which brings us face to face with our singularized ability-to-be, there goes an unshakeable joy in this possibility."[31] Joy is not to be mistaken for this contentment which too often we identify with happiness; rather, it is the feeling linked to the increase and the "acting out" of our ontological power (our *Seinkönnen*). To anticipate one's death, to envisage oneself as mortal is to live oneself in the mode of anticipation, as this being which is itself (which is a self, singular and yet multiple, triply ecstatic) only by being ahead of itself and which, in returning to itself from beyond itself, ek-sists being. Such is the privilege and the joy of being human: to be able to be (being): *Sein-können*. And if there is a single Heideggerian injunction, it lies in the continuation of this *Können* into a *Sollen: Seinkönnen-sollen*, a having to be, or to act our own ability to be. Since one *can* be it, one *must* be it. This is tantamount to bringing it to the second power. To persevere in one's being is to be in truth, to be truth truly.

Death, then, is not the negation or the opposite of life, but the condition of its affirmation, the freeing of its potential. So, in anticipation, it is a question of comporting oneself to death as a possibility, and as a distinct possibility, in that it is a possibility of which we do not expect that it be actualized. And it is on the basis of the anticipation of this non-actualizable possibility that Dasein as such has the general structure of anticipation, or of pro-jection of itself into a realm of possibilities which themselves can be actualized, which are indeed projects in the ordinary sense of the term. Death is not a project, but the horizon from out of which Dasein projects itself and frees possibilities for itself, frees itself as freedom for this or that possibility, this or that future. It is with "anticipation" that Dasein reveals itself to itself fully, that is, becomes transparent to its own being as the fundamental and originary operation of truth whence things appear in truth, disclosed in this or that way:

> Being-towards-death is the anticipation of a power-to-be on the part of that being whose kind of being is anticipation itself. In the anticipatory revealing of this power-to-be, Dasein discloses itself to itself as regards its uttermost possibility. But to project itself on its ownmost power-to-be means to be able to understand itself in the being of the being so revealed — namely, to exist. Anticipation turns out to be the possibility of understanding one's *ownmost* and uttermost power-to-be — that is, the possibility of authentic existence.[32]

What anticipation does, then, is to shift the focus from the result of the operation of truth — the disclosedness of things with the world — to the very operation of truth, that is, to the ecstatic clearing whereby things are made manifest. Such is the reason why Heidegger insists that "authenticity" is merely a "modification" of Dasein's being: it does not amount to a change of Dasein's being, but to a different way of being this being, that is, no longer on the basis of its lostness or alienation within the anonymity of the One, but on the basis of itself as this absolutely singular disclosedness, as the happening of truth. In and through anticipation, then, Dasein is revealed to itself in truth, as truth. And so, in thus relating itself to its own self, in becoming itself through the appropriation of that which is most proper to it, that which constitutes it as Da-sein or as the being that "is" or ek-sists being, existence exists more existingly. By existing differently, that is, by existing explicitly the ground or the origin from out of which existence exists, man exists more intensely; for now it is existence itself that is existed, it is the very disclosedness that characterizes existence which becomes the explicit possibility of existence. But to exist more authentically naturally means to be in the world more authentically, to be turned back into the world, returned to the world on the basis of one's ownness; it is thus to relate to oneself, to the world, and to others again and anew; it is a repetition of that which always and already is, but which, through this repetition, always already comes to be differently.[33] Heidegger does not venture into any detail concerning what this proper mode of relation to the world and others would be. Perhaps such a description did not belong in the analysis of existence as the average or everyday existence. But if there is an ethics that follows from the existential-ontological description, this is where it begins: at the point where, returning from itself as this self which is the site of truth, as this self which discloses on the basis of a radical and inescapable finitude, Dasein turns back to the world and to others in a way that no longer resembles the kind of relation that prevails in the One: "As the non-relational possibility, death individualizes—but only in such a manner that, as the possibility which is not to be outstripped, it makes Dasein, as being-with, have some understanding of the *Seinkönnen* of Others."[34] Solicitude takes on a different form; language becomes more discrete, almost silent (*Verschwiegenheit*);[35] the ordinary, manipulable relation to the world as the world of things there for me is suspended. Existence is now held in view as the ecstatic happening of truth, and one's being as being-towards-death is allowed to bear on how we see the world. And the look onto the world has shifted. It is no longer the technical look that guides the handling of things and practical affairs, but the more hesitant and altogether briefer glance, in which existence catches a glimpse of itself. To anticipate is to see oneself as such, or as existence, from the very limit of existence: it is to see oneself come or arrive from a distance, to see oneself approaching, and, in this approach, to witness the birth of the world, the burgeoning of being. For death is indeed there, absolutely real and yet entirely virtual, purely possible, and it is the presence of death that presides over the birth of the world and grants it value and intensity. It is by pressing against the present that death is able to inject it with a sense of fragility and urgency, thus turning it into a moment that matters, wresting it from evanescence and the destructive flow of time. By pressing against the today, as if the today were without tomorrow, death transforms the contingent into a necessity. It is no longer just I who is finite but the world as such, this world from which I cannot dissociate myself: this landscape, this love, this friend, or this smell—all are here as if for the last time. Death clarifies and brings all things into their proper light. In its wake, the false problems tend to vanish, and only the most salient points of existence remain.

34

In anticipation, existence frees itself *for* its own death, and this means for itself. It becomes free—free for its own freedom, free to *be* its own freedom. Its world is freed anew, and so are the possibilities contained therein. For existence has now "liberated" itself from its lostness in those possibilities which normally thrust themselves accidentally over it; and "one is liberated in such a way that *for the first time* one can authentically understand and choose among the factical possibilities lying ahead of that possibility which is not to be outstripped."[36] This liberation is a release, the release of a power or a potential linked to a giving up of itself as an absorbed self: to anticipate, in the case of a possibility which is irreducibly so, does not mean to intend in the traditional phenomeno-logical sense; it does not mean to expect, to look forward to; it does not reveal a certain impatience; for that which is coming is not something present-at-hand. It is something that exceeds the form of the present altogether. For what is coming is Dasein itself, the event or the happen-ing of truth: a reversed intentionality, in which the I is summoned and comes to be as such on the basis of something that happens to it. And to comport oneself to truth does not mean to await or expect; it means to hand oneself over to it. "Anticipation reveals to Dasein its lostness in the One-self, and brings it face to face with the possibility of being itself, pri-marily unsupported by concernful solicitude, but of being itself, rather, in an impassioned freedom towards death—a freedom which has been released from the illusions of the 'One.'"[37]

Resolve

The phenomenon that designates the operation through which exist-ence decides itself for its own being, for itself as singular existence, Heidegger calls *Entschlossenheit*.[38] To be resolute amounts to nothing other than to a mode of being, in which one is, or rather *I* am, necessar-ily and unavoidably, open to my own disclosedness: it amounts to living at the tip of existence, at its extremity, where it gathers itself and "is" truly, where its power is most visible and most penetrating. Thus, exist-ence is itself sharpened to a point, its extremity both at the end and at the beginning. It is an arrow thrown into the free space of being, which it discloses as it penetrates it. And so "resoluteness" amounts to nothing other than a sharpening of existence, as a result of which existence becomes more incisive, penetrates deeper into its own capacity and power to be, deeper into the flesh of being. If Dasein, as being-in-the-world, designates man's relation to being, resoluteness, in turn, desig-nates the operation through which one, or rather, *I*—but it is in that very operation that *one* is turned into an *I*—resolve myself for this rela-tion to being which Dasein always and necessarily is. It is therefore a double relation: a relation to one's relation to being. In this relation, which is not a relation to something other, or even a new relation, but a relation to that which, in and of itself, is always in relation, and thus a relation of relation, existence is as it were doubled, or repeated. It is re-entered and affirmed as such. And thus re-entered, it comes *properly* to be. What is being re-entered there is not the everyday existence, not the anonymous existence that is oblivious of itself, but existence as such, the existing of existence. This existence is thus at once the same and an other. It is the same, insofar as it is existence as such, and not this or that existent that is in question. And yet it is other, insofar as, in repeating itself, existence repeats only its own disclosedness as existence, only this very disclosing which it *is*. In this repetition, existence is brought to another power, for it has freed for itself its own (ontological) power. It has freed within itself this power which it has and is, this power of being or existing being as such.

Thus, existence is resolute when, turning back on itself *as* disclosedness, it decides itself in favor of existence, and thus lives its relation to the world, to others and to itself in the mode of singularity. So, far from designating a withdrawal into some pure interiority, in which *I* would no longer be concerned with others and with the world as such, resoluteness signifies a different way of being in the world, a way that is an essential modification of our everyday way of being in the world, and in which something like an "I," something like a first person singular, first becomes possible. And insofar as this way of being takes its point of departure in Dasein's ownmost power to be, it also designates the possibility of a proper or authentic relation to others, of a solicitude which is genuine insofar as it is itself centered around the ownmost possibility of who one is relating to:

> Resoluteness, as *authentic being-one's-self*, does not detach Dasein from its world, nor does it isolate it so that it becomes a free-floating "I." And how should it, when resoluteness as authentic disclosedness, is *authentically* nothing else than *being-in-the-world?* Resoluteness brings the Self right into its current concernful being-alongside what is ready-to-hand, and pushes it into solicitous being with Others. . . . When Dasein is resolute, it can become the 'conscience' of Others. Only by authentically being-their-Selves in resoluteness can people authentically be with one another—not by ambiguous and jealous stipulations and talkative fraternizing in the "One" and in what "One" wants to undertake.[39]

To the being-together of everyday existence, in which one forgets oneself as singularity and lives according to the mode of the empty majority, we thus need to oppose the community of singularities, the *being*-together of which would precisely be the meaning of existence as such, the community of mortal, factical existents.

The Augenblick

Yet resoluteness, as the specific mode of being in which the very being of Dasein is held in view, or as the doubling of existence in which existence comes to be as singularity, also and primarily defines a mode of temporalizing. Let us not forget that the operation of truth or clearing with which Dasein coincides (and it is as such, i.e., as clearing, that it is Dasein) is a function of the meaning of the being of Dasein as "ecstatic" or "rapturous" temporality. Like every instance or mode of truth, then, resoluteness clears a space and opens up a present from out of an originary and twofold throw: the pro-jected future of Dasein that approaches from the death of Dasein as its ownmost and uttermost possibility; the thrownness of Dasein, in which Dasein finds itself as the being that has always already been, and that has no other choice than to be this beenness so long as it is. Thus, from this twofold throw, and like every other mode of truth, resoluteness marks a site, a spatial and temporal clearing which is experienced and seen as presence in the present: resoluteness is a way of being "there," present to the world and to oneself.

But what present is opened up in resoluteness? How is Dasein *there* when resolute? The term that Heidegger reserves to designate the present of resolute Dasein is *Augenblick:* when resolute, Dasein is there in the "moment." Now, the present or the time which is thus opened up is to be radically distinguished from the present of this or that particular situation. It is to be distinguished from the kind of present that is linked to a punctual and practical situation, in other words, from the mostly "concerned" and "absorbed" present of our everyday life, the present of needs and ordinary dealings with the world. Furthermore, it is also to be distinguished from the abstract present (the "now") of the theoretical attitude, which we now unquestioningly consider to be the very form of the present, unaware of the spatial, and specifically linear, understanding of time such an attitude presupposes, the ontological-existential ground of which can be traced back to the ordinary or fallen nature of our relation to the world in everyday life. Rather, the present that is at issue in the "moment" is that present in which existence is present to itself as the very operation of disclosure, or as the very *there* of being. In the moment of vision, or the *Augen-blick,* Dasein "brings itself before itself":[40] it *sees* itself for the first time for what it is, that is, for the originary clearing, the truth or the "there" of being. Thus, the moment is not linked to the disclosure of a particular situation, but to the disclosure of situatedness as such. It is the present or the time of truth's disclosedness to itself as the originary event of being. As such, the *Augenblick* designates a different relation to time and to the present in general: it marks at once a rupture or a caesura (*Gebrochenheit*) in the continuum and the fascination of "fallen" time, and a return to the essence of time as ecstatic and rapturous, as finite and horizonal. This, then, does not mean that the moment marks the possibility of a flight from time into eternity.[41] On the contrary: it means that existence becomes *all the more* open to the world and to the situation in the essential modification that takes place in resoluteness. For the situation is now disclosed from out of Dasein's disclosedness to itself as originary disclosure:

> When resolute, Dasein has brought itself back from falling, and has done so precisely in order to be 'there' in the moment all the more authentically for the situation which has been disclosed.[42]

A few pages further down, Heidegger adds the following:

> That *present* which is held in authentic temporality and which thus is authentic itself, we call the *"moment."* . . . The moment is a phenomenon which in principle can not be clarified in terms of the "now." The "now" is a temporal phenomenon which belongs to time as within-time-ness: the "now" 'in which' something arises, passes away, or is present-at-hand. 'In the moment' nothing can occur; but as the authentic present [*als eigentliche Gegen-wart*], the moment makes it possible to encounter for the first time [*läßt er erst begegnen*] what can be 'in a time' as something at hand or objectively present.[43]

Nothing occurs *in* the moment: no single thing, no concrete situation, but the sheer power of occurrence which Dasein itself is. In the moment, time itself occurs as the suspension of the impersonal, anonymous, and objective dimension within which things, events, and situations are believed to take place. For these, as things to be handled or as objects to be contemplated, are first encountered from out of the event of time itself, which presents itself in the moment. Unlike the "now," as the empty form within which events and facts take place, the moment marks the very advent or gathering of time, the fold at which and within which past and future are folded into one another, thus transforming the present into a site of intensity, such that Dasein re-enters the world or repeats its own existential facticity with a renewed and heightened sense of itself as the power, and thus also the freedom to be (being), as the power and the freedom of being itself:

> Dasein is not something present at hand alongside other things, but is set in the midst of beings through the manifestness of the full temporal horizon. As Dasein it always already maintains itself in this threefold perspective. As that which rests in time it only is what it can be if in each case at its time — and that simultaneously means in each case here and now, with reference to these beings that are precisely thus manifest — it is there, that is, opens itself up in its manifestness, that is, resolutely discloses itself. Only in the resolute self-disclosure of Dasein itself, in the moment of vision, does it make use of that which properly makes it possible, namely time as the moment of vision itself.[44]

In resoluteness, existence liberates itself from its own entrapment in the absorbed life of everydayness. It frees itself for itself, as this ability to be or disclose being. Thus, the modification or conversion brought about by resolute disclosedness is also at the source of a renewed understanding of what it means to *act*, of the very possibility of action in the most essential sense, and, yes, of what I would be tempted to call, albeit under erasure perhaps, the very possibility and beginning of ethics: "The moment of vision is nothing other than the *look of resolute disclosedness [Blick der Entschlossenheit]* in which the full situation of an action opens itself and keeps itself open."[45] Thus, in the moment, Dasein has an eye for action in the most essential sense, insofar as the moment of vision is what makes Dasein possible as Da-sein. It is to this that man *must* resolutely disclose itself. Man must first create "for himself *once again* [my emphasis] a genuine knowing concerning that wherein whatever makes Dasein itself possible consists." And this, Heidegger tells us, is the "fact that the moment of vision in which Dasein brings itself before itself as that which is properly binding must time and again stand before Dasein as such."[46] Thus, in the moment of vision, existence resolves itself to itself, to itself as Da-sein, thus allowing it to become free for the first time—free not to *do* this or that, at least not primarily, but free to be its own being, free to *be* in the most intense and generous sense, that is, free to be for its own freedom or its own ability to be. Thus, "the moment of vision must be understood, and that means seized upon [*ergriffen*], as the *innermost necessity of the freedom of Dasein*."[47] And this, Heidegger adds, is tantamount to "liberating the humanity in man, to liberating the humanity of man, that is, the *essence* of man, *to letting the Dasein in him become essential*."[48] With resoluteness, then, as the mode of disclosedness in which Dasein is presented to itself according to its essence, that is, as this power and freedom to be, are we not also de facto presented with the essence and the possibility of action? In light of a possibility of existence itself, in which existence grasps itself as pure possibility, does action, and the demand to act in a certain way, or rather, the kind of demand that can be made of Dasein so that it will activate its ownmost and uttermost ontological potential, come to be redefined radically? With Heidegger, can we not begin to articulate an ethics that would be not of alterity but an ethics of the self (which does not mean an ethics of selfishness), or of the essence of man as power and freedom to act being? Is this not what Heidegger suggests when he writes that

> As resolute, Dasein is already *acting* [*Als entschlossenes* handelt *das Dasein schon*]. However, the term 'acting' [*Handeln*] is one which we are purposely avoiding. For in the first place this term must be taken so broadly that "activity" [*Aktivität*] will also embrace the passivity of resistance. In the second place, it suggests a misunderstanding in the ontology of Dasein, as if resoluteness were a special way of behaviour belonging to the practical fac-

ulty as contrasted with one that is theoretical. Care, however, as concernful solicitude, so primordially and wholly envelops Dasein's being that it must already be presupposed as a whole when we distinguish between theoretical and practical behaviour; it cannot first be built up out of these faculties by a dialectic which, because it is existentially ungrounded, is necessarily quite baseless. *Resoluteness, however, is only the possible authenticity of care itself, that is, the authenticity which, in care, and as care, is the object of care itself.*[49]

Thus, were it not for the classical opposition between theory and praxis, were it not for the way in which praxis and ethics are traditionally understood in opposition to thought, as action in opposition to contemplation, resoluteness could come to designate the origin of proper action and thus to delimit the sphere of ethics itself. Were it not that the very operation whereby existence as such, or care, becomes the very concern of care itself, simply takes place before any distinction can be made between the theoretical and the practical, between thought and action, resoluteness could indeed be seen as the movement that opens existence to itself as to the site or the place of its singularity, as to its *proper* place. And so, despite Heidegger's warnings in *Being and Time*, but still keeping them in mind, let me reactivate the old, Aristotelian word of φρόνησις (prudence) to designate the mode of disclosedness in which Dasein comes face to face with itself as the site or the truth of being: at that moment, the ἀληθεύειν and the ἀληθεύων, the disclosing and the disclosed, coincide absolutely, in what amounts to a doubling of truth. And we shall also offer to reactivate the ancient and noble word "ethics" to designate the kind of relation—to others: to the world, to men, to things, and to Dasein itself—that characterizes the man of prudence thus redefined. But this, of course, as we now know from the 1924–25 lectures on Plato's *Sophist*, is something that Heidegger himself suggested, in an effort to translate Aristotle's analyses concerning πράξις, φρόνησις, and βούλευσις back into their existential-ontological ground. In that text, which in many respects announces and provides a context for the analysis of *Entschlossenheit* in *Being and Time*, Heidegger suggests that the ἀληθεύειν or the mode of truth that is at stake in φρόνησις involves the being of Dasein itself: it is an ἀληθεύειν where the human Dasein tries to wrest itself from its own coveredness, tries to become transparent to itself through a constant struggle against its tendency to cover itself over. For, Heidegger argues, the human Dasein is for the most part concealed to itself in its proper being. It is so wrapped up in itself that it cannot even "see" itself for who it is. And so it must learn to *see*. This apprenticeship in seeing its own being, and in *being* it in the right and proper way, is what φρόνησις is all about: it is primarily a matter of seeing through, and thus of clarity (*Durchsichtigkeit*), and, subsequently, of consideration (*Rücksicht*).[50] It is only as phronetic or prudent that man can act accordingly, for only thus is the situation fully disclosed to him. And action itself, which, according to Aristotle, is the ultimate goal of the process of deliberation (βουλεύεσθαι) that characterizes the prudent man, presupposes this seeing as guiding the right and proper way to be Dasein. It is this seeing (also characterized as an *Erblicken* and a *Blick des Auges*, a "catching sight" and a "blink of the eye") in which Dasein catches sight of the momentary situation and decides or resolves itself (the Aristotelian βουλή is translated as *Entschluß*) for it on the basis of itself. All of this happens in a moment, in the blink of the eye that defines the moment, the time of action and ethics, and which Aristotle is careful to distinguish from the time of those beings that are forever, the time of eternity:

> Φρόνησις is the inspection of the this here now, the inspection of the concrete momentariness of the transient situation. As αἴσθησις, it is the blink of the eye [*der Blick des Auges*], the momentary look [*der Augen-blick*], a momentary look at what is momentarily concrete, which as such can always be otherwise. On the other hand, the νοεῖν in σοφία is a looking upon that which is ἀεί, that which is always present in sameness. Time (the momentary and the eternal) here functions to discriminate between the νοεῖν in φρόνησις and the one in σοφία.[51]

Thus, in Heidegger, there will have always been a place for ethics, a space for the properly human time of action and decision, as the fragile and always threatened time within which man lives. There will have always been a place for the affirmation and the enacting of man's essence as the ecstatic disclosedness to the truth of being. There will have always been a place on earth for man as the mortal, and, for that very reason, the most alive of all beings. Indeed, ethics no longer gestures towards a morality of good and evil, of the will as a capacity to choose between good and evil, or even as the ability to obey a law as the universal law of reason. Freedom is entirely disconnected from the will here, and rearticulated along the lines of an ontological power, which we always already are, and which can nonetheless be related to in such a way that it is increased, in such a way that it amounts to a general increase of one's beings as this *power to be* (being).

Homo Theoreticus

> Man himself has become more enigmatic for us. We ask
> anew: What is man? A transition, a direction, a storm
> sweeping over our planet, a recurrence, or a vexation for
> the gods? We do not know. Yet we have seen that in the
> essence of this mysterious being, philosophy happens.[52]

Heidegger's entire effort as regards philosophy will have been to return thought to the world whence it unfolds, to wrest it from the dangers of abstraction, or objective representation, and to return it to life. In other words, Heidegger's effort can be seen as turning philosophy into a vital activity once again, that is, as an activity in which the life or the fate of man as such and as a whole is at issue. It will have been, for Heidegger, a matter of taking philosophy seriously to the point where it becomes something extreme, absolutely singular:

> Philosophy—as we are presumably superficially aware—is not some arbitrary enterprise with which we pass our time as the fancy takes us, not some mere gathering of knowledge that we can easily obtain for ourselves at any time from books, but (we know this only obscurely) something to do with the whole, something extreme, in which an ultimate confrontation and dialogue takes place for man [*worin eine letzte Aussprache und Zwiesprache des Menschen geschieht*].[53]

Philosophy is thus engaged in an extreme and intense activity, in that, in it, what is at issue is the whole of what is: not just this or that being, or even this or that region of being, but being as such, and the very being of he or she who philosophizes. And if, Heidegger tells us, the Greeks came to value philosophy to the extent that we know, it is because, for them, the philosophical attitude meant this ability to dwell amid things as amid a meaningful totality, this extraordinary capacity to be in the world in such a way that the world itself could become an issue for man. More even: the Greeks understood that the very fate of man, what "man" meant and was capable of, was entirely a function of the way in which man would be affected by, and relate to, the whole of that which is. From then on, what the Greeks called φιλοσοφία, or θεωρία, had nothing to do with a pleasant and intellectually sophisticated form of leisurely activity. It was activity in the strongest and most noble sense. In an attempt to clarify the meaning of the Greek concept of θεωρία, Heidegger writes the following:

> But what is θεωρία for the Greeks? It is said that it is pure contemplation, which remains bound only to its object in its fullness and in its demands. The Greeks are invoked to support the claim that this contemplative behavior is supposed to occur for its own sake. But this claim is incorrect. For, on the hand, 'theory' does not happen for its own sake; it happens only as a result of the *passion* [my emphasis] to remain close to what is as such and to be beset by it. On the other hand, however, the Greeks struggled to understand and carry out this contemplative questioning as a—indeed as *the*—highest mode of man's ἐνέργεια, of man's 'being at work.' It was not their wish to bring practice into line with theory, but the other way around: to understand theory as the supreme realization of genuine practice.[54]

In repeating the Greeks—which Heidegger did in an idiosyncratic and truly original way—his aim was to return philosophy to its ancient nobility, to reactivate the sense of urgency and the passion linked to genuine philosophical questioning. But in what does this genuine questioning consist? In nothing other than a desire and an ability to open oneself and one's thought to the manifestness or the truth of being, to relate to the world in such a way that it comes to be recognized as the place of our dwelling. In other words, it consists in opening oneself to this world not as the world that stands opposite me, but as this world which I myself *am*, as this living fabric whose threads are ontological. Could one ever dream a more perfect life than the one engaged in that activity? Is it surprising, Heidegger asks, that Aristotle reserved the word εὐδαιμονία, or happiness, for the sort of attitude that would bring us infinitely close to the ever renewed and forever original epiphany of being?[55] "Everyone agrees," Heidegger writes in his 1924–25 lecture, that "the purest joy comes from being present to beings κατὰ τὰν σοφίαν,"[56] that is, according to thought. This "pure abiding-with," this "pure presence-to," Heidegger adds immediately, "is in itself the purest disposition."[57] It is primarily in this that Heidegger is Greek: in his concern to *live* philosophy as the most decisive and most extreme type of existence, that is, as the type of existence in which existence as such and as a whole is at issue and at stake. Philosophy, then, far from constituting an activity of disembodied contemplation oriented towards eternal substances, far from designating the operation of a faculty of a subject disconnected from the world and from things within it, marks a distinct possibility of existence, that is, a distinct way of being in which things and the world as such and as a whole come to be revealed as disclosed entities, and existence itself as the very operation of truth whereby such entities are disclosed. As Heidegger puts it concisely in the opening page of the "Letter on Humanism": "Thinking accomplishes the relation of being to the essence of man."[58] We should not be surprised, then, to see him reintroduce the word "ethics" to qualify the type of existence engaged in "theory," even if, in the following passage, he has not yet taken his distance from Aristotle with respect to the question concerning the metaphysical meaning of being as presence:

> For the Greeks the consideration of human existence was oriented purely toward the meaning of being itself, i.e., toward the extent to which it is possible for human Dasein to be everlasting. The Greeks gathered this meaning of being, being as absolute presence, from the being of the world. Accordingly, one cannot force Greek ethics into the mode of questioning of modern ethics, i.e., into the alternative of an ethics of consequences or an ethics of intentions. Dasein was seen simply there with regard to its possibility of being as such, whereby neither intentions nor practical consequences play any role. Even the expression ἦθος corresponds to this conception of the being of man; ἦθος means comportment, the proper way of being.[59]

It is this ancient, ontological sense of ethics that Heidegger is concerned to reawaken, or perhaps simply to awaken, if it is true that his understanding of "the Greeks" is primarily inspired by a highly personal and free interpretation of the words ἦθος and ἠθικός, whether in the context of Aristotle's *Nicomachean Ethics* or Heraclitus's ἦθος ἀνθρώπῳ δαίμων.[60] So what begins by way of a reading of Aristotle continues to develop throughout an entire trajectory: Heidegger will remain absolutely committed to the idea according to which the philosophical life, as the life open to the truth of being as such, is the highest and most intense of all possible lives, the truly ethical and active life (the life that *acts* the essence of man):

> If the name "ethics," in keeping with the basic meaning of the word ἦθος, should now say that "ethics" ponders the abode of man, then that thinking which thinks the truth of being as the primordial element of man, as one who ek-sists, is in itself originary ethics.[61]

I shall now try to show in greater detail how philosophy can be seen as *acting* in the most essential sense, or, to repeat Heidegger's own words, as *originary ethics*. For Heidegger, philosophy will have never been anything other than the question concerning being, whether that question bears on the "meaning," the "truth," the "history," or the "event" of being. Yet if being is a question, in other words, if there is philosophy, it is simply because being is always at issue for us. In our very being, being itself is at issue for us. Only because always and from the start is it at issue can it become an *explicit* issue, and indeed the decisive and uttermost issue. In other words, the "question" of being, as the question that belongs to philosophy most properly, is itself only a "response," an explicit and conceptual thematization of something which, from the start and always, is at issue — and in such a way that this question is not a problem constituted by a pregiven faculty of intellection, but by our very being: it is a possibility or a modality of existence, a *Seinkönnen*, that is, a way — and indeed the supreme way — for us of being (our) being. Thus, we could say, in what amounts to a reversal of the Cartesian *cogito*, that it is insofar as man ek-sists that man thinks. For to ek-sist means: to stand in the Open as such and as a whole, to abide by beings and dwell amid their presence. And thinking is one such way of standing in the Open, one way of being open. Thought is not an absolute point of departure, then, the origin of the question, but already a response, a response to the call of being, or to the fact that man is situated beyond all beings, as this or that being, and thrown in the openness of being. Thus, it is on the basis of man's ek-sistence, on the basis of his transcendence, which amounts to a specific stance, that something becomes an issue, that something becomes question-worthy (*fragwürdig*).

Were it simply for beings, and not for being as such, there would be no question, no problem. For there would be no ground on which to question, to reach this position of wonder (the ancient θαυμάζειν) with which philosophy proper begins. Yet insofar as man is always granted with more than just beings, insofar as man is from the start open to something in excess of beings and of himself, and yet a something that is neither a thing nor a supreme and superior being but being or truth as such, questioning can arise. The ability to question, and, correlatively, to think, does not arise from the fact that man possesses a faculty of intellection and representation (we already saw how *intelligere* or *comprehension* arises prior to any such theorizing, through the very existing of existence), but from the fact that there is something in question, and in such a way that this being in question emerges from out of the very existing of existence, and to such an extent that existence itself is called upon and called into question. Thus, to philosophize, or to create concepts, man first needs to be seized and gripped, as if by the throat. Existence, as the very "there" or truth of being, takes hold of you, grabs you and grips you, and concepts are like the thoughts which one spits out under the repeated attacks (*Angriffe*) of the bare fact of existence. Philosophy is born out of the assault of existence, and concepts are fragments of being itself:

> Philosophy is the opposite of all comfort and intensity. It is turbulence, the turbulence into which man is spun, so as in this way alone to comprehend existence without delusion.[62]

And some two pages further down, Heidegger adds the following:

> In the philosophical concept [*Begriff*], man, and indeed man as a whole, is in the grip of an attack [*Angriff*] — driven out of everydayness and driven back into the ground of things. Yet the attacker [*Angreifer*] is not man, the dubious subject of the everyday and of the bliss of knowledge. Rather, in philosophizing the Dasein in man launches the attack upon man. Thus man in the ground of his essence is someone in the grip of an attack, attacked by the fact 'that he is what he is', and caught up in all comprehending questioning.[63]

If there is the very form of the question, then, it is because man, in his very being, is called into question, summoned by something other than himself, yet something which is neither exterior nor superior to him (the alterity of the Other or of God), but co-extensive: man is folded into being, and being into man, both are one yet distinct—and it is in this fold, in this coming-together of man and being that thought takes place. It is through this opening or this fold that man is able to see further. If man looks afar, his gaze turned to the horizon, it is because his being unfolds at and from the horizon. It is from out of this horizon, and on its very surface, that man thinks, questions, philosophizes; not from within himself, or from some part of his physical body. Thinking is from the start cosmic, terrestrial, and nomadic. From the very start, man is already "there," in what amounts to a nomadism more nomadic than any journey, and thinking emerges in a movement of return to the things and beings from out of this horizon. It is insofar as existence always stands beyond beings, and beyond itself as the sheer immanence within beings; it is insofar as, for existence, to be means something more and other than to be just this individual being, namely, to be being as such; in other words, it is insofar as, for existence, this difference is always at stake, and insofar as, qua existence, it stands within this space or this split—that there is philosophy, or meta-physics in the literal and proper sense.

In and through thought, then, man testifies explicitly and thematically to the fact that, for him, there is more to being (human) than relating to beings; through thought, man testifies to the excess to which he is open from the start and in the openness of which he finds his place and his stance. What characterizes thought, then, is the ability to open itself to the ontological difference as such, to relate to this difference qua difference, that is, in such a way that the difference as such becomes the explicit object of the relation. Of course, in resolute disclosedness (in praxis), or even in its everyday absorption in the world, Dasein presupposes and understands the ontological difference. Whether proper or improper, Dasein's relation to the world and to its own being takes place within the temporal operation of truth. But only with thought—to which, starting in the 1930s, Heidegger will add poetry and art—does this operation become explicitly articulated, be brought to language or to work into the work, or the poem. Only with thought does the ontological difference, or the fold of being, come to the fore as such. Only with thought is Dasein brought back into the realm of its essence, thus becoming who it is: "It is philosophy which, in a concealed way for the most part, lets Da-sein first become what it can be."[64]

To exist, as I have repeatedly suggested, is to be open to being, or to the truth of being. Existence is nothing other than this opening, this gaping. Yet in thought, existence exists this opening in a way that is quite distinct, inasmuch as thought, like art perhaps, is not only *of* being, but also *for* being. In thought, man stands within being and holds onto being, in such a way that his belonging to and together with being becomes the explicit task of his being. Thinking remains a task in which my being, as well as the constellation man-being, is at stake. Thought alone, with art perhaps, inherits the becoming of this co-respondence and is responsible for it. In thought, the very destiny or becoming of man is at stake. If there is a question concerning being, or concerning the meaning or the truth of being, it is because, in our very being, being itself is in question; yet being itself can be in question only insofar as we are open to being, insofar as we are nothing other than this opening to being. In other words, what calls for thinking, what provokes thought, is the very fact of being, brute being, through which thought "can be" being; it is the fact that man, open to more than just this or that being, encounters beings from out of this excess which, because it exceeds him, whilepassing through him and traversing him, never becomes an object of knowledge and is never turned into a familiar relation. It is because, ultimately, man is in the world in a way that is never quite familiar, because he inhabits the world in a way quite different from a pilot aboard his ship, that he can wonder about the world, about the fact that there is a world, or that there is the "there is"—in other words, that he can think. It is not so much man who thinks as being that thinks in him. Only when thought frees itself from the grip of "knowledge," which always pushes thought to represent the world, and returns to existence as to the ground whence it unfolds can it designate this mystery according to which the difference or the gap that separates being from beings, while bringing them together, comes to language. It is there, in existence (Da-sein), that thought is being born. This is where it dwells. To think is to dwell, but in such a way that the operation of dwelling coincides absolutely with the dwelling as ek-sistence. Thought has nothing to do with representation (and this includes science) or with knowledge, for these forget that thought is incarnate and cosmic, that truth is carnal and of the world, and that the world itself, before it can be envisaged as surface, inert presence, and availability, is lived and alive with the rays of being. Thinking thinks insofar as it expresses life and thinks the world, and not just this other abstraction, the "I," with its ideas and its tranquil atomism. "I think, I am": it is not insofar as I think that I exist. Rather, in thought, this existing being which I am is redoubled, elevated to another power of existence:

> Plato says in one of his major dialogues[65] that the difference between the philosophizing human being and the one who is not philosophizing is the difference between being awake (ὕπαρ) and sleeping (ὄναρ). The non-philosophizing human being, including the scientific human being, does indeed exist, but he or she is asleep.[66]

Why does—should—one philosophize? Simply—but this simplicity is the work of a lifetime—"in order once again to 'see' all things more simply, more vividly, and in a more sustained manner."[67] Philosophy, for Heidegger, will have never been anything other than this awakening to the unfamiliar and literally extraordinary event of being, other than this ability to dwell amid things and others as if in the midst of this ever renewed epiphany.

PART II. HISTORY AND POLITICS

2

The Politics of Repetition

Under the authority of difference, a certain philosophical discourse seems to have taken hold of our time and marked our century in a way that no other has. Or is it that our time itself has deposited its essence in this discourse of difference—whether as fracture, fissure, rift, fold, or caesura? Yet difference, one might wish to retort, was not born yesterday, and philosophy did not wait for the sunderings and the wounds of this century to attribute it a place. But the question is precisely that of the place or the space which philosophy chose to attribute to difference. For if difference must be attributed a place within thought, where would such a place come from, if not from some primordial identity, the identity of thought itself? As soon as it becomes a question of making room for difference, or of attributing a place to it, is difference not already subordinated to a regulative principle, the ultimate horizon of which is identity? Is difference really at home in this thought? Or is it not rather from out of a primordial and irreducible difference, as well as from out of the space broached by such a difference, that thought itself comes to be determined, finds its own place and unfolds? If to philosophize after Hegel means something for us, it is as a result of this question concerning the possibility of thinking difference without the logical priority of identity. Will difference ever be thought prior to, outside, or independently of identity, or will it always be forced to reintegrate the ineluctable of what it itself calls its "principle"? If, in a way, we all come after Hegel, it is as the inheritors of a difference that is perfectly integrated, and of a content, or a thought, that is wholly differentiated. With Hegel, difference is absolutized, which means, precisely, ab-solved from its *mere* or immediate opposition to identity, in which it finds its truth, and which is itself infinitized in the very process whereby it reveals itself as *differentiated* identity, or as the identity that posits itself through its being op-posed to the self-positing of an other, which is *its* other. With Hegel, then, difference becomes the very way in which identity comes to constitute itself, the very way in which the content relates itself to itself and constitutes itself in the movement of opposition to itself. In other words, difference is opposition, and identity is self-differentiated. I do not wish, here and now, to sketch the characteristic features of that discourse which, having fully estimated the magnitude of this inheritance, attempts to develop a thinking of difference for itself, that is, a thinking wrested from the soil and the roots of Sameness. An abyssal discourse, I might add, since it ventures the reversal of a philosophical practice that goes back to Plato and that continues to nourish our thought, our knowledge, our institutions, our code, and our systems. To speak of this discourse in the singular is already to betray it, given the multiplicity and the variety of paths that it clears. Such diversity constitutes a further reason not to address it here and now.[1]

Yet if I mention such discourses—to which one could attach the names of Nietzsche, Derrida, or Deleuze—it is only with a view to singling out one aspect or question that seems to run through them all, insistently and obsessively, one theme that seems indissociable from the question of difference. This aspect, perhaps most thoroughly exhibited by Deleuze, yet also strongly emphasized by Derrida, is defined as repetition, recurrence, or iterability. Yet I would like to suggest that this complicity between the concepts of difference and repetition are already at work, albeit more implicitly, in the work of Heidegger, and specifically of the "early" Heidegger. And so the question with which I shall be concerned in this chapter is the following: To what extent does the thinking of the ontological difference command a renewed interpretation of repetition? To what extent does repetition itself open onto a difference that does not presuppose the constitution of any sphere of identity?

Repetition and the Ontological Difference

Philosophy's fundamental and only constitutive question is that of the being of beings, and of the decisive, yet unrecognized, difference between being and beings. If being is not in the way of a being, then what is its mode of being? To what extent can we say that being *is?* Being as such is neither simply present, nor present to itself, but is only in the movement of difference from itself, whereby it manifests itself as other than itself, thus concealing itself in something that it essentially is not. All there is is this "not" of being, which is presence itself. It is in the movement of this difference, in this originary hiatus, which is essentially temporal, that is, ekstatic-horizonal, that there is or that presence unfolds. Presence unfolds only as the covering up of this movement of presencing, of which it is nonetheless the trace. Presence, and all the be-ings that shine in its midst, are only the signs of an ongoing and archaic spacing which is older than any particular being and than presence itself. This originary hiatus, in which beings come to distinguish themselves from the movement of their presencing so as to occupy the scene of full presence, Heidegger calls the "ontological difference." This difference is peculiar in that it never appears qua difference in the realm of presence that it serves to open up, and that it escapes the law of presence which it itself has decreed. It unfolds in such a way that it reveals its own concealment rather than its differential power, in such a way that in it being as such withdraws, thus handing man over to the sole presence of beings.

One understands, therefore, how this difference can be "forgotten": man, as the being who stands amid beings understandingly and ecstatically, is overwhelmed by the sheer presence and ontical weight of beings. Man, as the being who is essentially open to the world, is, as it were, blinded by its sheer presence, his gaze saturated with the full presence of beings. The forgottenness of the originary difference whereby presence comes to be constituted as such from out of a movement of clearing which itself is not manifest is thus not a mere by-product of the difference, but belongs to it essentially. In other words, the forgottenness of the difference from out of which man is able to comport himself to his world and dwell in it understandingly belongs to the very way in which the difference unfolds. The difference unfolds in such a way that it effaces the trace of its passage as it inscribes it. This implies that forgottenness is not the result of some mnemic deficiency on the part of the being for whom forgottenness is at issue. It is not only as an object that man is excluded from this forgottenness. He is not even the subject of the forgottenness, the subject who forgets, for he is not a subject. Rather, he is a Dasein, that is, the being whose mode of being consists in dwelling within the space of this originary difference, albeit in such a way that the difference as such is never held in view. Yet the difference is not only originary; it is also irreducible. This, in turn, means that any concept of identity and any conception of sameness arise out of this originary difference, as an effect of the self-concealing nature of the ontological difference. For example, Dasein's interpretation of itself as ἄνθρωπος, as a unity of body and soul, as rational animal, in other words, as a form of self-identical and self-present ego, arises out of the forgottenness of the originar*y difference that has always and already opened such conceptions to the fragmented and disseminated life of ecstatic existence. Dasein can become a "subject" only from the historical and metaphysically determined unfolding of the forgottenness of his essence, only when, immersed in the ontical concretion of the world, it interprets itself as one of those beings present at hand that lies before its gaze.

To rescue the ontological difference from its structurally almost inevitable forgottenness, to become alive to questioning not only about beings, but about the presencing of that which is present, as the Greeks once did, thus implies a conversion or a transformation on the part of the questioner, one that would perhaps remind us of a transcendental ἐποχή, were it not such as to turn us away from the sphere of transcendental subjectivity so as to point to a more originary givenness of the world. Such a conversion points beyond metaphysics, which constitutes the formal thematization of the forgottenness of the ontological difference, back to the unthought of metaphysics, that is, back to the originary difference with the closure of which metaphysics begins. It takes the form of a comportment that exceeds the possibility of its metaphysical reappropriation while constituting an adequate response to what Heidegger designates not as a mere deficiency of thinking, but as a historical-destinal "event." "Repetition" (*Wiederholung*) is the historical comportment that constitutes the adequate response to the forgottenness of the question concerning being.

This category is so decisive that Heidegger places the whole of the project of fundamental ontology, as it is expressed in the first few pages of *Being and Time,* under its banner and authority. The time has come, as Heidegger suggests at the very outset of the book, to repeat and raise anew the long since forgotten question concerning the meaning of being. The time has come, once again, to become alive to questioning about why and how it is that we seem to understand what it means to be, that we always seem to move ourselves within a pre-understanding of the world and of our own being, without such an understanding ever becoming an explicit, that is, conceptual, object of investigation. The time has come, then, to reopen that question that was once broached by the Greeks, ever so tentatively, and then closed off, almost immediately, by the Greeks themselves, thus sealing the fate of Western thought, inscribing it as the path of metaphysics. But why has such a time finally come? Why now? Why today? Because that very path has come to an end, because those very possibilities that were originally laid out as the possibilities of metaphysical thought have been gathered in and around their end, infinitized and absolutized in that systematic discourse that we began by evoking. Thus, the need for repetition arises out of a sense of end, of completion and exhaustion of those metaphysical possibilities that have marked the history of Western thought. The need for repetition, therefore, arises out of a certain sense of urgency, out of a necessity to confront our time and to invent our future. It is under the pressure of the "today," to which Heidegger also refers repeatedly in the opening pages of *Being and Time*, that the repetition of that difference which, in its very forgottenness, allowed for metaphysics to emerge as such, and to come to be gathered in its most extreme possibilities, becomes a matter of urgency. In the repetition of that ontological difference, to which the West was once alive, it is not a question of returning to the Greeks as to a moment that would have remained secured in the depths of time, awaiting its own reiteration. Rather, it is a question of repeating those very possibilities of thought that once emerged qua possibilities, yet never became actual, or rather, became actual by canceling out the potential power contained in them, by opening up the path of metaphysics or representational thinking. But are possibilities not essentially futural? Does possibility not signify the very mark of the future in the present? And if the repetition of the question concerning being is essentially the repetition of a possibility, does repetition itself not become, paradoxically perhaps, a category of the future? In that sense, must we not also conclude that the task of repeating the question concerning the meaning of being presupposes that we have already answered what the horizon for the understanding of being is, namely, temporality? Does the call for a repetition of a possibility of thought not presuppose that we have already solved that which the repetition is supposed to open onto? In other words, is it not the account of the primordial temporality of Dasein in Division Two of *Being and Time*, and of Dasein's historicity, that allows Heidegger to call for a repetition of a historical possibility in the opening page of the book? Does that account not serve as the existential-ontological ground for the project of fundamental ontology as a whole? Conversely, we might wonder whether fundamental ontology itself is not an illustration of that proper mode of temporality which Heidegger designates as historical, not in the sense that it would happen in time, but in the sense that it would itself take its point of departure in history conceived as the temporalizing of temporality.

Repetition and the Temporality of Dasein

It is with these questions in mind that I now turn to what we could designate as the temporality of repetition, which Heidegger thematizes in various places in 1927–28.[2]

Since the ontological difference must be interpreted temporally, the repetition of that difference, as a mode of relating which is itself temporal, must itself be thought in connection with the temporality of the ontological difference. In other words, we must understand how repetition itself is first made possible and thus ultimately subordinated to the way in which the ontological difference happens as time, or rather as the temporalizing of temporality. Unlike remembrance or reminiscence, repetition does not presuppose the constitution of the being thus responding to the forgottenness of the difference as subjectivity. It is because the being for whom this difference is at issue is not a subject, or a soul, but a Dasein—and this means the being who, from the start, is made to dwell within an originary understanding of that difference, such that this being is always exposed as the site of this originary hiatus—that the proper response to the temporally differentiating power of the difference cannot be one of remembrance or reminiscence, in which the past is united with the present in the self-presence of the subject, but one of repetition, which is essentially ecstatic. What does this mean? It means that repetition, when properly understood, constitutes a primordial ecstatic dimension of the temporality of Dasein, that ecstasis whereby Dasein relates to its own past. Built into the very structure of repetition, then, is the ecstatic-horizonal structure of time itself. So, before the repetition can be anything like a philosophical program or project—as in the project of fundamental ontology that consists in a repetition of the *Seinsfrage*—it must be identified as an existential-ontological possibility that is grounded in and constitutive of the temporality of Dasein itself. It is only once repetition has been fully thematized as such a possibility that the stakes and the demands concerning the repetition of the ontico-ontological difference can become absolutely clear.

One of the fundamental discoveries of *Being and Time* is that Dasein always and already understands the being of beings, albeit pre-ontologically or pre-conceptually. Division Two of *Being and Time* identifies temporality as the "beyond" that allows for the understanding of being in general. The temporal nature of understanding is best revealed in the exemplary phenomenon of resoluteness, where it appears as essentially futural. Indeed, understanding appears to presuppose a relation to a possibility or a can-be which Heidegger designates as Dasein's ownmost, namely, death. Yet it is not only the future that is at stake in resoluteness, as well as in all modes of understanding that presuppose death as their ultimate horizon. If understanding is indeed primordially futural, it also bears immediately on the present as well as on the past. Indeed, in coming-towards-itself, Dasein has also taken itself over as the being that in each case has already been. In other words, this coming-towards-itself is also a coming back to itself and a taking itself over again as the being that it is. Dasein brings itself back again. Not simply as this entity that it was, and no longer is, but as this entity that it continues to be in the mode of having-been:

> But this coming-to-oneself does not, as such, stretch over a momentary present of my own; it stretches over the whole of my having-been. More precisely—and here is our claim—this having-been-ness temporalizes itself only from out of and in the future. The having been is not a remnant of myself that has stayed behind and has been left behind by itself.[3]

In other words, Dasein is or exists "authentically" only in the repetition of itself, not as the repetition of a moment *m* that it originally was, constituted as such in its entirety, in the way in which an entity would be repeated sequentially in time, but as the repetition of something that it comes to be in the process of coming-towards-itself. The coming-towards-itself that Dasein experiences in its proper and ownmost mode of being is a coming-back-towards-itself, not as the self that it was before facing its ownmost possibility, but as the self that it has become, this self that is other than itself: "The repeating of that which is possible does not bring again something that is 'past.'"[4] Repetition, then, far from reintroducing the same, only introduces difference. Far from constituting an abdication of one's freedom, or a passive obedience, genuine repetition marks the site of a temporal strife, which Heidegger designates as an *Erwiderung* (SZ 386/438), a retort, or a rejoinder. In other words, repetition becomes the place of a temporal confrontation, such that the "today" is neither the stake of a nostalgia for a time past nor the opening towards a bright future, but a constant back and forth, and, indeed, a struggle, between past and future, between an originary self-projection and a return to one's having-been, in which historical possibilities are disclosed and a heritage is made manifest.[5] Is this not what Heidegger means when he writes that

> Repetition does not abandon itself to that which is past, nor does it aim at progress. In the instant [the instant is the moment of decision that follows from resoluteness] authentic existence is indifferent to both these alternatives.[6]

This understanding of repetition is conceivable only to the extent that we no longer think of repetition as the recurrence of something in time, but as a mode of time itself, as the way in which temporality temporalizes itself. Furthermore, repetition can be understood as introducing difference when we cease to think of it as a category of the past, and think of it in its unity with the future: what is repeated is not something that is past, something that once was, and that is now preserved in some past, awaiting to be rescued or brought back to life, in a way quite identical to the way in which it used to be. Rather, what is repeated is something that is first revealed from out of a projection ahead of one-self into one's can-be. In other words, repetition presupposes a primordial projection into the realm of possibility as the condition of possibility of its own iterability. The past *is* insofar as it *can be* repeated. But the iterability of the past presupposes the difference introduced by the possibility from out of which the past emerges. Ultimately, the possibility of repetition lies in that possibility that always lies ahead so as to constitute the ultimate horizon from out of which time temporalizes itself, namely, death. Ultimately, repetition, as well as the possibility of the emergence of a past for Dasein, is made subordinate to the finitude of time. Is this not another paradox? Does repetition not traditionally involve the possibility of infinity? Is it not infinite repetition in the form of continued creation that allowed Descartes to secure his world from the threat of total collapse? Is finitude not ordinarily conceived as an obstacle to the unfolding of repetition? To summarize: repetition does not apply to things in time (intratemporal beings), but to the temporalizing of temporality; repetition is not a category of the past, but of the future; repetition presupposes the finitude of time. Finally, it is only because repetition presupposes ecstatic temporality that it is able to introduce difference and open onto the novel. As such, it is also a condition of possibility of transformation and action.

Repetition and Transformation

Having structurally, that is, ontologically, justified the conclusions at which we arrived at the beginning of the first part of this chapter—those tentative conclusions that emphasized the historical dimension of the project of fundamental ontology understood in terms of repetition—we can now return to this dimension in an attempt to take the full measure of its historicity.

The following passage might serve as an entry into the topic:

> Fundamental ontology is always and only a repetition of this ancient, early manifestation [of the many and essentially temporal senses of οὐσία]. But what is ancient gets transmitted to us by repetition only if we grant it the possibility of transformation. . . . And characteristically, the tradition, i.e., the externalized transmission, deprives the problem of this very transmission in a repetition. The external tradition, and its employment in the history of philosophy, denies problems their life, and that means it seeks to stifle their transformation, and so we must fight against the tradition.[7]

The tradition that is spoken of here, and which constitutes an obstacle to genuine repetition which, far from constituting a conventional attitude, is the condition for transformation, is to be distinguished from the other sense of tradition (*Überlieferung*), of which Heidegger says that it constitutes the result of a choice that arises out of Dasein's relation to its ownmost possibilities. All of this is to say that Heidegger's account of the tradition is not altogether negative and is at least twofold. Repetition is aimed at freeing thinking from the hands of those whom Heidegger designates as the "inept guardians of tradition,"[8] in order to promote a freer and more constructive relation to the past. This alternative conception of tradition is perhaps best expressed in the following, almost symmetrical passage from Heidegger's 1925 *History of the Concept of Time:*

The assumption of the tradition is not necessarily traditionalism and the adoption of prejudices. The genuine repetition of a traditional question lets its external character as a tradition fade away and pulls back from the prejudices.[9]

A few lines down, having declared his intention to "establish a genuine contact with the tradition," Heidegger distinguishes between two basic ways of relating to the tradition:

On the one hand, it can be purely a matter of traditionalism, in which what is assumed is itself not subjected to criticism. On the other hand, however, the return can also be performed so that it goes back prior to the questions which were posed in history, and the questions raised by the past are once again originally appropriated. This possibility of assuming history can then also show that the assumption of the question of the sense of being is not merely an external repetition of the question which the Greeks originally raised.[10]

As we clearly see from this passage, only the second mode of contact is said to involve repetition in the true sense, that is, repetition defined as original appropriation. What characterizes repetition thus defined is its ability to bring change about, its capacity for transformation. How far does this power go? What sort of transformation does the repetition of the question concerning being call for?

Far from being merely conservative, then, the thinking of repetition is oriented towards change, unlike the thinking of the return, which is doomed, simply because it returns only to that which once was and is no longer. This means that the second type of contact is not merely indifferent to the first one, or that it simply runs parallel to it. Rather, the very nature of repetition is such that to it belongs also the undoing or the peeling off of those layers of traditionalism that constitute an obstacle to the original retrieval of the past, and to the possibility of digging out new modes of thinking and acting. In other words, repetition is in itself essentially deconstructive, which does not mean simply destructive, careless, and dismissing, as Heidegger's long and sustained confrontation with the metaphysical tradition indicates. The repetition can be carried out only in and as the deconstruction of the history of ontology, since that history is precisely the *how* of the forgottenness of the question. The repetition, and that is the concrete working out of the question, cannot be carried out independently of the historical inquiry of the question, and that means the inquiry concerning its effacement. That history itself may be defined in terms of an effacement, an effacement which leaves traces, is precisely what is at the origin of the need for deconstruction. In that respect, deconstruction is to be understood as an exhibition of the process of self-effacement. It is a retrieval, a clearing of those traces which are inscribed in the movement of the self-effacement of the question. To destroy, then, does not mean to efface the traces, to scorch the philosophical earth so as to fertilize it anew. To destroy means to reveal the history of ontology as that field of traces, the tracing of which belongs to a peculiar effacement. Thus, it is a construction, insofar as it retrieves, reveals, and isolates an otherwise confused phenomenon (in that respect, the project of fundamental ontology remains phenomenological throughout):

> In thus demonstrating the origin of our basic ontological concepts by an investigation in which their 'birth certificate' is displayed, we have nothing to do with a vicious relativizing of ontological standpoints. But this destruction is just as far from having the *negative* sense of shaking off the ontological tradition. We must, on the contrary, stake out the positive possibilities of that tradition.[11]

Heidegger's relations to the tradition, to his own time, and to the historical possibilities of Western metaphysics are thus far from simple. On the one hand, the tradition is viewed as a rigid and mostly dogmatic relation to the past, one that needs to be dismantled and exposed in its conservatism. In his later work, Heidegger will go as far as to identify this tradition with nihilism proper.[12] On the other hand, the tradition is seen as that which is handed down over to us and which, as such, is worthy of repetition. Yet this handing down is made possible only on the basis of a certain historical conversion, only on the basis of a relation to the Greeks that arises from out of a sense of end and ultimate gathering of those metaphysical possibilities of thought that have traversed the history of the West.

In short, and with respect to the realm of praxis to which Heidegger's project of repetition of the forgotten question regarding the meaning of being opens, the category of repetition, and specifically the ecstatic conception of temporality that underlies it, seems to undercut two traditional ideological or metaphysical comportments: on the one hand, the reactionary, nourished by a thinking of the return (to the origins, to God, to values, to meaning, etc.), and, on the other hand, the progressive, whose conception of history as the arche-teleological unfolding of a meaningful process is rooted in a certain appropriation of the philosophy of the Enlightenment. While Heidegger's alleged anti-humanism and nihilism, so often pointed out by his detractors as the source of his involvement with National Socialism and his inability to speak up against the final solution, can at first glance be derived from his suspicion regarding the universal values of the Enlightenment and the liberal tradition inherited from Rickert, Wildenband, and Dilthey, his stance with respect to reactionary thinking seems to be overlooked. This brings us to the treacherous question of Heidegger's politics. Although the reasons and the circumstances for Heidegger's political engagement cannot adequately be dealt with here,[13] it nonetheless seems already clear, on the basis of the nature of Dasein's temporality and historicity, that they cannot be derived from what could be seen as a purely reactionary tendency of Heidegger's thought. In order to understand Heidegger's relation to history, to the past and to the tradition, it does not suffice to consider superficially his remarks concerning the necessity to deconstruct the history of ontology. It is of the utmost importance to understand that such a deconstruction is aimed at retrieving a constructive relation to the past, based on a proper (*eigentlich*) understanding of historicity as originary temporality. And if something is to account for Heidegger's involvement with National Socialism, it is certainly not some "nihilistic" dimension of his thought, one that would be the direct consequence of the "deconstructive" project. Rather, it is to be found in the truly *positive* historical content that Heidegger identified in the "movement," which, as a close reading of the Rectoral address would reveal, signified the possibility of that very repetition which *Being and Time* set out to thematize in its necessity. I would like to suggest that the repetition that is called for by Heidegger in the 1920s by far exceeds the realm of ontology proper, or rather, that ontology or theory in the highest sense is, as Heidegger never ceased to claim, de facto and from the very start praxical. The transformation that this project entailed was so radical and so profound that it became compatible with a revolution of the German Dasein as a whole. The problem is that Heidegger, at least for a while, mistook the Nazi revolution, which from the start meant nothing besides the sheer and unscrupulous destruction of Western history, with an authentic liberating that was to pave the way for an original appropriation of that history. Did Heidegger opt for the wrong revolution? The following passage, written in the winter of 1937–38, at a time when Heidegger had clearly become disenchanted with the actuality of Nazism, seems to point in that direction:

> The future is the origin of history. What is most futural, however, is the great beginning, that which—withdrawing itself constantly—reaches back the farthest and at the same reaches forward the farthest. . . . Therefore, in order to rescue the beginning, and consequently the future as well, from time to time the domination of the ordinary and all too ordinary must be broken. An upheaval is needed, in order that the extraordinary and the forward-reaching might be liberated and come to power. Revolution, the upheaval of what is habitual, is the genuine relation to the beginning. The conservative, on the contrary, the preserving, adheres to and retains only what was begun in the wake of the beginning and what has come forth from it.[14]

And Heidegger adds on the following page:

> What is conservative remains bogged down in the historiographical; only what is revolutionary attains the depth of history. Revolution does not mean here mere subversion and destruction but an upheaval and recreating of the customary so that the beginning might be restructured. And because the original belongs to the beginning, the restructuring of the beginning is never the poor imitation of what was earlier; it is entirely other and nevertheless the same.[15]

Is this not Heidegger's mistake, then: to have mistaken National Socialism for a revolution in the most genuine sense, to have misjudged it to the point of seeing it as an authentic relation to the power of the origin? To say, then, that underlying Heidegger's thought is a revolutionary concern is not an overstatement. Yet Heidegger's definition of what a revolution is, and by that we mean the temporality and the ontology that underlies it, is irreducible to any traditional model, including the fascistic or otherwise conservative one. To be sure, Heidegger did at some point see in the reality of National Socialism the upheaval necessary to reawaken the German people and possibly the West as a whole to its forgotten and abandoned essence. Yet the peculiar logic of the repetition that calls for the revolution, the way in which this revolution is bound to the beginning of philosophy and to the task of thinking, exceeds and, to a lesser extent, even suspends the model within which too often Heidegger's thought is being forced. And such an excess has everything to do with the way in which revolution is intimately bound up with genuine repetition. Beyond Heidegger's own political errancy, then, we may wonder whether genuine repetition might not be thought as a political alternative to revolution, whether the very temporality of repetition is not such as to have from the start opened onto another relation to praxis altogether.

If I now may gather the most decisive features of repetition as they emerge from a reading of Heidegger's early project of fundamental ontology, and in a way that would constitute the point of departure for a dialogue with those thoughts of difference and repetition that have marked our century so decisively, I would wish to emphasize the following points:

1. Repetition presupposes difference.
2. Repetition introduces difference.
3. Repetition cannot be understood on the basis of the recurrence of something in time, but only on the basis of the temporalizing of temporality. As a corollary of this point: repetition is a category of the future.
4. Repetition is a condition for action and transformation in the highest sense. In that respect, one might wonder about the extent to which Heidegger's conception of repetition constitutes an appropriation of the notion of μίμησις.
5. Repetition is not a metaphysical concept, but a deconstructive philosopheme (and this is what makes it paradoxical: that which is repeated is also undone in its very repetition).

3

Boredom
Between Existence and History

Soon after the publication of *Being and Time*, in a few enigmatic and highly complex pages devoted to a "Characterization of the Idea and Function of a Fundamental Ontology,"[1] Heidegger suggests that in redefining the task of philosophy as fundamental ontology, one cannot remain content simply with revealing the sense of being as time. For insofar as this task is carried out as a possibility of Dasein itself, it must itself be submitted to the rigor of the ontological analysis. Thus, in what amounts to the ultimate phase of the project of fundamental ontology, the analysis is to turn back upon the way in which the transcendence of Dasein is involved in the very elaboration of that project, back upon the way in which this task is made possible and limited at the same time by the very way in which the factical existence of Dasein is folded into it. For what characterizes Dasein in its factical existence is precisely the fact that it is always and from the very start confronted with nature, or with the totality of beings. Heidegger introduces this problematic of *das Seiende-im-Ganzen*, or of "beings as a whole," under the name metontology (*Metontologie*), and the latter constitutes the very heart of his reflection in the years 1929–30.[2] It is only with the exposition of the way in which ontology runs back into the metaphysical ontic in which it is caught from the very start that philosophy radicalizes itself and is turned over into meta-ontology. Heidegger announces the programmatic nature of this fully developed concept of metaphysics towards the end of the *Kantbuch*, claiming that

> fundamental ontology, however, is only the first level of the metaphysics of Dasein. What belongs to this [metaphysics of Dasein] as a whole, and how from time to time it is rooted historically in factical Dasein cannot be discussed here.[3]

Whereas the 1928 lecture course still conceived of philosophy as a whole, including its last phase (i.e., metontology), under the name "fundamental ontology," the texts and lecture courses written and delivered immediately thereafter identify fundamental ontology with only the first phase of what came to be characterized as metaphysics. Yet in no way does this slight fluctuation in Heidegger's vocabulary call into question the centrality of the problematic concerning the whole of beings. Can we assume that the second level of the metaphysics of Dasein, merely gestured towards in §42 of the *Kantbuch* and only partly exposed in the 1928 lecture course on Leibniz, is actually carried out in the remaining three texts that address this question of metaphysics as the question concerning Dasein's relation to beings as a whole, viz., "What Is Metaphysics?," "On the Essence of Ground," and the immediately following lecture course of 1929–30 entitled *The Fundamental Concepts of Metaphysics?* If the first two texts, both published in 1929, have been subjected to many analyses, the latter, published in 1983 and translated only recently, has perhaps not received the attention it deserves.[4]

Naturally, it cannot be a question here of offering a detailed and systematic analysis of this rich—albeit incomplete—lecture course in its entirety. Instead, I wish simply to take up one aspect of this lecture course, one of two original aspects that perhaps distinguish these remarkable lectures from the texts Heidegger published around the same period. In a way, by focusing on this single aspect, which constitutes the object of the entire first part of the lecture course, I shall barely touch upon the question of metaphysics as a radicalization of fundamental ontology. For the goal of this first part, entitled "Awakening a Fundamental Attunement [*Grundstimmung*] in our Philosophizing," is to unveil the ground or the truly existentiell soil from out of which philosophizing might be possible. In other words, this first part is supposed to bring us to the very threshold of metaphysics and of its fundamental concepts by turning to the buried source of a concrete disposition of our existence. Thus, the preliminary task to which Heidegger devotes himself in that lecture course is the awakening within us of a metaphysical disposition which, as existents, is proper to us, and on the basis of which the entry into metaphysics should take place. But things will turn out to be more complicated. Indeed, the analysis of the fundamental disposition which is supposed to take us to the very threshold of metaphysics, or, to be more precise, the historical diagnosis to which Heidegger submits this disposition, is introduced at the cost of a tension which the 1929–30 lecture course is not in a position to reduce. The solution to this tension—such is at least the thesis that I wish to put forward—will be found only when Heidegger will reformulate the project of the question concerning the *sense* of being and transform it into the question concerning the *history* of being. In passing, we shall also see the extent to which this tension is at the very source of some of the remarks of a quasi-political nature Heidegger makes in the course of his lecture course, thus throwing considerable light on his subsequent engagement in favor of Nazism. In other words — and this constitutes the truly paradoxical nature of Heidegger's enterprise — the progressively revealed access to the fundamental concepts of metaphysics is eventually inscribed in a context which itself is such as to call into question existence as the primal and originary source of metaphysics. Thus, while confirming some of the decisive traits of the analysis of *Befindlichkeit,* and specifically of anxiety, as developed in *Being and Time* and "What Is Metaphysics?" the analysis of profound boredom (*die tiefe Langeweile*) announces the great historical *Grundstimmungen* that Heidegger will identify throughout the 1930s, when philosophizing, or thinking, will no longer be ontology so much as co-respondence with the truth of being in its epochal unfolding. More specifically, "profound boredom" remains stretched between a thinking of mood that remains largely indebted to the early analyses of existential facticity, and a thinking of fundamental attunement that is to serve as the ground for an epoch and a "we," and the provenance of which is itself no longer clear. True, it is still a matter of time, of the essence of time. But the decisive question concerns precisely and primarily the essence of time itself. Is time essentially temporality (*Zeitlichkeit*), as *Being and Time* argued, and as the 1929–30 lecture course sets out to confirm, or does it unfold from an even more originary source, the source of being itself, hitherto understood as sending and destiny, in other words, as history?

The Analysis of *Stimmung* Prior to
The Fundamental Concepts of Metaphysics

As is well known, the term "mood" (*Stimmung*) appears in at least two strategic moments prior to *The Fundamental Concepts of Metaphysics.* The first occurrence is to be found in Heidegger's *Hauptwerk,* and the second in his inaugural address to the University of Freiburg in 1929, entitled "What Is Metaphysics?" I wish simply to mark those two occurrences briefly and economically in order to show that the 1929–30 lecture course throws yet another light on this phenomenon.

Within the context of metaphysics as a whole, and that is to say as including both fundamental ontology and metontology, a first analysis is devoted to the phenomenon of mood in *Being and Time.* There a precise position is ascribed to what Heidegger calls *Befindlichkeit* or "disposition." Section 29 identifies *Befindlichkeit* as one of the two fundamental ways in which, prior to any act of cognition or rational articulation, Dasein is or exists its own "there" or disclosedness, and thus understands its own being. Disposition is the ontological characterization of what is ontically referred to as mood or being-disposed, as *Stimmung* and *Ge-stimmtheit*. Heidegger emphasizes three essential characteristics of disposition thus defined. First of all, disposition discloses Dasein in its facticity; then disposition discloses being-in-the-world as a whole; finally, disposition discloses the world from a specific angle (for example, *fear* will reveal the world as something threatening). By virtue of its being thrown in the world, Dasein is always disposed in the world in a particular way. The world is always given to it as a world that is determined (*bestimmt*), and this determination is the result of Dasein's primordial facticity. Through *Befindlichkeit*, Dasein is revealed as the being whose being consists in existing this *fact* that it itself *is*. As thrown, Dasein is always situated, and consequently always disposed towards the world in a specific and concrete manner.

Later in the text (§40), when it has become a question of identifying a distinctive mode of existence in which Dasein is disclosed as such, or as being-in-the-world, Heidegger turns to *anxiety*. This is a distinctive attunement in the sense that in anxiety one comes face to face with being-in-the-world as such, and not with this or that particular being, or region of being, in what amounts to a traumatizing and abyssal experience: what is actually threatening is nowhere to be found, and yet it is already there, almost palpable. In Heidegger's own words: "It is so close that it is oppressive and stifles one's breath."[5] Here what is disclosed is the sheer facticity of existence, the raw fact of human existence. What is most striking about anxiety, perhaps, at least with respect to the 1929–30 lecture course, is its power of individualization:

> In anxiety what is environmentally ready-to-hand sinks away, and so, in general, do entities within-the-world. The 'world' can offer nothing more, and neither can the Dasein-with of Others. . . . Anxiety individualizes Dasein and thus discloses it as *'solus ipse'*. But this existential 'solipsism' is so far from the displacement of putting an isolated subject-thing into the innocuous emptiness of a worldless occurring, that in an extreme sense what it does is precisely to bring Dasein face to face with its world as world, and thus bring it face to face with itself as being-in-the-world.[6]

Thus, if anxiety does refer Dasein back to itself as to a *solus ipse*, Dasein, as factical, always refers back to the world within which it is thrown.

Equally decisive is the link that Heidegger establishes between anxiety and the *Unheimlichkeit*, that is, this uncanniness linked to the fact that, in anxiety, the world no longer appears as the familiar world of our everydayness, but as this fate from which there is no escape, this dimension within which we find ourselves inexorably thrown, and which precedes and makes possible any dealings or familiar relations with the world, and not-being-at-home, not feeling at home or familiar with the world. This uncanniness of the world, this relation to the world in which, all of a sudden, one no longer feels at home with it or within it will be reinscribed in the analysis of boredom, where it will be envisaged as a disposition opening onto metaphysics understood the ability to question beings in their totality: when, Heidegger claims, Novalis describes philosophy as *Heimweh*, or as "homesickness," in other words, as this "drive [*Trieb*] to be at home everywhere,"[7] he presupposes that we have experienced our being as open to the whole of being, and thus the journey out of the familiarity of the world and into its uncanniness. Also, the thematic of the *Unheimlichkeit* runs through the whole of Heidegger's thought and constitutes the ground whence Heidegger thinks the phenomena of being-in-the-world, dwelling, having a home, and, on this basis, the ideas of homeland, nation, and community.[8]

As for the temporality of anxiety, as well as that of attunements in general, it is revealed on the basis of the ecstasis of *Gewesenheit* (§68). If understanding is grounded primarily in the future, disposition temporalizes itself primarily in having-been-ness. This does not suggest that it does not also implicate the other two ecstases of temporality. It simply means that the ecstasis of having-been-ness is such as to carry the weight of that particular moment of the being of Dasein. But insofar as the temporality of attunement reveals existence in its facticity or in its having always and already been thrown into the world, it does not coincide with the most authentic mode of temporality, that mode in which the whole of Dasein's being comes to be *for* Dasein itself, thus revealing Dasein to itself as this being which *can* and *must* be its own being:

> But even though the present of anxiety is *held on to*, it does not as yet have the character of the moment of vision, which temporalizes itself in resolution [*Entschluß*].[9]

In other words—and Heidegger will reproduce this thesis in his analysis of boredom—the phenomenon of disposition provides the ground from out of which the resolution and the instant can emerge, but in itself does not suffice for Dasein to become transparent to itself and assume its own being.

Whereas the analysis of *Befindlichkeit* in *Being and Time* aimed to reveal one's moods as an existential based on facticity, one of three moments of Dasein's being, and was thus subordinated to the overall task of revealing the ontological structure of Dasein as well as the meaning of this structure, "What Is Metaphysics?" takes the analysis of attunement—and specifically of anxiety—in a slightly different direction. With respect to its relation to the 1929–30 lecture course, suffice it to say that it announces it in the following way: it is developed not with a view to investigating further one of Dasein's existentials, but with a view to providing an access to the question concerning the nature and essence of metaphysics. It is therefore treated as a way of being disposed in which one can come to read or decipher the truly meta-physical or trans-natural essence of existence itself, thus revealing the ontological ground of this primordial theoretical attitude traditionally referred to as "metaphysics." In anxiety, one experiences the total withdrawal of beings, the absence of all things. Yet this absencing of all things remains the experience of something: not of some definite thing, but of the no-thing that sustains the presence of everything, this thing which is not a being but beings as a whole. Thus, anxiety reveals Dasein as the being who, holding itself out into the nothing, is always already beyond beings, confronting beings as a whole in the very withdrawal of beings. In other words, anxiety reveals existence as transcendence, or as metaphysics. And in that respect, the analysis of anxiety is inscribed within the problematic of fundamental ontology.

Stimmung in
The Fundamental Concepts of Metaphysics

What of the analysis of *Stimmung* in the 1929–30 lecture course?

Before turning to the analysis of profound boredom as a distinct and privileged mood with respect to the possibility of laying the ground for a metaphysics of Dasein, I wish to formulate the following few preliminary remarks.

To begin with, the *Stimmung* is now specifically referred to as Grund-*stimmung*, as fundamental or grounding attunement. In what sense is it grounding or fundamental? What does it serve to ground? The ground is here to be understood in the following threefold sense. First, the *Stimmung* is fundamental in that it reveals the ground of Dasein who, as transcendence, is its own groundlessness, or its own abyss, its own being as being open onto the abyss or the nothingness of being. And we shall have to see how this ground itself begins to shake in the course of the analysis. But the *Stimmung* is also fundamental in that in it the very possibility of philosophizing is rooted: the very entry into metaphysics presupposes the prior awakening of a disposition as the very soil whence metaphysical questioning grows. This second sense of ground coincides with the explicit intention of the first part of Heidegger's lecture course, which is to provide an access to metaphysics and to its fundamental concepts on the basis of the "awakening of a fundamental disposition." Naturally, the first two senses of ground are coextensive. Metaphysics, Heidegger tells us in §44, is a comprehensive questioning, in the twofold sense that, first of all, it is at every moment concerned with the whole of being, and, second, whoever is involved in metaphysical questioning is caught up in the question and thus affected by it in his very being. But,

Heidegger adds, man can be thus caught up and affected only to the extent that he is "gripped" by what he questions, only to the extent that his being is attuned to what is being questioned. This accord, this attunement is that on the basis of which metaphysics unfolds. The goal of the first part of the course is thus to generate the possibility of such a being-gripped whence the metaphysical questioning regarding beings as a whole can unfold. And it is only once this fundamental attunement will have been awakened that the analysis will be in a position to turn to the fundamental metaphysical questions regarding world, finitude, and solitude. And profound boredom is itself only *one* attunement among others, *one* point of entry into the domain of metaphysics. In principle, many more attunements could claim to open onto metaphysics. Yet, in fact—and such is the reason why the choice of profound boredom as the *Grundstimmung* that is supposed to facilitate *our* awakening to the fundamental concepts of metaphysics is not simply arbitrary, or even simply strategic—it would seem that we are always historically disposed, that the dispositions of existence are themselves primarily rooted in the history of Dasein, and that the possibility of a turn to beings as a whole is always a matter for a decision that has exceeded that of existence. Yet if, Heidegger tells us, the fundamental tone belonging to a mode of questioning concerning beings as a whole—in other words, the way in which and the extent to which it sets the tone—is always a matter of destiny, that is, a tone that is transformed according to the epochs, and that does not necessarily prevail at every epoch, philosophizing as such, that is, as the questioning that unfolds on the basis of an opening to the whole of being, is itself marked by this nostalgia or this longing which Novalis captured in the term *Heimweh* and Aristotle in the term *melancholia*.[10] It is because, at the very heart of our existence and our destiny as men, there is this longing for homecoming, this nostalgia, that there is philosophy.

This second sense in which the *Stimmung* can be said to be fundamental naturally leads to the third, with which I shall be concerned henceforth. This third sense is actually already entirely implicated in the second, and in a way that is rather problematic. It coincides with this historical ground or foundation of which we have already seen how it permeates the task that consists in awakening ourselves to metaphysical questioning. It is in the context of this discussion concerning the disposition or the mood that is most conducive to philosophy that the recourse (albeit only implicit) to a philosophy of history seems necessary and inevitable. For if the Dasein is "gripped" and "situated," in other words, stamped, in a way that is no longer characterized simply by a practical context, and the scale of which is no longer determined simply by this concrete and singular existent, but by a more general and shared context—if, in other words, the possibilities of the Dasein, and this includes its possibilities of thought and of openness to its own essence, are a function of a history and an epoch within which it is situated, then the question concerning the provenance of this history and the limits of this epoch begins to linger on. Whence, by what, and for how long is the historical Dasein thus situated? If the Dasein is a destiny, whence does the latter unfold? Does the fundamental tone originate in the Dasein itself, or is the Dasein itself always disposed from out of a more ancient horizon and from a deeper time? We are indeed always concretely caught up and situated in the world. We always relate to it in a particular way. But this relation, this situatedness, are they of Dasein's own doing, or is Dasein always thrown and disposed on the basis of a foundation other than that of its own transcendence, and which determines its destiny? Is this not what we need to understand by "epoch": this world-configuration that happens to us, this presence of the world that is *our* share and that we inherit, this inheritance that delimits and limits the field of possibilities for us? And would philosophy, metaphysics itself, not be subjected to the law of this sending? Is it not itself, and thus its very possibility, a matter of destiny? And if such is the case, would the time of existence, as the ecstatic, finite, and horizonal time, not need to be turned back to history as to this deeper time and this more originary ground?

Profound Boredom as the *Grundstimmung* of Our Time

What is most striking about the analysis of boredom proper, the ultimate goal of which is, once again, to awaken us to the question concerning beings as a whole as to the fundamental question of metaphysics, is that it is subordinated to a task which is historical in nature. It is a matter, Heidegger suggests, of isolating a profound boredom as a fundamental attunement of "our contemporary Dasein," and, in so doing, of opening ourselves to the fundamental concepts of metaphysics. But could it not be objected that this is precisely what the opening page of *Being and Time* was already attempting to achieve? There, by referring to an extract from Plato's *Sophist,* Heidegger attempted to awaken within us, his readers, the necessary perplexity (*Verlegenheit*) required even to begin to raise the question concerning the sense of being, and thus to transform philosophy into fundamental ontology. Thus, perplexity could very well be counted as one of the many fundamental dispositions that can pave the way to genuine philosophizing. It even seems to announce the θαυμάζειν, or the "wonder," of which later on Heidegger will say that it constituted the truly Greek *Stimmung,* in other words, the attunement that corresponded with the "first beginning."[11] Yet perplexity is left unanalyzed in *Being and Time:* It is envisaged neither as a

Stimmung revealing a moment of Dasein's being as care, nor as a *Grundstimmung* defining our contemporary Dasein. As a result, *Being and Time* remains sheltered from the questions that begin to be articulated in the lecture course from 1929-30 and from the unsolved tension which characterizes it. Consequently—and to return to the lecture course— the goal of the analysis of profound boredom is to grasp the "fundamental meaning of our being" (*Grundsinn unseres Dasein*), and to do so not with a view to developing an "anthropology or philosophy of culture [*Kulturphilosophie*], but as that which opens up the proper questioning of philosophising for us."[12] We must therefore not lose sight of the ultimate goal to which the analysis of profound boredom remains subordinated, that is, the access to the essence of philosophy as the questioning rooted in the ontological difference. For it is precisely in that regard that Heidegger's enterprise would differ from all the variations on the theme of the *Kulturphilosophie*, which all claim to reveal something about the essence of our time and the foundation of our existence on the basis of vague and often vacuous considerations concerning the *Zeitgeist*. That being said, and as I have already suggested, it is precisely in attempting to identify a disposition which would characterize *us*, today, that Heidegger renders problematic the passage which this disposition was supposed to enable. Indeed, insofar as *Being and Time* has already identified the "fundamental meaning" of Dasein as temporality—a "meaning" which the 1929-30 lecture course has every *intention* of confirming—why begin to search for the fundamental meaning of *our contemporary* Dasein? Must we conclude that to the meaning of Dasein's being as temporality we need to juxtapose another fundamental meaning of Dasein, when the latter is envisaged as people, community, and epoch? In the end, we shall have to wonder the extent to which the identification of profound boredom as the attunement that is proper to "our" "today" differs from this philosophy of culture which Heidegger is so eager to overcome, and the extent to which anthropology is simply avoidable when, leaving the neutral and descriptive shores of fundamental ontology, it becomes a question of venturing into the turbid waters of historical diagnosis.

Before turning to the structure of this profound boredom which Heidegger describes as "ours" and as "contemporary," it is perhaps necessary to look at the way in which Heidegger identifies boredom as the fundamental attunement of our time. Taking his clue from four interpretations of our contemporary situation,[13] which all frame the epoch as a struggle between spirit and soul, Heidegger develops a critique of the essentially diagnostic-prognostic nature of *Kulturphilosophie*: "This philosophy of culture does not grasp us in our contemporary situation, but at best sees only what is contemporary, yet a contemporaneity which is entirely without us, which is nothing other than what belongs to the eternal yesterday."[14] If the philosophy of culture fails to delimit our epoch adequately, if nothing can be expected from it from the standpoint of the essence of philosophy, it nonetheless reveals something essential about the epoch: that it is the epoch in which such books can be written, that these diagnoses of culture seem to correspond to what we today would call the demand of the time, that we ourselves seem to want such slogans. The decisive question then becomes: Where does it all come from? Whence this longing for quick answers and journalistic clichés, for empty talks about the decline of the West and the loss of our soul, for superficial remarks regarding the erosion of culture in global trade, technology, and the urban environment? In Heidegger's own terms:

> Why do we find no meaning for ourselves any more, i.e., no essential possibility of being? Is it because an *indifference* yawns at us out of all things, an indifference whose grounds we do not know? . . . Must we first make ourselves interesting to ourselves again? Why *must* we do this? Perhaps because we ourselves have become *bored* with ourselves? . . . *Do things ultimately stand in such a way with us that a profound boredom draws back and forth like a silent fog in the abysses of Dasein?*[15]

Yet before answering this question, before even considering the question of a profound boredom that would characterize our contemporary Dasein, Heidegger analyzes boredom for itself, that is, as the disposition in which the essence of time, in its purity as it were, transpires, thus also confirming the sense or the horizon of being as Da-sein. And this analysis is in many ways exemplary, magisterial even: More complete, more detailed, more convincing even than the analysis of anxiety developed in previous texts. As such, it does seem to provide a privileged access to the problematic of metaphysics and to its "fundamental concepts," thus also securing a positive outcome for the completion of fundamental ontology as metontology. To say nothing of what the analysis confirms regarding existence as the locus or the medium of the temporalizing of temporality, and the essence of time as the finite and ecstatic sense or horizon of being. Never, perhaps, will Heidegger have come closer to realizing the Proustian ideal of isolating and describing "pure" time. Insofar as it cannot be a question here of rendering the detail of Heidegger's analysis, I shall limit myself to the description Heidegger makes of boredom in its most profound sense, and with respect to which all the other types of boredom identified in the course of the analysis serve as preparatory sketches.

In profound boredom, one can no longer say that it is this or that thing which one finds boring, or that one is bored because time drags, as when stuck at X's train station, a small provincial town, awaiting for a train that will arrive only hours later. It is not even as if one is bored in the face of this or that event, a film, for example, or a dinner party. The truth is that one does not even know that one is bored, so diffuse is the boredom. And yet, it is there, absolutely, omnipresent, enveloping us in its invisible thickness: one is bored.

There is indeed, as in those types of boredom previously described, a feeling of emptiness, of being left empty (what Heidegger calls a *Leergelassenheit*), but not as the negative of a plenitude: one would be at a loss identifying what it is that is actually missing. And yet one is left as if drained, all attempts to relate to the world by way of dealings having failed, all access to the world as this familiar world made of familiar things having been suddenly denied, all relation to ourselves as relating to beings in the world as this or that kind of person, as philosopher or as sports journalist, as jealous or as in love, etc., having been severed. Suddenly, this world leaves us indifferent:

> What emptiness is it, when we do not become bored by particular beings, and are not bored ourselves either, as this particular person? It is an emptiness precisely where, as this person in each case, we want nothing from the particular beings in the contingent situation as these very beings.[16]

In the face of boredom, everything becomes equal, equally indifferent. Yet this wresting from the power of this or that being, from the hypnotic attraction of immanence, is at the same time the surging forth of beings as such and as a whole, and of existence as being-in-the-world. Here a power of an entirely different kind begins to reveal itself. It is a power that exposes us in the inescapable necessity of our having to be our being in the mode of *power*. Boredom reveals us to ourselves as this pure power or pure possibility, as the necessity of our being as free being: freedom to be or to exist being, freedom of the possible as such. The necessary and inescapable freedom of man, as the being who has the power to be being, is revealed precisely in the state of limbo, which Heidegger characterizes as *Hingehaltenheit*, in which profound boredom leaves us, precisely insofar as it denies us any concrete possibility. When no longer holding on to the world, when severed from its concrete and factical possibilities, existence discloses itself as pure possibility, or in its being as *sein*-können. In denying existence access to beings in this or that particular mode, boredom refers existence back to itself, turns it back upon itself, precisely as this pure possibility, as this thrown being that always projects its own thrownness, and the possibilities of whom, at that particular instant, have been suspended. Boredom refers Dasein back to itself as to its own task: as this *sein-können* which it has to be, as this freedom which it must exercise, or as this existence which it must exist. Boredom reveals existence to itself as this power of being, which is a power to be being: existence *can* be, it can be being, and is nothing outside this power; it is only this power-to-be (being). And it is in that respect that it is Da-sein, the "there" of being, the openness to the Open as such. And so this openness, which is the whole of its being, is also the duty of existence, the task that belongs to it most properly: we must *be* our being (since it is pure potentiality), and we are never done with it: so long as we are, we must continue to be, and to be this potentiality: this potentiality to be being. As profound attunement, boredom is thus quite particular, in that it gathers existence onto itself: not within itself, in what would amount to an interiority severed from the world and from others, but as ex-istence, as ecstasis or transcendence attuned to being, attuned to being *because* it is ecstatic. Existence, Heidegger tells us, gathers itself onto itself as onto its extremity, or its tip (*Spitze*): it is there, at the extremity of its being, that its power is exercised and its essence revealed; it is there that it truly *can*. Not unlike the thrust of a ship, gathered in its prow, in order to break through the ocean, the existent, precisely insofar as it ex-ists, or races ahead, is a "breakthrough" towards being:

> To such coming to be left in the lurch [*Im-Stich-gelassenwerden*] by beings' denial of themselves as a whole there simultaneously belongs our being impelled toward this utmost extremity [*diese äußerste Spitze*] that properly makes possible Dasein as such.[17]

Yet if this extremity is indeed the point at which existence as such is gathered, it means that the extremity is the possibility of Dasein as potentiality, what makes it possible as such, or frees its possibilities. The prow is indeed the completion or the realization of the ship, its end (its *telos*); but, as such, it is also its origin or its condition of possibility, its essence. This is where the existent stands, where it "is." And it is precisely insofar as man is this forward thrust, insofar as its place is not "here" but "there," that it is open to the world as such, that is to say, as this horizon whence beings unfold and come forward, that it is from the start "situated" in this difference, a source of wonder and awe, and of which philosophy is the most immediate and raw expression. What the Greeks called ἐνθουσιασμός, and to which Heidegger tries to awaken us, is precisely this "bliss of astonishment—being torn away in that wakeful manner that is the breath of all philosophizing."[18]

And this extremity at which existence, thus sharpened, is gathered is none other than time itself. It is time insofar as it is gathered in the "instant." How exactly? How does the essence of time illuminate and make possible the twofold state in which boredom forces us, that is, the state of being left empty and that of being held in limbo?[19] From the point of view of the being left empty, first of all. What happens there? In profound boredom, present, past, and future beings are denied and withdraw in a sort of indifference. They withdraw precisely as this or that being, no matter the way in which they may be envisaged. It is the nature of this seeing (*Sehen, Sicht*), made possible, at bottom, by the essentially temporal structure of existence and which here no longer has any hold on beings, that Heidegger has in mind when he claims that beings withdraw from it completely:

> All beings withdraw from us without exception in every respect [*Hinsicht*], whatever we look at [*worauf wir hinsehen*] and the way in which we look at it; everything in retrospect [*Rücksicht*], all beings that we look back upon [*alles Seiendes, worauf wir zurücksehen*] as having been and having become and as past, and the way we look back at them; all beings in every prospect [*Absicht*], everything we look at prospectively as something to come, and the way we have thus regarded them prospectively. Everything—in every respect, in retrospect and prospect, beings simultaneously withdraw.[20]

Thus, Dasein, cut off from any concrete and particular relation to beings, is referred back to itself as Dasein, that is, precisely as the temporalizing of temporality whence all relations to beings unfold, as the disclosedness to beings as such and as a whole on the basis of the essence of time. That which, in boredom, turns Dasein away from beings is precisely what makes this relation to beings possible, that is to say, time. Yet in boredom Dasein is as it were hypnotized, entranced, and paralyzed by time itself. In other words, if boredom does indeed reveal Dasein in its essence by denying it the dealings which this essence ordinarily makes possible, Dasein nonetheless remains cut off from this essence, which it experiences, however. In order for existence to "enact" this essence, in order for it to appropriate what it experiences, the entrancing of time must be ruptured, and existence, from an object of fascination, must become the object of action. Now, this is precisely what takes place in the "instant," that is, in the temporal expression of the *Hingehaltenheit*. In profound boredom, the Dasein suddenly comes face to face with the essence of time: not with this time that is so slow in passing and that is the sign of my boredom, nor with this time that co-incides with the punctual moment, the precise instant when boredom takes over, but with this time that I am, this instant which is something like pure time and which, far from being a mere punctual moment, a point of my linear existence, is, as it were, the gathering, the extremity or the hinge, of my threefold ek-sistence, the fold or the binding at the heart of which the ecstases are articulated. In it the ecstases are gathered and touch themselves. This is the sense in which my existence is the origin or the source of my being, of my *power*-to-be. This is the sense in which, in it, the possibility of existence as such reveals itself, that is, precisely, existence as pure possibility, or as freedom to be. In boredom, time reveals itself as the enabling power, as that which makes possible

Dasein as possibility, as that which frees the freedom of Dasein, or frees Dasein *as* freedom. And if time is the origin and the source of freedom, it is not as eternity, but precisely as finitude. Thus, to liberate the Dasein in oneself, to liberate oneself for the essence of time or freedom as such, is tantamount to liberating oneself for the finitude in which an "I" comes to be constituted. Already in *Being and Time*, in a neologism and an analysis too often misinterpreted, Heidegger designated this possibility as *Entschlossenheit*. To resolve oneself (*sich entschliessen*) does not mean to becomes resigned to a destiny given in advance, to something like a *fatum*. It means, rather, to resolve oneself for oneself, where the self in question designates precisely the essence or the opening whereby "there is," the advent or the event of being in the opening cleared by time. It also means—in what amounts to a modification or a mode of *Erschlossenheit*: to open oneself to the fact that something is opened within us. In other words, to resolve to be in the mode of freedom, or to let existence exist as the truth of being:

> Only in the resolute self-disclosure of Dasein to itself, in the instant [*Augenblick*], does it make use of that which properly makes it possible, namely time as the moment of vision itself. The instant is nothing other than the *look of resolute disclosedness* [*Blick der Entschlossenheit*] in which the full situation of an action opens itself and keeps itself open.[21]

The action that is in question here is not action in the ordinary sense, but the enacting of the essence of man, the freeing of man for his essence.

Everything, in the analysis of profound boredom, thus seems to confirm the fundamental thesis of *Being and Time*, according to which the meaning of being is indeed time, and where time coincides with existence itself, which, as a result, is best understood as the clearing or the "there" of being, the actual temporalizing through which "there is." Furthermore, profound boredom, as a fundamental disposition, seems to provide the very possibility of metaphysics with a concrete ground, and thus introduce to its fundamental concepts. We are thus on the right track. And on one level, this analysis will not be called into question. Yet, despite its obvious success, the analysis carries its own overcoming. Or, rather, the analysis, and the project of a metaphysics that is to culminate in a metontology, reveals its own limitations when it becomes a question of identifying a disposition that would no longer be simply "mine," but also "ours," no longer simply trans-historical, but historically rooted. And it is this very concern that will be at the source of the transformation of Heidegger's own thought, of the turning which that thought will undergo in the 1930s, a turning that will not be entirely unrelated to the sinister episode of the Rectorate. How exactly?

Having completed his existential-temporal analysis of boredom, Heidegger is now in a position to return to the question formulated at the outset of the lecture course, and which concerned boredom as the fundamental disposition of our time. It is, as we recall, this very question which led Heidegger to develop his detailed analysis of boredom, culminating in the analysis of profound boredom and of its temporal essence. The problem, therefore, has to do with the "passage" from boredom as a temporal-existential disposition to boredom as an attunement that would characterize "us" "today." It is with the difficulty—actually unresolved—of this passage that I shall be concerned with henceforth. Now, by way of warning, it cannot be a question of arguing that it is impossible to account for the phenomenon of history from the standpoint of existential temporality. This would go directly against the explicit purpose of §§72–77 of *Being and Time*, and against the way in which, in those sections, Heidegger grounds the historicality of Dasein in *Zeitlichkeit*. That being said, we must distinguish between two problems: it is one thing to ground the historicality of Dasein, the possibility of a common destiny and a community, even the possibility of a historical science, on the basis of time as temporality; it is quite a different matter to identify an epoch, and to define a mutual belonging (something like a "we"), on the basis of a fundamental disposition, or, in what would perhaps amount to a "vulgar" characterization, one would be tempted to refer to as the *Zeitgeist*. For there, certain questions of method need to be raised: how does one identify such a tone? How can we be assured of its validity? How can we delimit the epoch that this tone is supposed to express? Where does the "we" attached to this epoch begin, and where does it end? Furthermore, as soon as one begins to talk in the name of a "we" and on the basis of an epoch, are we not already venturing into the vague, and actually dangerous, terrain of *Kulturphilosophie*, this very philosophy which Heidegger warns us against and with which he contrasts the genuine task of philosophy as metaphysics? Can such a philosophy continue to unfold from existential temporality in its desire to reveal its essence, or will the delimitation of a "we" and an "epoch" not force Heidegger to rethink the very nature of time itself? As much as the analyses of boredom may seem useful and convincing, the diagnosis of our epoch as an epoch bored with itself, and of a boredom that would define "us" in our historical being, may strike us as eminently problematic from a methodological point of view and vague from a substantial point of view.

This is how Heidegger justifies his diagnosis.

Despite the hustle and bustle of contemporary man, despite the general restlessness and feverishness in the face of contemporary "issues" and "crises" of all kinds, this man is bored. He is bored to and with himself, and his boredom is co-extensive with his own existence: he is his own boredom. This means that the contemporary Dasein is cut off from himself as Dasein (as the ek-sistent being, or as the being who *is* being, who is the "there" or the clearing of being), oblivious to the Dasein in him, and this means to his essence, to the point of no longer being able to "act" his essence or his freedom. Hence the feeling of emptiness, this "what for?" and this "where to?" characteristic of nihilism. And what is lacking, the reason for our boredom, is not this or that thing, this or that being, but the absence of a constraint and a distress (*Not*), of an essential oppression (*Bedrängnis*) of our Dasein as a whole, where the entire weight of existence as openness to the world could be felt, and this despite the general distress that surrounds "us," and of which the "social misery," the "political confusion" (these are, after all, the years of the Weimar Republic), the "powerlessness of science" are only examples among others.[22] This lack of distress is what is really suffocating; this is what puts us to sleep and numbs us, despite ourselves, as it were. Therein lies "our" emptiness. And because of the lack of such an oppression, we err through existence as if through a wasteland, distraught and dispersed. And what results does this produce? A flowering of activities, of programs and essays of all kinds, in short, "a universal smug contentment in not being endangered,"[23] a situation where

> no one stands with anyone else and no community stands with any other in the rooted unity of essential action. Each and every one of us are servants of slogans, adherents to a program, but none is the custodian [*Verwalter*] of the inner greatness of Dasein and its necessities.[24]

One can only be surprised by the speed at which things seem to be happening. In no time, without any particular caution, Heidegger moves from the singular Dasein to "our" Dasein, and from the necessity to act my freedom, of which philosophical questioning would be the ultimate expression, to a shared (and already political) acting under the custody and guidance of a single man. It is now a question, if not quite of a *Führer*, at least of a custodian able to appeal to the Dasein in us and to reawaken us to our essence. Against the problems, the concerns, the difficulties, and the solutions of the Weimar Republic (indeed, in a state of complete crisis and virtual implosion at the time of the lecture course), a certain preference, a certain inclination for an authoritative and saving figure begins to emerge. As if the "hero" evoked in §74 of *Being and Time* began to take shape and be given a face. On the other hand, at no time is it a question of government, of representation, of legislation, in short, of politics in the traditional sense of the term. Our epoch, Heidegger argues, is indeed "able"; it even raises many interesting questions and problems. But "competencies" and "talents" are not what we need. What is lacking is the strength (*Kraft*) and the power (*Macht*, and no longer simply *Können*), which all the competencies in the world cannot replace.[25] And if anything is achieved with this accumulation of competencies, Heidegger argues, it is rather "the suffocation of all such things."[26] Away, then, with this expertise and this competence, let us now seek to bring about peril, strength, and power: in a word, oppression. But how could the latter be "administered" (*verwalten* carries this meaning of administering)? How can Heidegger have considered devolving to this *Verwalter* that which concerns existence in its most intimate being and determines its destiny?

To this generalized and shared emptiness, to this lack of oppression in the strict sense of the term also corresponds the announcement of an "instant" as that which truly enables the return of Dasein to itself in an exemplary "decision," this very return on the basis of which the Dasein becomes a task for man. From the very depths of our boredom, from the heart of our absolute destitution, a voice can be heard. It is the voice that appeals to our essence and that demands of man that "he necessarily shoulder once more his very Dasein, that he explicitly and properly takes this Dasein upon himself."[27] Yet, Heidegger is quick to add, this demand has nothing to do with putting forward something like a human ideal, or with reviving a moribund humanism. Unless, of course, one understands humanism differently, as Heidegger himself did, most explicitly perhaps in his letter to Jean Beaufret from 1946—that is, unless one understands humanism as the "liberation of Dasein in man."[28] Yet, as I already suggested, this liberation hardly amounts to getting rid of something within Dasein. Least of all does it amount to wresting Dasein from its own condition. Rather, it is a matter of freeing Dasein with a view to its own freedom for being, or for its disclosedness to the world as such. And so it is a question for Dasein of assuming its own Dasein as "an actual burden," as this never ending task and demand. It is in this very decision for existence—"resoluteness"—that Dasein is first opened to its ownmost possibilities of thought and action, that it becomes free for its own freedom. And it this very state of urgency and neediness which, indirectly, the contemporary boredom establishes.

Now, if questioning, thinking in the most genuine sense, is indeed for Heidegger the ultimate expression of this oppression in which Dasein is revealed to itself as metaphysical animal, it would also seem that philosophizing has its limitations and that this urgency may be introduced through other means, among which politics would figure prominently. As soon as it becomes a matter of awakening to its essence no longer just a singularity, but a community or an epoch, the limitations of philosophical questioning become apparent, and the latter could then very well do with the help of something else, or even *someone* else. And this is where the *Verwalter* reenters the scene:

> If, in spite of all our neediness, the oppressiveness of our Dasein still remains absent today and the mystery still lacking, then we must principally concern ourselves with preparing for man the very basis and dimension upon which and within which something like a mystery of his Dasein could once again be encountered. We should not be at all surprised if the

contemporary man in the street feels disturbed or perhaps sometimes dazed and clutches all the more stubbornly at his idols when confronted with this challenge and with the effort required to approach this mystery. It would be a mistake to expect anything else. We must first call for someone capable of instilling terror [*Schrecken*] into our Dasein again.[29]

Thus, Dasein is no longer alone, absolutely individualized in the task of reawakening itself to its own essence. The task has become historical. And, where history is concerned, as Hegel already made it clear, there is so much that questioning can *do:* terror, revolutions, and the unleashing of passions can sometimes achieve far more. Of course, Goethe's valet, or the Heideggerian equivalent, namely, the "contemporary man in the street," might be somewhat disoriented and lost when confronted with the challenge of history. But never mind the man in the street. Never mind his idols and his existential gadgets. With a bit of terror coming from the right leader, everyone will get his share of the burden — although, as we all know, when the *Führer* eventually arrived, some were made to take upon themselves a burden with allures of death and ashes, and the terror that spread over Europe had little to do with the *Entsetzen* or the becoming seized by terror which Heidegger advocates as the precondition for the "bliss of astonishment" or the sense of wonder before beings as a whole. Can Heidegger really have been mistaken to such a degree? Can he really have picked the "wrong man," welcoming Hitler himself as the genuinely historical figure whose destiny was to liberate us from our existential torpor by introducing oppression, danger, incertitude, strength, and power in politics? Can Heidegger really have believed in the National Socialist terror — in spite of the absolute transparency in its ultimate goals and its lack of the most rudimentary philosophical ambition — as in this historical breath that was to sweep through Europe and announce a golden age for this existent being who we are? Can Heidegger have genuinely seen in Nazism the possibility of freeing the essence of Dasein and of constituting it in an authentic community? I believe so. It is striking to see the extent to which the terms with which Heidegger embraces the forcing into line (*Gleichschaltung*) of the German university in his Rectoral address are virtually identical with the ones developed in the 1929–30 lecture course. In both cases it is a matter of extracting the epoch from its torpor and its indifference to the ontological difference, a matter of once again opening history to the power of the whole of being, of holding it and maintaining it there, in short, of acting in such a way that the epoch become philosophical again by reawakening itself to the sense of wonder and awe before the fact of being. To believe, if only for a second, that Hitler and his "movement" may have had the slightest intention of realizing such an ideal amounts to an obvious and particularly worrying form of blindness. But equally worrying is the fact that, at least for a while, Heidegger believed that such a historical turning could be brought about by a political regime, whatever its nature. To expect from any movement, party, or government that they reawaken us to our essence as ek-sistent beings amounts to a political fault: it is at once too ambitious and naïve, too theological and messianic. But this is perhaps, for us, the political lesson that can be drawn from this past century, who will have believed in politics as in a saving and redemptive power. And Heidegger himself will not be caught at this twice: having burnt his fingers in politics, his hopes will turn to thought, and to the still buried resources of art and poetry, all deemed to carry a historical and destinal power far greater than that of politics.

Let us now close this political parenthesis and, by way of conclusion, return to our guiding question. If philosophy is defined primarily in terms of a certain opening to the disclosedness of being, or of the world as the ground from out of which beings emerge and on the basis of which our relation to beings is made possible, the question is to know whether such an opening is primarily a matter of tone and attunement. Rather, the question is that of the status of the fundamental disposition as the tone, the attunement, or the rhythm on the basis of which such an opening takes place and the ultimate aim of which is to determine Dasein no longer simply in its singularity, but as historical and communal. Is such an attunement ultimately a matter for the existential ground, and for the temporality that is coextensive with it, or is it more akin to the very breath or rhythm of being itself understood as a configuration of presence, as the epochal arrangement or constellation of being? In other words, does history unfold primarily from Dasein itself, as Heidegger suggested in *Being and Time*, and as the *Fundamental Concepts of Metaphysics* (§76) continue to assert, or is the existent not always and already historically stamped by a ground which it does not master, to which it responds and with which it corresponds, and in the midst of which each time it finds its own place? And as soon as the *Stimmung*, or the attunement, is understood as a "response to" and a "correspondence with" the *Stimme*, or the voice, of being, does philosophy itself not receive its determination (*Bestimmtheit*) from this primal opening to the being of beings as a whole, in what amounts to a sort of prelude where thought and being are harmonized, reciprocally in tune and attuned to one another? In a somewhat enigmatic passage, pregnant with thoughts to come, Heidegger expresses his own uncertainty: the question concerning the essence of time is, indeed, the founding metaphysical question, and thus the origin of all questions. However,

> whether in fact the problematic of metaphysics must always be developed
> on the basis of the temporality of Dasein, cannot be objectively decided for

the whole of world history, as it were. The possibility of a different kind of necessary grounding for metaphysics must remain open. However this possibility is not some empty, formal or logical possibility; rather, what is possible regarding this possibility depends entirely upon the fate of man.[30]

Thus, we cannot determine a priori what such a possibility may be, or under which conditions philosophy may take place. It is a matter of history and destiny, and, as such, it is not within our scope, even if it does concern us most intimately, even if this is where our fate as men is decided. But does this not suggest that the metaphysical problematic, or the problematic of thought as the thought of the ontological difference, remains inextricably rooted in the essence of time, yet no longer understood on the basis of the temporal being of Dasein, but on the basis of that which disposes us towards difference, or on the contrary turns us away from it, that is, on the basis of the history of being, which is none other than the history of the epochs of difference itself? But then the task of thinking would no longer be summarized so much under the title "being and time," as under the—still programmatic—title of "truth and history." And if such is the case, the search for the *Grundstimmug* of an epoch will find its anchor point not so much in an analysis of everyday existence as in the great metaphysical and poetical texts, these historical documents, these testimonies in which the truth of a constellation of presence is deposited, every *Grundstimmung* marking a passage, a turning within the history of being. As to know which disposition or which attunement is best suited to orient us towards the thinking of being as being, in this epoch which, more and more, Heidegger will see as abandoned from being and from the gods, one will have to wait for the great works and lecture courses from the 1930s. If the θαυμάζειν or "wonder" indeed corresponds with the fundamental disposition of metaphysics in its Greek beginning, and if "doubt," and most of all the "certainty" that is coextensive with it, indeed characterize modern thought, "terror" (*Schrecken*), Heidegger tells us, is the mark of the completion of metaphysics as technics, in that, in it, the uncanny abyss of being that escapes calculating thought begins to take shape and can be intimated. Henceforth, Heidegger will ground the very possibility of a turning of metaphysics into a new beginning and the very gathering of thought in its essence on this fundamental attunement, and on the "delicateness" and the "sacred horror" (*Scheu*) it inspires.

PART III. SCIENCE

4

Science, "Servant of Philosophy"?

The title is, if not polemical, at least deliberately provocative, even though the expression after which it is modeled is Heidegger's own. Equally, the general context within which this expression arises is in no way neutral. It already stages the encounter between philosophy, art, and science and defines the conditions of this relation, which, despite some minor alteration, will remain in place right until the very end. In his 1929-30 lectures on *The Fundamental Concepts of Metaphysics*, Heidegger provokes us "merely to recall that art — which includes poetry too — is the sister of philosophy and that all science is perhaps only a servant [*ein Dienstman*] with respect to philosophy."[1] Now, even though Heidegger goes perhaps further than he ever subsequently will in the tone of his formulation,[2] this very formulation defines the terms of the relation between philosophy and art on the one hand, and between philosophy and science on the other: whereas the first is marked by a proximity or an affinity, the second is marked by a radical distance. Ultimately, this a situation that I wish to analyze and question, wondering about the extent to which Heidegger's conception of contemporary science is not too monolithic, all too quickly identified with the event of technology, with respect to which "thinking" is to serve as a counter-essence. The general question underlying my concern, and to which I shall turn at the end of this chapter, can be formulated as follows: why is it that, while a considerable strand of philosophy (let us say, to put it schematically, "analytic" philosophy broadly defined) reorganized philosophy around the sciences, phenomenology, beginning with Heidegger himself, while engaging with the sciences in different ways, reorganized philosophy around the arts? What is it that pushes phenomenology towards art, and away from the sciences? This is my long-term and far-reaching question, the implications of which are discussed also in the following chapters: "Art, 'Sister of Philosophy'?" and "The Place of Architecture."

More immediately, and by way of examining Heidegger's relation to the sciences in general, and the natural sciences in particular, I wish to begin by situating the place of the sciences in Heidegger's thought, focusing on his remarks and analyses contemporaneous with the thinking of being in its truth and historical unfolding. As a second stage, and by way of laying out the ground for the question to which I was referring a moment ago, I would like to address a few questions to Heidegger, which can all be reduced to one: is Heidegger's description and diagnosis of modern science simply confirmed and accentuated in contemporary science — and by contemporary I mean twentieth-century physics and biology — or has science since Descartes, Galileo, and Newton undergone a transformation that is not simply epistemological, but also ontological? In other words, does Heidegger's description of "modern science" apply to contemporary science? A further concern, which is intimately linked with the first, has to do with the irreducible link that Heidegger establishes between the event of modern — and this means experimental and practical — science and technology as marking the metaphysical destiny of Western history. The two concerns come together in the following question: if Heidegger's diagnosis concerning the "mathematical project of nature" as opening onto the total control, domination, and subjectification of nature as a whole indeed finds its most obvious attestation in seventeenth- and eighteenth-century physics, does it still portray adequately science's relation to nature *today?* In other words, is science essentially and necessarily — fatally — bound up with such a project? Is it itself the servant of technology, or can it serve as a counter-measure to technology by revealing the extent to which its relation to nature, far from being one of mastery and domination, can only ever be one of *dialogue,* and one which, furthermore, can only take place from within nature itself?[3] And if such is the case, should philosophy see in contemporary science the greatest and highly dialectical danger of a servant turned master and possessor of not just philosophy, but nature as such and as a whole? Or should it see science as an ally with respect to the possibility of thinking the ontico-ontological difference anew and engaging in a dialogue with nature? Remarkably, we shall see how, on at least one occasion, yet at length, Heidegger considered that very possibility, broaching an intriguing relation between philosophy and biology.

Science in the Light of Its Essence

> Insofar as, in pursuing our way, we must speak of the sciences, we shall be speaking not against but for them, for clarity concerning their essence. This alone implies our conviction that the sciences are in themselves something positively essential. However, their essence is frankly of a different sort from what our universities today still imagine it to be. . . .the sciences today belong in the domain of the *essence* of technology, and only there.[4]

The above quotation describes with great accuracy and great economy the fundamental nature of Heidegger's relation to the sciences. It is not for philosophy to elevate itself to the status of a science, and this means to model itself after the mathematical-physical paradigm that seems to have fascinated so much of philosophy since Kant. Nor is it a question of simply declaring that science and philosophy have nothing to do with one another. For philosophy, or thinking in Heidegger's sense, has everything to do with science, with science understood as an event and a phenomenon—as something positively essential. If it speaks of science, it does not speak against it, but *for* it—not in the way of the philosophy of science, whose role it is to expose the findings, methods, and tools of the various sciences, but only to the extent that it speaks for its *essence*. Philosophy's relation to science is one of essence: in its relation to science, philosophy is philosophy only to the extent that it thinks science with respect to its essence, and to its essence alone. Whereas science itself can transform itself into a philosophy of science, it is simply unable, qua science, to think the essence from which it unfolds. Thus, if the sciences call for *thinking*, and not simply for debates or discussion, if they constitute a *positive* phenomenon, it is insofar as they themselves cannot "think." They can, of course, represent, describe, calculate with great accuracy, and reflect on their own procedures and presuppositions, but they cannot think, at least in Heidegger's sense. For thinking is always the thinking of *essence*. This is where thinking takes place, and nowhere else. There very well may be questions raised and problems articulated outside of the question of essence, not just in the sciences, but in philosophy itself, yet such questions and problems have not even begun to enter the domain of thought proper. We shall have to see, of course, what Heidegger means by essence. But at this stage, let us simply note that the sciences call for thinking, and precisely insofar as they cannot think. Thought does not think against science, then, but in its name, or in the name of its essence. This means, of course, that the essence of sci-

ence is itself nothing scientific, that it cannot be investigated scientifically. It means that science emerges and unfolds from a ground
that is altogether heterogeneous to the scientific practice it has become.
And therein lies Heidegger's greatest difficulty, one encountered in every
phenomenon or event that calls for thinking: actually to show this emergence and unfolding, actually to reveal how a positive phenomenon such
as the advent of modern science is the effect or the outcome of an event
which is itself nothing scientific and that Heidegger characterizes as the
essence of technology (and not technology per se). But what is the
essence of technology in which the essence of science is grounded?

Whence does the event "modern science" unfold, if not from science
itself, from an evolution or even a transformation of science as previously conceived? This event, Heidegger claims, has its origin in the essence of technology. Not in technology per se — for do we not *know* from
an historical perspective that modern science precedes technology, and
by that we mean the birth of mechanized industry in the late eighteenth century? — but in the *essence* of technology. And so we now need
to ask: What is the essence of technology? The birth of modern science
is only, on Heidegger's reading, a derivative phenomenon, the origin of
which is to be found in the essence of technology. Similarly, however,
the essence of technology is itself nothing technological. Science and technology must be thought together, but on the basis of an essence that is
heterogeneous to both. And if thought has to do with essence and essence
alone, it means that it itself is entirely different from, or entirely heterogeneous to, science and technology. It is separated from them by an abyss,
the abyss of essence. Yet this abyss is precisely what grounds science and
technology, it is precisely what allows them to be or unfold as such.

In his *Contributions to Philosophy*, Heidegger describes what he calls
"machination," which designates the event and essence of technology,
as the "epoch of the total lack of questioning" (*Zeitalter der völligen Fra-
glosigkeit*). This does not mean that, these days, questions are not asked.
On the contrary. But we need to distinguish between questions that are
responses in disguise, questions that are formulated retroactively, from
the answers themselves — this is the quiz question, whether at school or
on television — and those questions, few and rare, which question in the
direction of a dimension that is far in excess of any response, for such
questions belong in the realm of the questionability of that which is in
question, and need not be formulated by way of question marks. There
are false questions in the same way in which there are false answers. But
genuine questioning coincides with the operation of thought as such.
Such is the reason why Heidegger calls questioning "the piety of
thought." Now, as we have already begun to see, the question in Heidegger's sense always bears on "essence." Thus, the *question* (or the problem) concerning technology and modern science is a question regarding

its essence; the question concerning the thing is a question regarding its essence, etc. But "essence" here is not to be understood in the Aristotelian, and subsequently scholastic and modern, sense of *quidditas*. I would even claim that the entire difference, the difference between metaphysics or representation and thought, is concentrated in the space between those two senses of "essence." For where metaphysics asks the question τί, *quid,* the thing that is in question with respect to its essence is already given in its thingliness, and it is only a question of representing it on the basis of its presence. Thus, the essence always ends up resembling the thing in question; as a re-presentation, it is always modeled after the thing in its presence, and this precisely when it is supposed to account for the thing in its very presence and identity. Between the conditioning essence (*Be-dingung*) and the conditioned thing (*das Be-dingte*), there is always a relation of image, of semblance and likeness, and therefore of identity, even if and when this likeness is most remote, even if and when the relation of semblance has been loosened to a maximum. Now, the entire force of the ontico-ontological difference in Heidegger's sense is to show how the relation between condition and conditioned is, first, not a relation between a thing or a being, or even a principle, and another thing, but a relation between a process, or a verb and a being, or a participle, and, second, not a relation of likeness and identity between a universal law or kind and a particular instance, but a relation of difference between a pre-individual singularity and an individuated thing. Thus, from quiddity, the sense of essence becomes event: *Wesen* henceforth points to a process, a becoming or a genesis, which is precisely not that of creation, or of production understood as reproduction of the same in beings. Between essence and the thing there is indeed something like a genesis, or a coming into presence, but the essence does not serve as the model—which is always a model of self-presence and self-identity—or the originary manifestation after whose image the thing itself would appear. The essence of a thing is its mode of coming-into-presence and presupposes difference: beings are nothing like being, yet unfold from its unfolding. This is even what so many find upsetting in Heidegger's approach: the essence of technoscience is nothing techno-scientific, the essence of the thing is nothing thing-like, and the essence of essence, as indicated in "On the Essence of Truth," is nothing other than its non-essence, which is not to be equated with its mere negative, or its inverted image, but with its counter-effectuation.[5] If the question in Heidegger's sense bears on essence, and on essence alone, it is because it alone bears and sustains the truly questionworthy or problematic dimension of the real. All questions bearing directly on things, to which scientific questions already belong, are already responses to a prior question bearing on the essence of such things; such questions bearing directly on things are thus already the impossibility of any essential questions, that is, questions bearing not on the representation of things given in advance in their presence, but on the eventfulness of things, on the non-present horizon from out of which they present themselves as things. If machination signifies the degree zero of questioning, then, it is not in the sense that it does not formulate any questions or articulate any problems. Rather, it is in the sense in which that on the basis of which these questions and problems are formulated, namely, given presence, is itself already a response to a question that is far more decisive, for it addresses being in its eventful unfolding. And the question of essence, which drives the entirety of Heidegger's thought and marks the possibility of thought itself, is formulated in the following terms: *Wie west das Sein?*—How does being unfold according to its essence? It is a question concerning being in its *how,* not its *what.* Needless to say, then, essence, to which thought belongs, and from which science and technology unfold, is itself nothing human: thought, science, and technology are not primarily, essentially, human activities; as human activities, they point to a non-human origin. In every human activity there is something older than the human.[6]

In order to follow the movement of essence, I wish to begin by looking at a lecture Heidegger delivered in 1938 under the title "The Epoch of the World-Image," in which the relation between science and technology is addressed most clearly in terms of their common essence. The lecture opens with the following statement:

> One of the essential phenomena of modernity is its science. A no less important phenomenon is machine technology. However, we should not mistake it for the mere application, in praxis, of the mathematical sciences of nature. Rather, machine technology is itself an autonomous transformation of praxis, and this is in such a way that it is rather it, praxis, which demands the use of the mathematical sciences of nature. Machine technology remains the hitherto most visible continuation of the essence of technology, which is identical with the essence of modern metaphysics.[7]

Thus, to the essence of science and the essence of technology, we now need to add yet another essence: the essence of metaphysics. Science, technology, metaphysics all share the same essence. This, of course, does not mean that they are identical, or that they can be reduced to one another, but simply that they unfold from the same ground, are born of the same process or event. The addition of this latter essence, though, is possibly more surprising, insofar as while the connection between science and technology seems inevitable, the connection between techno-science and metaphysics is certainly not. Particularly if we recall that, prior to the introduction of the entire problematic of machination and technology, and most typically in "What Is Metaphysics?," "On the Essence of Ground," and *The Fundamental Concepts of Metaphysics,* "metaphysics" designated precisely the transcendent ground or the essence of science itself, understood both as *die Wissenschaft,* or philosophy as *Urwissenschaft,* and as modern techno-science. The very place and the very meaning of metaphysics itself has shifted, in light of the question regarding the meaning of being having been recast as the question concerning the essence and the truth of being in its historical-destinal dimension. Thus, metaphysics is no longer so much the ground and essence of science and technology, as it is itself a derivative phenomenon to be thought alongside the advent of techno-science in modern times. The question of essence now bears also on what was once thought to be the essence, and that is human transcendence. The question of essence points beyond the human, even reinterpreted as ecstatic transcendence, into the otherwise than human.

The question that now needs to be raised in connection with these phenomena, a question that designates them in the unity of their provenance, is the following: "What conception of beings and what interpretation of truth underlie these phenomena?"[8] In other words: at the very heart of the advent of modern science and technology lies a pre-understanding regarding the being of beings, or regarding the way in which beings as a whole are or present themselves. This event takes place within a pre-conception of truth to which these phenomena have no access as such, and which philosophy alone can access. The question regarding the essence of techno-science is a question regarding a specific configuration or economy of truth, a question regarding a specific disposition or pre-orientation towards things, and subsequently a specific interpretation of truth. How can such a conception be defined? It is a conception marked by "research" (*Forschung*), and by that we need to understand a particular "project" (*Entwurf*), which needs to be understood both in its ordinary meaning, as expressing a specific goal or plan, albeit a pre- or unconscious one, and in the sense of a particular mode of being, of a particular stance taken amid things in the world. This project is further characterized as that through which a fundamental plan or base (*Grundriß*) is projected onto a domain of beings, most significantly nature. At the heart of modern science, then, there is a plan that guides and orients the research. Modern man, insofar as he is under the grip of techno-science, orients himself within nature on the basis of a pre-given project. This project precedes and allows for the event of techno-science, delimits and frames the realm of the possible for the human in modern times. Nature itself is this delineated, circumscribed, and framed area. This is the extent to which the project is mathematical. Mathematized nature refers first and foremost to nature having become the object of this project, having the distinct trait of the *Grundriß* according to which and on the basis of which the human orients itself. Nature is never neutrally given, is always pre-given, historically pre-understood, and mathematized, planned, and projected nature characterizes our current pre-understanding of it. Beings as a whole are oriented in a particular way, pre-disposed and pre-oriented as falling into and finding their place within a pre-allocated frame (which Heidegger will later on call the *Gestell*, or the frame).

A few consequences follow from this, in terms of what is ordinarily seen as distinctive traits of modern science. If such traits are indeed distinctive, they are nonetheless not *essential*, but only secondary and derivative with respect to the essence of techno-science as carried out in the mathematical project of nature. Two such traits are most often associated with the advent of modern science: first, it is said that science, and physics in particular, is mathematical, or calculative; second, that it is experimental. Now, if it is undeniable that modern physics is entirely dependent on mathematics (and on Euclidean geometry and differential calculus in particular), and no longer, as was still partly the case in ancient physics, on metaphysical speculations regarding the structure of matter, as in Greek and Roman atomism, or on the hierarchical structure of the universe, as in Aristotelian physics and cosmology; if, in other words, the success of modern physics can be attributed to its ability to verify its hypotheses mathematically, the origin of such a "mathematical" turn in physics refers back to a much older event, which is not calculative in essence, yet which allows for discoveries such as differential calculus and Newton's equations. It is because physics takes place within a more general project, mathematical in essence, whereby nature is determined and envisaged in advance, already known to some extent (the extent in which it is to be encountered as an object of scientific investigation and research), that physics can become mathematical in the restricted sense, and this means an "exact" science, the exactness of which is a function of the precision of mathematical calculation:

> The strength of mathematical natural science is exactness. . . . But the mathematical exploration of nature is not exact because it calculates correctly. Rather, it must thus calculate, because what binds it to its domain of objectivity has the character of exactness.[9]

In other words, by mathematics in the primordial sense, Heidegger means the specific "decision" within which the encounter with nature takes place in modern times. And in this specific project nature appears as "the self-enclosed nexus of spatio-temporally related movements of different mass-points" (*der in sich geschlossene Bewegungszusammenhang raum-zeitlich bezogener Massenpunkte*).[10] Now, this general definition of modern physics does indeed apply to Newtonian physics, and the further details and explanations given by Heidegger and immediately following this definition seem to cover the main points of classical dynamics. But it integrates neither the laws of thermodynamics—the second of which has decisive consequences with respect to the reversibility of time postulated in Newtonian dynamics—nor relativity, which called into question the Newtonian principle according to which space and time were two entirely unrelated and independent phenomena, nor, finally, quantum mechanics, which simply formalized mathematically an entire new domain of nature that seemed to escape, at least in part, the basic laws of classical dynamics. Allow me to leave to one side the question as to whether Heidegger's description of the mathematical project of nature accurately portrays the state of physics in the twentieth century, and whether a closer analysis of such a state would in a sense call into question Heidegger's entire diagnosis regarding the fate of science in its correlation to technology. What matters at this stage, and following Heidegger's analysis, is that a phenomenon can become visible as such, and thus qualify as a phenomenon, only insofar as it conforms to this plan, and this means only insofar as it is determined in advance as a spatio-temporal magnitude. To the extent that nature can still be thought it is perceived as having to conform to the criteria and standards developed by modern physics. Outside the rigor and exactitude of this discipline, best suited to teach us what nature is and guaranteed by mathematics, there is only the non-scientific and highly subjective interpretation of poetry, or of religion. The true is now associated entirely with the objective, and if other conceptions of nature are recognized, it is only in the name of the subjective, which is a matter for personal taste and preference. As for the second alleged distinctive trait of modern science, namely, the turn to the experimental verification of mathematically formalized hypotheses, it too is only a derivative phenomenon with respect to the founding metaphysical event of modern times, namely, the mathematical project of nature:

> Yet it is not through experimentation that the natural sciences essentially become research; on the contrary, experimentation becomes possible where and only where the very knowledge of nature has transformed itself into research. It is only because modern physics is essentially mathematical that it can be experimental.[11]

In other words, the experiment is itself guided and sustained by a hypothesis, the outcome of which will be determined by an ability (or not) to follow a series of movements in the necessity of their development, and to formalize this necessity mathematically. But the hypothesis itself reveals and presupposes a metaphysical pre-orientation within nature, and a theoretical decision regarding the status of nature itself.

How can such a pre-conception of beings as a whole and such an interpretation of truth be further qualified? What concept of truth and what image of nature lie at the heart of the mathematical project characteristic of modern science? The response to this question lies perhaps in just one word, although this word carries with it an entire cluster of philosophemes that run through the whole of Heidegger's thought from the 1930s onward. The word is "Representation." And here one has no other choice but to refer to the German concept of which "representation" is a translation: *Vorstellen*. For it is the root-verb *stellen* (to posit) that is of paramount importance here, a root-verb around which Heidegger gathers many other verbs, past participles, and nouns: *vorstellen* (to represent), *herstellen* (to produce, to make, to establish in the sense of bringing to stand), *erstellen* (to erect, to construct—a verb, in fact, very close to *herstellen*), *sicherstellen* (to take possession of), *das Gestellte* (what is posited), *das Gestell* (the frame, the stand). All these terms help characterize the essential trait of the relation between man and nature in modern times, and the way in which this relation crystallizes in modern science and technology. By following this semantic thread we should be able to delimit the modern conception of truth, and take the full measure of the event of modern science.

Insofar as it is "research," modern science comports itself to nature as what can be represented. It directs itself towards nature in terms of the extent to which it can be made available for representation and mathematical formalization. In this process of formal representation and calculation, nature is as it were summoned and forced to reveal itself as the representable pure and simple. It is in this process that nature becomes objectified, that phenomena become objects. Only what thus becomes an object is considered to be, is recognized, and identified as *being*. Beings are now objects. Science has become objective and is driven by the search for the objectivity of objects. This objectification of beings is announced and completed in a representation, whereby beings are posited before one's theoretical-scientific gaze:

> The whole of beings is now taken in such a way, that it first is and can only be to the extent that it is posited by the human as representing and producing [*sofern es durch den vorstellend-herstellenden Menschen gestellt ist*]. . . . The being of beings is sought and found in the representability [*Vorgestelltheit*] of beings.[12]

It is only when beings cannot be grasped in the event of their being or in their essence, it is when they are perceived as given and already individuated within presence, that they not only can but must be re-presented. Representation becomes the only way in which they can be addressed and investigated. For "thought," whether philosophical or scientific, it becomes a matter of producing images of beings, of mapping their presence and their comportment in formal representations. The world itself, beings as a whole, come to be seen as that which can be represented: "is" what can be "represented." Implicit in beings, then, or rather in this interpretation of their being, is their reproducibility: beings can be reproduced in thought understood as a power of representation. And, indeed, from this side of itself, from this *present* side of itself, every being *is* representable. Science testifies most clearly and most exemplarily to this representability. From this side of presence, all beings are in principle reproducible. Reproducibility, from which production, and specifically industrial and mechanical reproduction, follows, is co-extensive with representation.

To the ontological status of beings as always and already given in their presence, evident and unquestionable with respect to their coming-into-presence, and therefore as available for representation and repro-duction, there corresponds a new way of being amid beings, on the side of the human. For the transformation takes place not just on the side of what has now become an ob-ject (*Gegenstand*). It also and co-extensively takes place on the side of what or who, in the process, in this mutation of truth, has become a subject. To the stance that now properly belongs to what is present (*Vorhandene*) as *Gegen-stand* or ob-ject corresponds a stance of the one who represents as sub-jectum, as providing and sus-taining the ground for the object in its objectivity, as the being whose being consists primarily in its ability to represent, formalize, calculate, anticipate, etc. For only a subject in the modern sense of the term can represent. What does representation signify if not this ability to bring or posit before oneself (*vor-stellen*) what is simply present (*das Vorhandene*) as something standing opposite or against (*als ein Entgegenstehendes*)? What does representation entail, if not this bringing or this positing of the present before oneself by bringing it to oneself? Thus, to the *Stellen* of *Vorstellen*, to the presentation that characterizes representation, there corresponds a particular stance. It is no longer the Greek stance, the ecstatic ex-sistence of the one who dwells amid things in their originary presence, and in the event of their presencing, but the sub-sistence of the one who brings the world to him- or herself by positing him- or herself as the ground for the presence of all present things, as the ground for the objectivity of objects. To be in the world for the modern man, and, in an exemplary way, for the man of science, means to stand within in such a way that the world as such and as whole within which that stand is taken becomes an object for representation, formalization, and, ultimately, appropriation and domination:

> To represent [*vorstellen*] means here: to posit something before oneself from out of oneself [*von sich her etwas vor sich stellen*], and to take possession of the posited as such [*und das Gestellte als ein solches sicherstellen*]. . . . Representation is no longer the hearing [*das Vernehmen*] of what unfolds in presence [*des An-wesenden*], in the unconcealment of which the hearing itself belongs, and this as a mode of coming-to-presence proper to what unfolds in presence as the unconcealed. Representation is no longer a matter of disclosing oneself to . . . [*das Sich-entbergen für*], but of grasping and conceiving [*das Ergreifen und*

Begreifen von]. . . . It is no longer the reign of what unfolds in presence [*das Anwesende*], but the domination of the attack [*Angreifen*]. Beings are no longer what is simply unfolding in presence [*das Anwesende*], but what is first posited over against in representation [*das im Vorstellen erst entgegen Gestellte*], what is standing over against as an ob-ject [*das Gegen-ständige*].[13]

Greek man encountered nature as φύσις, or as birth to presence, and medieval man experienced nature as permeated by the eternal presence of god. Modern man, however, in facing the world as that which faces him from out of his capacity to represent it, encounters only himself, even when encountering the world, for this encounter takes place from within representation alone. Man has become the *subjectum* or the ὑποκείμενον itself, and by this we need to understand: the ground onto which every thing is gathered and allowed to unfold in its being and its truth. As a power of representation, man has become the absolute — an absolute that, in the end, reveals itself as will to power.[14] It is, in Heidegger's view, the unquestioned and unchallenged centrality of the figure of the human, the essentially anthropocentric metaphysics of our age, that is the decisive phenomenon behind modern and contemporary culture, characterized by the ever increasing presence of science, technology, and mass consumption. As such, our techno-scientific age signifies the consumed reign of a humanism coextensive with the very birth of modernity.

Now, representation is a trait that modern science shares with metaphysics: the world "is" only to the extent that it can be "represented," whether mathematically, by way of functions, theorems, axioms, equations, or philosophically, by way of concepts. But thought as such, what Heidegger at times calls "originary thought" (*anfängliche Denken*), is concerned only with presentation, and this means with the coming into presence of the present, prior to any representation. Thought is concerned with presence as such, or with the event of presence in what is present, an event which itself is simply in excess of and irreducible to the present.[15] In order to take the full measure of the difference between scientific representation and thought, let us turn to the following common experience, which Heidegger allows to unfold before us as it takes place, and through the phenomenological method that demands that we efface ourselves before the phenomenon, allowing it to unfold from its very place, which is not human consciousness, as a site of representations, but the earth, as the originary site of presentation:

If we nonetheless leave science aside now in dealing with the question regarding what representation [*das Vorstellen*] is, we do not do so in the proud delusion that we know better, but out of circumspection for not-knowing [*die Vorsicht eines Nichtwissens*].

We stand outside of science. Instead we stand before a tree in bloom, for example — and the tree stands before us. The tree faces us [*er stellt sich uns vor:* it presents itself to us]. The tree and we stand opposite one another [*stellen uns einander vor:* we are present to one another], as the tree stands there [*dasteht*] and we stand over against it [*ihm gegenüber stehen*]. As we are in this relation of one to the other and before the other, the tree and we *are*. In this presentation [*Vorstellen*], it is not a matter of "representations" [*Vorstellungen*] buzzing about in our heads. . . . Judged scientifically, of course, it remains the most inconsequential thing on earth that each of us has at some time stood facing a tree in bloom. After all, what of it? . . .

What happens here, that the tree stands before us, and we come to stand face-to-face with the tree? Where does this presentation take place, when we stand face-to-face before a tree in bloom? Does it by any chance take place in our heads? Of course.[16]

In a sense, then, the difference between the metaphysical-scientific attitude and the thoughtful and still phenomenological attitude is played out in these two senses of *Vorstellen:* as the ability, first, simply to stand within the space of that which stands before us, as the event of a co-originary and co-extensive presence; or, second, in a way that is irreconcilable with the former modality of presence, as the ability on the part of the human to represent, to turn into an ideality and an object that which is first born of the earth and belongs to it essentially. There is an event, then, the event of presence as such, in the face of which science remains speechless and powerless. This is the event in which the human, far from producing representations of the tree, far from mapping it mathematically and physically, or even conceptually, lets that tree be there, precisely where it is, in the very way in which it presents itself, in the very *place* in which it stands and its presence unfolds. If science does not think, it is only in the sense that what calls for thinking is precisely the simplicity of this event, which goes unnoticed in modern science, which cannot come to the surface by way of representation, and yet which is presupposed in every representation, in the very advent of modern science as such:

If the being—τὸ ἐόν—were not already manifest as something present, it could never appear as object. If the εἶναι (being) did not reign as the event of presence [*als Anwesen*], then we would not even be in a position to ask about the present [*Gegenwart*] in the Object [*Gegenstand*], and this means about its objectivity [*Gegenständigkeit*]. . . .

If the being of beings did not already reign in the sense of the event of presence of what is present, then beings could never have appeared as what stands over against [*als Gegenständinge*], as what characterizes the object in its objectivity. . . . If the being of beings were not already manifest as the presencing of the present, then electrical atomic energy could not have been born, nor indeed enroll men in the pan-technological form of work.[17]

Philosophy, science, technology all presuppose this event of presence in the midst of present beings; if they can go about with their business—

representing things in their objectivity, representing beings in their beingness, or in their being-natural, or being-life, or being-historical—it is always from this horizon of presencing, which they ignore and forget. They all begin with beings already present, without questioning them in their coming into presence, in their essence or provenance; from then on, they proceed with the metaphysical representation, and subsequently the physical-mathematical representation of beings. This question concerning the presencing of the present is a genetic question, that is, a question concerning the source or the origin from out of which the presencing of beings takes place. This is a question to which a temporal dimension belongs, yet one that is entirely in excess of the temporality of the world itself, of beings as already present, and to which metaphysics does not have access. Science cogitates, science represents, science explores and invents, science puzzles and disturbs. But science does not think. For thinking, at least on Heidegger's own terms, marks the ability to allow the event of presence itself to finds its way through language; it marks a possibility and a certain mode of standing amid things—the stance whereby things are allowed to unfold from their horizon of non-presence. The difference between thought and science is this abyssal difference separating the event of presence from the operation of objectification, the difference between *Gelassenheit* and *Vorstellung*. To claim that science does not think is simply to claim that science is not thought, that the two are separated by a difference in nature, that thought can never be scientific, and this means ultimately technological, but that the event or the essence of technology is precisely its object. For if, as Heidegger puts it, "thought has nothing to do with science," science, "on the other hand, and in its own way, always has to do with thought." The difference between thought and science is also the difference between "learning" and "knowing," a difference that Heidegger develops at some length in the opening pages of *What Is Called Thinking?* Thought knows literally nothing, it is this "knowing-less" than science; but it learns. Science, on the other hand, knows (almost everything), but does not learn. For one learns only in the proximity of the question, which remains in excess of any answer, but one knows only answers, which always presuppose the question, or what is most worthy of questioning.

However, even with the discovery of the essence of modern technoscience in the mathematical project of nature, even with the identification of the character of beings or things as objects, and of the human as subject, from which the modern conception of truth as certainty and the ideal of representation as exactness follows, we have not reached the full essence. For this phenomenon must still be accounted for as a possibility. More specifically, we need to ask about the slip from presentation to representation. How are we to interpret the *historical* turn? Was there, after all, an epoch or a moment in which the event of presence was truly experienced, devoid of representation? If not, does it not mean that science always was the measure of thought, that no clear boundary ever existed between thought and science? Has the conception of nature mutated in the way in which Heidegger describes it, or has it always lent itself, from the very start, to representation? Behind or beneath the essence of techno-science as the mathematical project of nature there lies an even deeper phenomenon: *Seinsverlassenheit*.

The concept of *Seinsverlassenheit*, to which that of *Gelassenheit*, inherited from Meister Eckahrt, will respond a few years later, is developed at length in Heidegger's *Contributions to Philosophy*, written between 1936 and 1938.[18] In that manuscript Heidegger devotes a few sections to the question of science, which he already thinks within the larger context of technology, or "machination" (*Machenschaft*). Yet machination itself, as the reign of full presence in which things have become objects, simply present and constantly available (*Bestand*), is coextensive with another phenomenon, or rather the same phenomenon, but already somewhat clarified as to its essence: *Seinsvergessenheit*, or the forgottenness of being in its truth (*Wahrheit*) or its essential unfolding (*Wesen*). This forgottenness is precisely what leads to the metaphysics of representation, insofar as one begins with already individuated things in their presence, with beings, without ever being in a position to question such beings with respect to the event of being or presence though which they come to be, but which is itself nothing like a being, a substance, an object, or even a subject. If metaphysics is a thought-of substance, it is primarily because the world it encounters and portrays is cut off from its non-substantial, truly event-ful or verbal origin, a world severed from the eventfulness of being. Yet *Seinsvergessenheit*, as the distinctive trait of metaphysical thought, has itself its root in yet a more originary phenomenon, the "abandonment of being" (*Seinsverlassenheit*). *Seinsverlassenheit* points to the origin of the forgottenness of being, and reveals this origin as structural, and this means ontological. So it is not as if the forgottenness of being were a matter of some mnemic deficiency on the part of the human psyche or brain, of some accidental moment within history up until then marked by a close proximity to the event of being. Rather, if the forgottenness of being calls for remembrance, it is only insofar as remembrance alone is adequate to the matter, only insofar as it coincides with thought as such. For the matter is precisely the event of being as the event of a turning away from presence within presence, the event of an abandonment or an erasure constitutive of presence and of history as such. Nowhere is this emphasis on the connection between thought and remembrance stressed with greater emphasis than in *What Is Called Thinking?* where Heidegger simply equates the possibility of genuine thought itself with the ability to remember an event that never took place in the present, but that is constitutive of the present as such, that opens it up and withdraws in that very opening. And if science is said not to think, it is precisely to the extent that the operation of thought for Heidegger is intimately and irreducibly bound up with the possibility of turning to that which, in beings themselves, has always turned itself away from them, and this at the precise moment when it allows them to unfold in their very essence, as those very beings that they are. The abyss separating thought, or meditation (*Besinnung*), from science is the abyss separating two temporal orders: a past that never was present, and so never calls for re-presentation, but for memory alone; a present, the essence of which can be grasped only in being re-presented. What science cannot think is its non-scientific origin or essence, one that is based on the founding and forever recurring event, the event of being in excess of, yet withdrawing in, beings. And yet, precisely for that reason, science demands to be thought, calls for thinking: for the non-scientific essence of science continues to echo at the heart of science, and only from out of this echo can science be genuinely understood as an event. So long as the advent of modern science is not placed back in the historical-destinal (*geschichtlich* and *geschicklich*) context from within which it is made possible, namely, machination, it is simply not *thought*.

How is machination described in *Contributions to Philosophy?* Machination is said to designate the *Unwesen des Seyns,* the non-essence of being. Now, *Unwesen* can and must be understood in two different ways here, granted that those two ways belong together and ultimately cannot be thought independently of one another. We can begin by stressing the "non-" in non-essence. In that sense, machination is the covering over or the erasing of the truth of being, of the event of presence that is in excess of anything simply present. As such, machination knows of presence alone, a presence that is further qualified as *beständige Anwesenheit,* both in the sense of constant, continual, or permanent presence, and in the sense of stock, readily available stuff, a twofold sense already announced in the interpretation of being as οὐσία. As Un-*wesen,* machination designates the process of the event whereby the essence or the unfolding (the *Wesen*) of being itself, what Heidegger calls the "truth" of being, is indeed covered over and forgotten. Machination, in which the fate of this erasure or this forgetting is played out, is nothing other than the history of this non-essence of being. It is the history of how the *event* of presence is erased in favor of presence alone, the history of the becoming-present in which the event of being is implicated from the very start. But, equally importantly—and one cannot emphasize this point enough, for it is too often ignored or forgotten, and is the source of much confusion and basic misinterpretations—*Un*-wesen is also Un-*wesen.* Certainly, machination is the *non*-essence or the counter-essence of being. But it is also its non-*essence* or its counter-*essence.* What does this mean? It means that between the event of being, to which Heidegger's thought as a whole is directed, and its own forgottenness or erasure in machination, there is a *structural* unity. Not an accidental relation, linked to some historical contingency, but an essential or intimate relation, precisely, which amounts to nothing other than the necessity of history. History is history of this necessity: it is the unfolding or the happening of the becoming-presence (and present) of the event of presence. Machination, as the non-essence of being, is precisely the non-essence *of* being. With the decisive consequence, then, that this non-essence is our only access to its essence or its truth. We cannot even begin to think this essence—and, for Heidegger, as we have already seen, this means simply to *think,* as opposed to *representing*—without thinking the way in which, structurally and necessarily, this essence unfolds as its non- or counter-essence: as metaphysics, and its continuation in contemporary science and technology. In other words, to think the essence or the truth of being is to think the way in which this essence or this truth has always and already begun to unfold in and as its non-essence or untruth. The essential unfolding of being is the unfolding of its non-essence. *Unwesen* is the "echoing" (*Anklang*) of *Wesen.* Tuning into this echoing provides the only access to the event of being and the only possible broaching of a counter-history, or a history "after" or, rather, perhaps simply parallel to the history of metaphysics—what Heidegger calls "the other beginning":

> Abandonment of being means that being abandons beings and leaves beings to themselves and thus lets beings become objects of machination. All of this is not simply "decline" but the earliest history of being itself, the history of the first beginning and of what is derived from this beginning—and thus necessarily stayed behind. But even this staying behind is not something "negative." Rather, in its end it merely brings to light the abandonment of being, granted that the question of the truth of being is asked from within the other beginning and so begins the move towards encountering the first beginning.[19]

Needless to say, then, there is no residual history, no other historical moment "in" history that would escape this structural erasure. Rather, the residual counter-history is there at every moment in history, precisely as residue, or as this potential that remains shy of full presence. As a result, there is no epoch, no place to which one could return as if to a lost possibility of thought; thought—as Heidegger insists throughout, but most obviously in *What Is Called Thinking?*—is always to come, yet precisely insofar as what calls for thinking and gives food for thought is something that has turned away from us from the very start, the event of the pure past as well as the pure future, in excess of the present in presence. One must surrender to this "evidence" (far from any evidence) that the event of being withdraws and erases itself in that which it opens up: presence as such, the world and the things populating it. History, understood from the unfolding or the event of being, is nothing besides this

inscription that is the mark of a withdrawal or an absencing: "Abandonment of being must be experienced as the basic event [*Grundgeschehnis*]
of our history."[20] Fundamentally, the event "modern science" is only the
effect of this structural historical-destinal trait. It is an event that shelters
its possibility and its authority from the inevitable becoming-presence of
the event of presence, or the withdrawal of the event of being in beings:
"That being abandons beings means: being *conceals itself* [*verbirgt sich*] in
the openness [*Offenbarkeit*] of beings."[21]

It is on the basis of machination thus defined that a true encounter
with science can take place. In §73 of *Contributions to Philosophy,* entitled
"The abandonment of being and 'Science,'" Heidegger claims that such
an encounter can only take the form of a meditation (*Besinnung*) of science, and this means a form of non-technological, non-machinic questioning that questions and thinks, if not *from* the other beginning, at
least from the space opened up by the question regarding the possibility
of this other beginning — if not from the perspective of a straightforward
overcoming (*Überwindung*) of machination, at least from the perspective of re-entering its essence (*Verwindung*). Through this "meditative"
mode of encounter with modern science, the echo (*Anklang*) of the non-
scientific, *seinsverlassene* essence of science will perhaps be heard
through the event of science itself:

> Because, in and *as* modernity, truth stands fast in the shape of certainty in
> the form of a thinking of beings as re-presented ob-ject, because the ground-
> ing of modernity consists in the establishing of this standing fast, and
> because this certainty of thinking unfolds as the institution and pursuit of
> modern "science," the abandonment of being is essentially co-decided by mod-
> ern science. And this [is so] always *only insofar as* modern science claims to be
> one or even *the* decisive [*maßgebende*] knowing. *Therefore* the attempt to
> point to the abandonment of being as the echo of beyng [*Seyn*] cannot
> avoid the meditation regarding modern science and its essential rootedness
> in machination.[22]

And so, from this quotation and from everything that we have said
so far, it is clear that Heidegger does not view modern science as an
insignificant event, as an event that does not call for thinking. Quite the
opposite. Thinking as such, the very possibility of thought, cannot do
away with an encounter with modern science, precisely as a significant
aspect of the non-essence of being. But the question is: on whose
terms? Must a dialogue or a confrontation with modern science take
place on those terms defined by science itself, which is about to impose
itself as the sole, or at least the most effective, rigorous (because exact)
mode of investigation and questioning? Does modern science exhaust,
not knowledge as such, not *what* there is to know, but *how* there is to
know, what "knowing" might mean? Is there another measure for what
it means to know, or has modern science provided the ultimate and
henceforth unquestionable standard after which all else will be mea-

sured? This is a danger Heidegger felt from his very early years, and one that only increased throughout his life. The increasing technologization of the world, and the spread of the mathematical paradigm in all sectors of human knowing, meant that another mode of questioning was becoming less and less probable. The field of question and knowledge was and is in danger of becoming entirely saturated with knowledge and information (and information technology has only added to this phenomenon), to the point where "knowing" (*Wissen*) or "science" (*Wissenschaft*) in the most originary sense of the term needs to take the direction of a "less-knowing" and an essential lack of certainty, which has become the sole measure of truth. Only from out of such an impoverishing of the cognitive apparatus will the questionworthiness of that which continues to be in question be able to come forth. For the question in the most rigorous sense—and this does not mean in the sense of "exactness"—is the question concerning the dimension of being prior to and in excess of actuality itself, and with respect to which actuality is already a response. In the end, it is simply a question regarding levels of questioning, and simply a question of asking: Where, at what level, is philosophical questioning played out? Is there, after all, a specific level at which philosophy takes place, one that would need to be radically demarcated from the techno-scientific level of questioning? Heidegger always believed there was, at least in principle, even at the time when such originary questioning had become almost impossible:

> With our question, we situate ourselves outside the sciences, and the knowing to which our questioning aspires is neither better nor worse, but *wholly other*.[23]

Only by isolating a level of questioning that is proper to philosophical thinking—a level that is never reached once and for all, but that needs to be continually freed—can philosophy avoid being swept away by the techno-scientific becoming of knowledge. And yet at no point is it a question of wanting to slow down technological progress, of regaining some lost paradise, of denying the sciences their ability to disclose and reveal. Not only would this be reactionary; it would be utterly useless.

Towards a New Dialogue?

I want now to take a step back from Heidegger's analysis as presented thus far, and to formulate a few questions with a view to reestablishing the possibility of a productive dialogue between philosophy and science. The question, with respect to some more recent, post-Newtonian developments, is whether they simply confirm science in its classical direction, accelerating its process, and thus reinforcing the general metaphysical process within which they take place according to Heidegger, and that is machination or technology, or whether such developments also mark some sort of rupture or caesura, one that is not simply epistemological, internal to physics itself, but perhaps metaphysical, and thus historical. Can we speak of contemporary science in a way that is *substantially* different from modern science, and in a way that modern science did not announce? In other words, I wonder about the extent to which the fundamental and irreducible *metaphysical* origin of the event of modern science is not one that was largely analyzed and called into question by the sciences themselves, thus suggesting that the sciences, while not immediately concerned with the *philosophical* question regarding the ontico-ontological difference, have opened, perhaps almost despite themselves, onto a nature, and a sense of nature that is significantly different, thus also altering sense of the relation between man and nature, moving perhaps from the Cartesian-Newtonian paradigm of mastery and possession to a far more tentative and reciprocal relation, one perhaps best described as a *dialogue*. To be sure, we cannot help noticing that man's grip on nature has never been more secure, that our technological age appears to have put us in control of the very fate of nature and of the earth in a way that we have not hitherto experienced. In a way, then, we cannot help but think that the completion of the modern project of a nature entirely domesticated and mastered is being fulfilled. At the same time, however, and in the light of the scientific discoveries of the last two centuries, from evolutionary biology to quantum theory and relativity, we might well be forgiven for thinking that the place of the human amid the infinity of the cosmos, nature, and life has ever been less secure, such is the radical decentering to which the human has been subjected. But the question is to know whether such a decentering is not itself the result of an increasing awareness of the place of the human within nature, which is precisely not a central, privileged one. What this means is that the human is no longer capable of adopting the position once imagined by Laplace, no longer capable of being this *subjectum* guaranteeing the objectivity of objectal nature. The question, in other words, to use the language of Merleau-Ponty's ontology, is to grasp the extent to which contemporary science has not come to recognize that the human is itself *of* nature, inscribed within it, thinking and reflecting it from within, and this in such a way that its vision of it is always partial and fragmentary, and in need of constant revision and questioning. Yes, science has become first and foremost descriptive, and often driven in an interventionist and techno-capitalist manner. But it has also not given up entirely on its ability and its calling to explain, to think, and this means to consider nature not just objectively, objectally, but to think the very relation that binds it to nature, the very way in which we, as human beings, are implicated in such an explanation, the very way in which science itself can be envisaged only as an ongoing dialogue with the laws and forces of nature. The question, in short, is one of knowing whether, alongside the technological absolute and unreserved domination of the human amid nature, there is not the recognition of an intrinsic fragility of the human, one that would be the very mark of our perhaps intrinsically ambiguous or duplicitous age? In other words, is our contemporaneity, our postmodernity, if we want to retain this term, not characterized, on the one hand, by the completion of a certain technological project, at the very heart of which stands the self-grounding of the human as the absolute ground onto which a relation to nature is constructed, and, on the other hand, by an increasing sense of absolute foundationlessness or groundlessness, by the abyss broached beneath our feet, by the withdrawal of ground, the very sense of which, particularly in relation to science, perhaps still remains to be explored? And is contemporary science not situated at the forefront of this withdrawal of ground? Is science itself not intrinsically duplicitous, at once serving as the ground for the ever increasing grip of technology, and revealing the utter groundlessness and fragility of the human within the history of the universe and of life, if not the groundlessness of nature itself? In other words, does the genuine relation to nature, which Heidegger himself, after Hölderlin, characterizes as a dialogue,[24] take place in *Denken* and in *Dichten alone,* or can it *also* take place in a science no longer marked by the imperatives of transparency, control, and domination imagined by Descartes and Newton?[25] And is there not, at the very source of such a renewed dialogue, a very different sort of attunement, not so much a will to domination as a sense of wonder and awe, which Heidegger himself began by recognizing as belonging to all sciences?[26] Can this relation to nature not serve as the ground for a renewed dialogue between philosophy and science?

Remarkably, on at least one occasion, Heidegger envisaged the possibility of such a dialogue with natural science. Admittedly, this is a possibility that predates the historical-destinal diagnosis regarding the essentially technological provenance of modern science, and so does not serve to call it into question. Yet it is precisely to the extent that it was developed before the problematic of "machination" and the *Gestell* were introduced that it is of interest. Heidegger did conceive — at least at one stage — of the possibility of a productive and genuine relation with the *content* of the natural sciences, and set out accordingly to define the terms and conditions under which this singular cooperation was to be conceived. Most remarkably, he set out to do so in the very lecture course in which science is introduced as the "servant of philosophy." If that lecture course, and the general period in Heidegger's work in which it was written, is so intriguing, it is partly due to the fact that so much seems unsettled and undecided, particularly so as regards philosophy's relation to art and science. Having, at the start of the lecture course, declared science to be the "servant of philosophy," he proceeds, in the latter part of the course, and in connection with the fundamental metaphysical concept of "world," to establish the ground for a genuine and productive relation to zoology and biology.

The general question with which this latter part of the course is concerned is that of the difference between what is often referred to as the "world" of the animal, and that of the human. Are they "world" in the same sense? Or is the world of the human, so rigorously thematized by Heidegger in *Being and Time, essentially* different from that of the animal? At stake in this question is nothing less than the possibility of securing the project of a phenomenological ontology as it had been developed in the years immediately preceding the lecture course. After all, *should* we be attempting to establish such a difference of essence between man on the one hand and animals on the other? Is man himself not an animal? Can we simply set aside the fact that the human is nothing other than an hyper-developed nervous system, a super-neocortex mounted on a reptilian brain? Is it possible that Heidegger is distributing life along lines that would isolate the human, on the one hand, and all other living organisms, on the other, from the amoebae and the most rudimentary organisms to the most evolved types of mammals with which man is known to share a common heritage and a common code? Can the possibility of ontology be ultimately rooted in a distinction as insecurely established and constantly under threat from an empirical point of view as the one between man and animal? Can we simply declare philosophy to be in principle protected from such threats, from the threat of the ontical or the empirical? What would justify such a clear distinction between the human and animal realm if not some metaphysical presupposition, some desire or need to divide the realm of life in this way? And, despite Heidegger's resistance to the so-called classical determination of man as rational animal, despite his rejection of this determination as intrinsically metaphysical, does he not remain indebted to metaphysics by insisting that we retain the distinction itself, by going to a great deal of trouble to show that between animality and humanity there is a difference that is not just of degree, but of kind, that the two are actually separated qualitatively by the abyss of the ontological difference itself, as if the very possibility of philosophy itself, as phenomenological ontology, rested on such a distinction being secure? The difference is (only) a difference of essence, a metaphysical difference: while on one level (on the level of its genetic code, for example, or on the level of its embryological development, say) the human is infinitely close to other living organisms, it remains separated from them, and infinitely so, by the abyss of the ontico-ontological difference. Genetic or evolutionary proximity does not preclude ontological distance. But is the ontological distinction ultimately secure? Does it not, in the final analysis, presuppose the very thing that it was supposed to ground, namely, the empirical, biological distinction itself? This, as we shall see, is something which Heidegger recognizes implicitly, without drawing the potential consequences of such a conclusion for the very project of philosophy as rooted in an existential analytic. In a different context, one in which we would need to follow Heidegger's analysis very closely, my approach to his treatment of life in the 1929–30 lecture course would be motivated by the suspicion that the distinction that is dismissed outright as a proper way into the question of life is actually presupposed in his supposedly purely ontological-existential analysis. In other words, the suspicion would have to do with the empirical overdetermination of a discussion that wishes to locate itself at a purely metaphysical level. In the context of this chapter, however, I am more interested in pursuing and extending Heidegger's attempt to establish a working and productive relation to the natural sciences, independently of the many problems and questions one might have as regards the ways in which it is carried out and the specific context in which it takes place.

What is remarkable about Heidegger's analysis of the question concerning the relation between human and animal life is his recognition that, contrary to what was asserted in §3 of *Being and Time*, philosophy's comportment to the positive sciences cannot be one of grounding alone, but has to be one that involves a certain *circularity* and an irreducible *ambiguity*. To a certain extent, albeit only in passing and obliquely, this is something Heidegger had already recognized in *Being and Time* itself, thus nuancing and complicating what was first announced as a relation of grounding between fundamental ontology and the positive sciences. In §10, entitled "How the Analytic of Dasein Is to Be Distinguished from Anthropology, Psychology, and Biology," Heidegger had already identified the singular and specific status of "life" among the various ways in which beings can be said to be: as a "science of life," biology "is founded upon the ontology of Dasein, *even if not entirely.*"[27] This is because life is recognized by Heidegger as being a mode of being in its own right, albeit accessible only in and through existence. Life, in its specific mode of being, and as a positive phenomenon, is envisaged only negatively in *Being and Time:* it is neither *Dasein,* nor simply *Vorhandensein,* nor, of course, *Zuhandensein.* Similarly, Dasein itself is not to be understood in terms of life, as a life-form plus something else. But what is life as a positive phenomenon? What is its relation to Dasein? These questions, left unanswered in the context of *Being and Time,* are addressed in the lecture course from 1929–30.

I shall be concerned to emphasize the way in which Heidegger thematizes the relation between Dasein and life, and subsequently between philosophy and biology in that lecture course, in an attempt to free up, from within Heidegger's own thought, the possibility of a relation to science that will not have yet settled in the diagnosis concerning its onto-historical provenance and its technological destiny. In other words, focusing on the example of "life," doing so in a way that I would ultimately like to see extend to all other fields and their empirical concepts, I shall be concerned to emphasize the order of co-implication between philosophy and science, which must not so much replace as counterbalance and complement that between philosophy and art.

Heidegger insists that we address the question of the distinction between animal and human life in terms of the *essence* of the animality of the animal, and the *essence* of the humanity of man. The phenomenon of "life" will be addressed not from the point of view of evolution, and even less from the point of view of morphological taxonomy, but from the point of view of *essence*. The goal will be to grasp "the original and essential character proper to the living being."[28] But should there be just one character? Is there an "essence" of the living organism? Or is the only "essence" of life this eminently plastic and adaptive force, this force capable of endlessly modifying and complicating itself? This force of which we can at no stage identify the sense and direction of its history, which it alone invents as it unfolds? And is this not the difference between the essentially open genetic program of life and the essentially closed program of the (early) computer, between self-organization as an open system and computation as a closed system? Life is a process that is by definition open ended, incomplete, and this incompleteness is its very perfection, its force, for it alone allows it to invent for itself solutions to new and unanticipated problems brought about by changes in its environment.

The question of essence is pursued through the concept of *world*. This is the concept on which the entire analysis rests. Man, Heidegger claims, is world-forming (*weltbildend*), whereas the animal is poor in world (*weltarm*). But poor in comparison with what or whom? The world of man. The animal is thus situated between the world-forming nature of man and the worldlessness of the stone. Heidegger is adamant that his thesis regarding the poverty-in-world of the animal is a statement of essence, and thus applies to all animals, irrespective of their behavior, evolution, or genetic complexity. It precedes any zoological investigation, and so zoology presupposes it.

Yet something quite remarkable takes place at this stage—the beginning of this "cooperation" I began by evoking, or the impossibility of simply cutting off the realm of essence from that of empirical data and the sciences organizing it. Having apparently secured the realm of essence from the threat of contamination from the empirical, and having thus distinguished the philosophical investigation from all other modes of questioning, and from zoology in particular, Heidegger immediately proceeds to nuance and complicate it, without going as far as to call it into question:

> Accordingly, if our thesis already contains a presupposition of all zoology, we cannot expect to derive the thesis from zoology in the first place. This seems to imply that in elucidating the proposition we will simply dispense with all the detailed wealth of acquired knowledge in the field, knowledge that can no longer be mastered even by the experts in it. So it seems. . . .
>
> The proposition ['the animal is poor in world'] does not derive from zoology, but it cannot be elucidated independently of zoology either. It requires a specific orientation toward zoology and biology in general, and yet it is not through them that its truth is to be determined.[29]

It would seem, then, and contrary to all expectations, that the empirical sciences of nature, and biology in particular, cannot be so easily neutralized or dismissed. It would seem that they cannot be ignored when it becomes a question of pondering the nature of life. But then why did Heidegger feel the need to introduce the question of essence in the first place, and to mark a clear and qualitative difference between man and the animal, when this difference is not recognized as such by the sciences in question? The proposition according to which the animal is poor in world, and which is going to serve as a way into the clarification of the difference between animality and humanity, is not a zoological proposition. Nor, however, is it a proposition that might come to be "elucidated independently of zoology" either. Should we understand Heidegger as wanting to define the terms of a possible encounter and dialogue with zoology and biology, as agreeing to negotiate a ground with them on the basis of a conception of life and world constituted in advance, and which would not be derived from the sciences themselves, yet in the development of which they would play a crucial part? This, I believe, is what comes out of a reading of Heidegger's lectures, in which philosophy finds itself in a singular and unique dialogue with the life sciences.

This relation is explored further under the banner of "ambiguity." If philosophy is to intervene in the sphere of life and animality, or in any sphere for that matter, insofar as all spheres have already been delineated and taken over by the positive sciences, then philosophy can find itself only in a relation of ambiguity with these areas and their concepts. For it is always from a metaphysical position that it wishes to intervene. However, given the fact that the phenomena under investigation are already the object of investigation of specific sciences, it always finds itself engaging with them. What is at issue in this engagement are the terms of the engagement itself. This is where the negotiation takes place for philosophy. And this negotiation is increasingly difficult, given the specialized nature of the fields in question, and the wealth of knowledge they provide. But philosophy cannot shy away from such a negotiation, and from the irreducible ambiguity in which it finds itself in relation to these sciences.

Given Heidegger's central concern in the second part of the lecture course, and given also his early interest in "factical life," we can understand his desire to define the terms of a possible productive relation to biology. Yet Heidegger is concerned to develop a *metaphysical* interpretation of life, and not simply to expose the findings of biology. That being said, the two find themselves mutually implicated:

> Taking all this into consideration, we can now appreciate the magnitude of the difficulties surrounding a *metaphysical interpretation of life*. We can understand how hard it is for biology to assert its own essence within the domain of natural science.
>
> However, inasmuch as the existence of every science, and thus that of biology as well, is historical, we cannot comprehend the occurrence of science or establish its relation to metaphysics by expecting biology to postpone the labors of positive research until a satisfactory metaphysical theory of life becomes available. Nor, indeed, can any purely autonomous and free-floating metaphysical theory, developed subsequently as a so-called synopsis [*Zusammenfassung*], have any significance in this regard. We cannot separate metaphysics and positive research, playing them off against one another in this manner.[30]

In what, then, must the relation consist? The answer Heidegger provides to this question is very much the result of the specific situation of his thought at the time, and of the lecture course as a whole. By that, I mean the definition of the task of philosophy, over and beyond fundamental ontology, as preparing the terrain for this second phase of the metaphysics of Dasein which, around that time, Heidegger designated as "metontology." The first part of the lecture course is intended to carry out just such a preparatory analysis.[31] It is in this context that philosophy is envisaged as performing "the incalculable task of preparing Dasein for that readiness" on the basis of which an originary relation to a given field is possible, and advances in science made. In other words, between metaphysics and science there is a relation of *fate* [*Schicksal*], understood as the historical convergence of an originarily metaphysical awakening in the face of nature and a passion for research, characterized as a "free possibility of existence."[32] How exactly, and under what conditions, this convergence comes about is something rather mysterious, and something that Heidegger is not yet in a position to answer. For the answer to this question, if such proves to be at all possible, presupposes the sort of fully worked out concept of history that Heidegger developed only later on in conjunction with the transformation of the question regarding the meaning of being into that regarding its historical essence (*Seinsgeschichte*). However, when this concept has been worked out, science will no longer be envisaged in association with philosophy, or with what will come to be called "thinking," but as an effect of the technological destination of being. This is the movement laid out in the first part of this chapter. What is most striking in relation to this later development, then, is the extent to which, at this point, Heidegger sees no real opposition between science and metaphysics. On the contrary: they are said to be united by a community of *fate,* or "reciprocity" [*wechselseitige Gemeinschaft*][33] — in other words, by a spirit of cooperation:

> Assuming that we find ourselves placed within this fate, we shall discover a proper stance with respect to the connection between living philosophy [*lebendiger Philosophie*] and living science [*lebendiger Wissenschaft*] only if we can sow among us the seeds of an appropriate mutual understanding [*wenn wir ein entsprechendes Verständnis bei uns pflanzen*]. This is not a thing that can be taught. It is a matter of an inner maturity of existence [*ist Sache der inneren Reife der Existenz*].[34]

This situation, however, is precisely the situation Heidegger sees as lacking in the university of his time, a lack and, indeed, a frustration that will precipitate his political engagement in 1933. Philosophy and science coexist in a sort of blissful ignorance of one another, each convinced of the secure nature of its own ground, whether in "concepts" in the case of philosophy, or in "facts" in the case of the positive sciences. For the most part, philosophy is not "living philosophy," and science is not "living science."

What exactly does Heidegger see in biology that would allow him to hope for this coming dialogue and understanding between science and philosophy?

First, the possibility of restoring, within science itself, a certain autonomy to the singularity of "life" "against the tyranny of physics and chemistry."[35] Heidegger is reacting here not only to early attempts in the eighteenth century to think the realm of life on the basis of the laws of nature revealed in classical mechanics, but also to a significant transformation in the field of biology towards the middle of the nineteenth century, when the emphasis began to shift from the mere *observation* of organisms taken as totalities to the analysis of their constitutive chemical elements. Whereas the former operated with the concepts of natural history, the latter began to draw on physiology and analyze the chemical reactions belonging to living organisms. The boundary between matter and life began to blur, and progressively began to be envisaged as a difference not in kind, but complexity. The cell revealed itself in relation to the molecule as the molecule in relation to the atom. According to this model, if the organism must still be envisaged as a totality, as Heidegger wants it to be, it is only to the extent that the regulation of chemical reactions and the coordination between cells amounts to a synthesis. The birth of biochemistry and genetics in the beginning of the twentieth century is the result of this trend initiated some fifty years before. With this "turn," biology also ceased to be a mere science of *observation*, and became experimental; physiology ceased to operate within nature, the museum of natural history, or the botanical garden, and entered the laboratory. Now, in the face of these developments, which were only confirmed in the course of the twentieth century, we need to ask why Heidegger is so insistent that life be freed "against the tyranny of physics and chemistry." This does not mean that biology must simply do with away with physics and chemistry. But it does mean that, from its perspective, the phenomenon of life as such needs to be recognized in its singularity, and cannot be addressed solely in physical-chemical terms. Biology is the science which, in Heidegger's mind, must be attentive to the specificity of this complex phenomenon we call "life." And this it must do against a twofold threat: that of mechanism, which threatens to reduce this complexity to an assemblage of constitutive elements or parts which in and of themselves are nothing life-like; and that of vitalism, which attempts to counterbalance the reductive approach of mechanism by introducing a force at the heart of organized matter. Whereas the former approach is reductive, the latter is speculative and threatens to reintroduce elements of anthropocentrism, teleology, and supra-mechanical considerations in the science of life. In the end, however, vitalism is as mechanistic as mechanism (since it simply rectifies mechanism without calling it into question). Drawing on the work of biologists such as Hans Driesch and Jacob von Uexküll, Heidegger will attempt to show how recent developments in biology provide resources for the constitution of a science of life that avoids the twofold threat of mechanism and vitalism.

Let us begin with the "threat" of mechanism. Heidegger sees a natural ally in this strand of biology—and, indeed, physiology—that opposes the purely mechanistic interpretation of life inherited first from Newtonian dynamics and then, in the eighteenth century, from chemistry, this modified form of mechanism, which fashioned the description of nature as a whole, including this peculiar mode of organized nature subsequently identified as life, up until the nineteenth century:

> In accordance with this method it was believed that—and in part is still believed today—that we can build up the organism through recourse to its elementary constituents without first having grasped the building plan, i.e., the essence of the organism. . . . It is only during the last couple of generations that biology in the proper sense has worked to overcome this approach. . . . The fact that such overcoming has happened through concrete investigation and experiment is all the more valuable.[36]

Heidegger hails as a decisive step in the history of biology the recognition of the holistic character (*Ganzheitcharakter*) of the organism, at the forefront of which we find the work of Hans Driesch, who, in isolating a cell from the fertilized egg of a sea urchin, obtained a full development that produced a small but complete organism.[37] By wholeness, we need to understand the fact that the organism is not "an aggregate composed of parts," but that "the growth and the construction of the organism is governed by this wholeness [*Ganzheit*] in each and every stage."[38] More recent theories of information and genetic coding would confirm this holistic approach, yet insisting that this "wholeness" is itself entirely contained within molecules and genes. This is precisely what is designated by the terms "organism" and "organization," namely, a capacity for internal order and general coherence. In his approach to the question of life, Heidegger seems to privilege what François Jacob describes as an "integrationist" model, which places the emphasis on organisms as part of a larger system, and views organs and functions only from within a larger constituted totality, not just that of the organism, but that of the species, with its sexuality, its preys, enemies, communication, rites, etc. Today, integrationist biology refuses to accept that *all* the properties of a living organism, its behavior and its achievements, can be explained through its molecular structures alone.[39] This is the very view Heidegger espouses when he opposes the conception of the cell as the primal and purely chemical element of living things on the basis of which the organism as a whole may be reconstituted. From a more contemporary perspective, we can only subscribe to Heidegger's concerns regarding the state of mechanism in eighteenth-century natural history and physiology, and even his opposition to Wilhelm Roux's research on the developmental mechanism of organisms: "we must attempt to make biology and zoology recognize that the organism is not merely a machine."[40] With the advent of cybernetics and "complex" machines, however, the machine and the animal have become models for one another, and contemporary biochemistry can be seen as mechanistic, while emphasizing that no single "part" of the whole can be considered in isolation from the organism itself, which is implicated in its totality at every stage and in every cell.[41]

The problem with the model alternative to that of mechanism, Heidegger goes on to argue, is that it proves able to think the organism holistically only at the cost of introducing a vital or supra-mechanical force, as in the vitalism of a Bichat, Cuvier, Goethe, or Liebig.[42] The vitalism Heidegger has in mind, though, is that of Hans Driesch, who postulates a vital force or entelechy within the organism. So Heidegger does put his finger on what constituted the apparent contradiction of biology, up until the advent of molecular biology and the idea of a genetic program applied to heredity: either a mechanism, which is rigorous and scientific, but does not account for the complexity of living phenomena, and for its apparent purposiveness; or a vitalism, which provides a principle of explanation of purposiveness, but by reintroducing the realm of final causes and entelechy, and thus of anthropology and theology. Prior to this discovery, one can understand and share Heidegger's concerns: vitalism seems to introduce some unaccounted for agency at the heart of life, and introduce a teleological principle that cannot be verified. But we should perhaps distinguish here between what we could call a metaphysical vitalism, which Heidegger is justified to reject, and the more scientific vitalism that raises the question regarding the singular character of life as a natural phenomenon, and to which Heidegger himself will turn ultimately. Self-organization, selection, adaptation, and self-perpetuation are the characters proper to life which, today, at a molecular level, justify perhaps the use of the concept of vitalism.

Since neither mechanism nor vitalism can answer in a satisfactory a manner the question regarding the singularity of life as a natural phenomenon, another approach is required. This is the metaphysical approach, which is nonetheless distinct in that it feels the need to find its own confirmation in the scientific literature. What Heidegger is seeking, therefore, in some aspects of zoology and biology from the beginning of the last century is the empirical *confirmation* of the essentially metaphysical thesis regarding the poverty-in-world of the animal. The specific manner in which Heidegger interprets carefully chosen developments in zoology and biology is crucial here. For this turn to science is entirely contained within the discussion of animal life, and thus within the metaphysical difference established at the outset between animal life, understood in terms of world poverty, and human life, understood in terms of world constitution. In other words, the turn to zoology and biology is ultimately not allowed to threaten the metaphysical distinction itself, not allowed to overflow into the essentially metaphysical characterization and destination of the human. The results of empirical research (which Heidegger is careful not to identify with the mere presentation of facts and evidence, as if these could ever be presented independently of an interpretation) are mobilized solely with a view to confirming a metaphysical thesis. Heidegger's major source of information in this regard is the work of Jakob Johann von Uexküll.[43]

The question, then, is to know how the thesis regarding the poverty-in-world of the animal measures up to what zoology and biology have to say about the nature of the organism—whether the organism "is the condition of possibility of the animal's poverty-in-world; or whether on the contrary it is not precisely the animal's poverty-in-world which enables us to comprehend why a living being can and must be an organism."[44] What is the essential trait of the organism? As we have already begun to see, Heidegger opposes the interpretation of organisms as machines, where organs are treated as instruments or parts of the machine. He actually goes to great trouble to establish a difference between the instrument as *readiness* [*Fertigkeit*] for something, and the organ as *capacity* [*Fähigkeit*] for something: organs have capacities, but they have them precisely as organs, that is, as something belonging to the organism; this is in contrast with the instrument, the pen, for instance, which excludes that kind of belonging to something else through which the character of capability is acquired. Strictly speaking, then, it is not the organ that has a capacity, but the organism that has capacities.[45] Further still: it is not so much that the organism has capacities; rather, capacities develop organs. One could interpret this vocabulary as suggesting that capacities designate virtualities, or virtual tendencies that develop organs as solutions to given problems: an eye is a solution to a problem of light; organisms invent themselves as the problems occur; they evolve in the face of changes, they capitalize on tendencies they possess; we cannot say that animals "can" see, that they have this as a possibility, and then actualize it through the constitution of eyes; but we can say that some organisms, in the face of a problem, have developed the same response, the conditions of existence of which were distributed virtually across a pre-organic space. This, I believe, is what Heidegger means when he writes the following:

> The organism does not have capacities, i.e., it is not an organism which is then additionally supplied with organs. Rather, to say that 'the animal is organized' means that the animal is *rendered capable* [*befähigt*]. Being organized means *being capable*. And that implies that the animal's being is potentiality, namely, the potentiality to articulate itself into capacities, i.e., into those instinctual and subservient ways of remaining proper to itself. These capacities in turn possess the ability of allowing certain organs to arise from them. *This capability articulating itself into capacities creating organs* characterizes the *organism* as such.[46]

The dimension of virtuality, never acknowledged as such, is even more visible in the following passage:

> In the last analysis, potentiality and possibility belong precisely to the essence of the animal in its actuality in a quite specific sense—not merely in the sense that everything actual, inasmuch as it is at all, must already be possible as such. It is not this possibility, but rather *being capable* which belongs to the animal's *being actual*, to the *essence of life*. Only something that is capable, and remains capable, is alive. . . . Being capable is not the possibility of the organism as distinct from something actual, but is a constitutive moment of the way in which the animal as such *is*—of its being.[47]

What Heidegger is recognizing here is crucial: it is the fact that the animal's *being* is not reduced to its *actual* being, that this being is best described in terms of its virtuality (its "being capable"), or its ability to evolve and mutate, to change and adapt, not on the basis of a predefined program, and pre-inscribed possibilities, but on the basis of an open capacity for change. But is this not tantamount to saying that there is no essence of life, at least no essence other than its ability to reinvent itself in the face of unforeseen events? For how could we know what life is capable of, what a given organism is capable of, once capability is understood precisely not in terms of a set of pre-given possibilities, but as involving a temporal process, as implicating evolution? Furthermore, once life itself has been opened onto a certain sense of time, and of history, must human life itself not be considered in relation to it, as itself partaking in that other history? We shall return to these decisive questions — which Heidegger does not ignore — at the very end of our discussion.

Despite these lurking questions, Heidegger insists on the abyss separating the animal from the human Dasein. This is the abyss of the ontico-ontological difference. Among other things, this means that, unlike man, the animal is never present to things as such, in their presence. This, Heidegger is quick to clarify, does not mean that life "represents something inferior or some kind of lower level in comparison with human Dasein."[48] He goes even as far as to recognize that "life is a domain which possesses a wealth of openness with which the human world may have nothing to compare."[49] It does not mean, however, that, while "possessing a wealth of openness," life is never open to openness itself. Animals are never present to things in their presence, whether as *Zuhandene* or *Vorhandene*, as objectively present or conveniently present. Rather, things as such, or in their being, are refused to animals, and this precisely to the extent that animals are absorbed by things. Such is the reason why animals do not comport (*verhalten*) themselves to a world (*Welt*), but behave (*benehmen*) within an environment (*Umgebung*). Their behavior is driven by instincts, by drives and needs, and this in such a way that the beings they relate to are not so much encountered, or disclosed as present, as they are captivating and absorbing. *Benommenheit* and *Hingenommenheit* are the essential features of the animal's relation to its environment: the animal is *absorbed* by those beings within its own environment, *taken in* by them. The bee is simply taken (*hingenommen*) by its food, captivated (*benommen*) by the sun that guides it in its search for the hive. In the bee's relation to its feeding place, or to the sun, there is not an apprehending (*Vernehmen*) of these things *as* feeding place, or *as* sun. Rather, there is only a behaving (*Benehmen*), "a driven activity which we must grasp in this way because the possibility of apprehending something as something is withheld [*genommen*] from the animal."[50] This possibility of apprehending, and this means of relating to something present as such, to presence itself, is simply refused to the animal. It is, Heidegger says, taken away [*benommen*] from the animal. Because the animal cannot relate to what is present at hand as such, the animal's relation to things is purely one of captivation and being taken by those things. Ultimately, to claim that captivation is the essence of animality means:

The animal as such does not stand within a manifestness of beings. Neither its so-called environment nor the animal itself are manifest as beings.[51]

Unlike man, who ek-sists, and this means who relates to manifestness as such, to whom beings can be disclosed (or concealed), animals simply in-sist. They are characterized by this state of *Benommenheit*, by the fact that they are entirely absorbed within themselves, within their own instincts and drives. Captivation, Heidegger declares, is "the inner possibility of animal being itself."[52]

It would be a mistake, however, to believe that the animal's absorption in the totality of its instinctual drives occurs within a self-enclosed capsule. On the contrary, in being taken by . . . , the animal is always related to something else, open to its environment. "Absorbed as it is into this drivenness, the animal nevertheless always pursues its instinctual activity in being open to that for which it is open."[53] The animal, Heidegger claims, following von Uexküll, is constituted not by its mere morphological aspect, but by something like an intrinsic "encircling ring" (*Umring*) within which all its affects take place. The organism is primarily this capacity for self-encirclement, on the basis of which all its other capacities emerge. This is where its ability to be affected or stimulated is located. It is through this "ring" that the organism is bound to its environment, with which it interacts. And the life of the animal is precisely nothing other than the struggle (*Ringen*) to maintain this encircling ring. As such, this ring is not be understood like "a rigid armor plate fitted around the animal," but as the very life of the animal. It is within this ring, which circumscribes the totality of its instinctual drives, that its struggle for preservation, reproduction, and maintenance takes place. This means that the central concepts and ideas of Darwinism are seen not as primordial, but derivative. By pointing to selection and adaptation as the two essential traits of evolution, Darwin did not unveil the mystery of life as such. Heidegger does not refer to Darwin's theory of natural selection specifically, but refers repeatedly to the Darwinian (and, in fact, Spencerian) idea of adaptation and struggle for life. These characters, Heidegger insists, are insufficient, in that they perpetuate the idea of an organism existing prior to its need to adapt, and thus in relative isolation from its environment. Only a theory of the organism as captivation, and this means as bound to its environment from the start, through an operation of encircling, can account for the essentially plastic, or organized, nature of the organism. The organism must not be understood on the basis of self-preservation; on the contrary, it is self-preservation that must be understood on the basis of the essential trait of the organism, namely, captivation. This, according to Heidegger, means that the organism cannot be understood purely in terms of adaptation. Although the Darwinian category of adaptation recognizes something decisive, it fails to understand its essence, insofar as it understands the organism as something merely present at hand which in addition happens to stand in relation to the environment. We should not understand the organism as something independent in its own right, which then adapts itself. Rather, Heidegger insists, drawing on von Uexküll's own analysis, the organism must be seen as adapting a particular environment *into* it—as "ring." Heidegger sees in Uexküll a total confirmation of his own thesis regarding the disinhibiting ring of the animal, and the abyssal difference separating the animal from the human. Today, complexity theory, while ignoring completely the vocabulary of encircling ring and captivation, also believes that natural selection and adaptation, while providing powerful tools to understand the phenomenon of evolution, do not account for the emergence of life as such. Another concept of self-organization is required, one involving the idea of "order at the edge of chaos."[54]

Heidegger concludes his analysis of the organism by recognizing a certain *incompleteness* at the heart of his interpretation. This interpretation is therefore not definitive. Yet it is not "in some external respect" that this interpretation is incomplete, but "from a perspective which brings us once again before the decisive problem in determining the essence of life."[55] In other words, the interpretation of the essence of animal life as captivation is *structurally* incomplete, incomplete as a direct result of the essence of life itself. The essence of life is incomplete, because it is an open *process*, a *movement* of which we can say that it is complete only in death. The movement proper to life is actually best described as "motility" (*Bewegtheit*), in other words, as capacity for movement or transformation, as what, today, science would call an open system:

> Captivation is not a static condition, not a structure in the sense of a rigid framework inserted within the animal, but rather an intrinsically determinate motility which continually unfolds or atrophies as the case may be. Captivation is at the same motility, and this belongs to the essence of the organism.[56]

What is quite remarkable, then, is the way in which the very notion of essence, of which we began by saying that we should expect it to come into conflict with the determination of life as evolution, is ultimately reconciled with evolution, and this means with a conception of life as intrinsically temporal. By recognizing the intrinsically temporal and historical dimension of life, Heidegger not only singles out the singularity of life processes over classical physical systems, but reveals the community of fate or destiny binding the human and the rest of animal life: "Birth, maturing, aging, and death all too obviously remind us of the being of man, which we recognize as being historical."[57] The historicity of the human being as Dasein, Heidegger tells in *Being and Time,* is a function of its essentially temporal, ecstatic being. But animal life itself, the being of which is not ecstatic, is also granted with a certain temporality, and a historicity. Not simply in that animals are born, live, and die, but also in "the fundamental fact of genetic inheritance."[58] And in this respect, Heidegger agrees with those biologists, like Boveri, who speak of organisms as "historical beings."[59] The history that is in question here, first exposed and analyzed by Darwin, is of course the history of *species*. The species in question, Heidegger is right to point out, is no longer the genus, under which individual animals were subsumed hitherto, but the very past, or the very historical being of the animal. This is a dimension that belongs intrinsically (or essentially) to the individuated life form, and which is consequently entirely implicated in the being of the animal as captivation, or as inseparable from its environment.

While remarkable, and potentially remarkably fruitful, Heidegger's emphasis on the historical being of life remains puzzling. Not to just to his reader, but to Heidegger himself, who wonders about the sense of history implicit in evolution:

> What sort of history then does the species possess and what sort of history does the animal realm as a whole possess? Can we and should we speak of history at all where the being of the animal is concerned? If not, then how are we to determine this motility? You can see that one question gives rise to others, that one question is more essential than another, that each question is poorer with respect to its answer than the next.[60]

Up until this lecture course, history was a domain reserved to the human Dasein. Having a history, being historical was considered the "privilege" of a being whose being was temporal in a very specific sense, namely, in the sense of a co-existence of ecstases rooted in the being-towards-its-own-death of existence. This singularity of human life, as implicating a distinct relation to death, irreducible to that of the animal, is reasserted in the context of Heidegger's lectures:

> Because captivation belongs to the essence of the animal, the animal cannot die [*sterben*] in the sense in which dying is ascribed to human beings but can only come to an end [*verenden*].[61]

Still, we are faced with the possibility of understanding history differently, and with the need to account for a sense of time that is neither the human time of ecstatic temporality, nor the chronological, measurable time of classical mechanics. More importantly still, we are faced with the difficult and perhaps aporetic necessity to think together ecstatic temporality and the time of evolution. Indeed, if the human Dasein does in some way partake in this other time, the time of evolution, as biology claims, must we posit ecstatic temporality as the condition of access to this other time? But, then, are we not in danger of positing a metaphysical time over and above the time of nature, of introducing from the start and perhaps arbitrarily a difference in kind between the human and the animal, as the very condition for the characterization of the essence of animal life? Should we instead understand ecstatic temporality as somehow engendered by this other, deeper history, which the human Dasein would have in common with the rest of animal life, and thus think the difference of being human from within the identity of life in its historical unfolding? But, then, would we not have to acknowledge a history more secret than that of the human Dasein, and a question more originary than that of the ontico-ontological difference? Would philosophy not have to undergo a certain transformation, from the existential analytic back into a sense of being as life? This, I believe, would have been a possibility. It would have brought Heidegger in greater proximity to thinkers like Bergson or Deleuze. Instead, soon after the lectures from 1929–30, Heidegger will begin to think of being itself as intrinsically historical, and modern science as the ultimate manifestation of the forgottenness of history in the most fundamental sense. But at least once, in a series of lectures that are as exceptional as they are intriguing, Heidegger will have thought of philosophy in a state of absolute proximity with the life sciences.

In the end, it is perhaps not the *content* of what Heidegger has to say regarding biology that we need to emphasize first and foremost. Biology is a science that has evolved considerably since the 1920s, and it is difficult to imagine what Heidegger would have thought of all the developments in molecular biology, genetics, and complexity theory that inform contemporary biology. Rather than the *content* of what Heidegger says in relation to biology, we should emphasize, and possibly generalize, Heidegger's demand that philosophy enter into a sort of dialogue with natural science, if it is not to remain naïve and isolated. What I want to emphasize is this need, over and beyond Heidegger's own analysis in the 1929–30 lecture course, over and beyond his own diagnosis concerning the technological provenance and destination of science in the later work, to define the terms and conditions of a genuine relation to science. How can philosophy engage with the natural sciences without becoming philosophy *of* science? How can it constitute itself as philosophy in and through this very relation? Heidegger, on at least one occasion, gave us a glimpse of what this productive relation might look like. On at least one occasion, and in relation to the question of the living organism, he alluded to the possibility of a real impact of the natural sciences on metaphysical positions.

PART IV. AESTHETICS

5

Art, "Sister of Philosophy"?

My aim here is to look into the nature of the relation between philosophy and art in Heidegger's thought, and to investigate the remarkable affinity Heidegger sees between philosophical thought and the work of art.[1] Yet since this relation is not monolithic or clearly articulated from the very start, it will have to be a question of adopting a genetic approach towards it, of tracing the very origins and evolution of this relation. As a result, the following pages will not be concerned with any detailed textual work, but more with a trajectory that runs through some thirty years of Heidegger's path of thinking. The danger associated with such an enterprise is, of course, one of oversimplification. Yet the hope is that, in isolating the genesis of the encounter between philosophy and art and in sketching its evolution, greater clarity will be gained as to the very image and goal underlying Heidegger's own thought, as well as to the role played by art in the development of that thought. Although concerned with tracing an itinerary in the development of Heidegger's thought, and so to a large extent chronological, the following pages unfold according to a structure that is not simply linear. Specifically, they will involve a certain circularity, a circularity inscribed within Heidegger's own development. As for the general title, under which they will unfold, it is there to mark and privilege a certain moment in the evolution I have just mentioned—yet not just one moment among others: a pivotal and programmatic moment, a moment indicative of a decisive shift in Heidegger's thought.[2]

The Initial Aristotelian Framework

Quite apart from the few references to art and artworks, mostly prose and poetry, to be found in Heidegger's early work, and in a way that does not seem entirely compatible with such references, the first systematic treatment of the meaning of art is to be found in the context of Heidegger's long engagement with Aristotle, whose work served as the very ground from out of which Heidegger developed his own question concerning the meaning of being (*Sinn vom Sein*). This general Aristotelian conceptual background cannot be underestimated. I would go as far as to suggest that, despite a certain natural affinity on the part of Heidegger's conception of philosophy (as a process of re-vitalization) with art, despite the fact that, from the start, the elements for a thematization of this affinity between art and philosophy were already in place, the Aristotelian problematic remains so securely established in the early work that it is precisely such as to unable a genuine encounter with art. What later on will become a source of questioning and puzzlement, and will lead to reestablishing the problematic of art, remains strictly impossible in the context of an ontological problematic rooted in Aristotle. What remains inconceivable at this stage is the subsequent demand that we distinguish clearly and decisively between art and craft, or between the *work* of art and the *product* of the artisan, as well as meditate on the metaphysical nature of art as *aesthetics,* and this means, according to Heidegger, as through and through *productive* or *poietic.* The possibility of a genuine thinking of art will be indissociable from an overcoming of the thinking of art as aesthetics, and of the metaphysics of production sustaining it.

Let me focus on some of the most relevant aspects of Heidegger's reading, mostly contained in the lecture course delivered in the winter semester of 1924–25.[3] Although devoted to a phenomenological interpretation of Plato's *Sophist,* the lecture course begins with a long introduction of over a hundred pages devoted to an interpretation of Aristotle's *Nicomachean Ethics,* Book VI. This anachronistic and retrospective reading is justified in the following way:

> Previously it was usual to interpret the Platonic philosophy by proceeding from Socrates and the Presocratics to Plato. We wish to strike out in the opposite direction, from Aristotle back to Plato. This way is not unprecedented. It follows the old principle of hermeneutics, namely that interpretation should proceed from the clear into the obscure.[4]

Now, this questionable methodological and hermeneutic choice is nonetheless interesting, in that it testifies to the overwhelming impact of Aristotle's thought on Heidegger's own, and to the tendency of the latter to read the history of philosophy through the eyes of the former. Naturally, these "eyes" are as much Heidegger's as they are Aristotle's, inasmuch as, through the methods of phenomenology and hermeneutics, Heidegger was able to bring the Aristotelian text to a new life, and wrest it from the grip of neo-Thomism.[5] Rather than call into question the principle of interpretation being evoked here, rather than challenge the view that the Aristotelian text is clearer than the Platonic dialogue and opens it up, when it could be argued that it also seals it, at least closes it off with respect to some of its most decisive possibilities, I wish to focus on the treatment of "art" or τέχνη that we find in that Introduction. Yet before turning to this analysis, the following and most decisive point should be emphasized.

The general context, which serves as a preparation for a reading of Plato's *Sophist* and *Philebus,* and in which a first relation between art and philosophy is established, is that of the connection between language and truth or, if you will, between λόγος and ἀλήθεια. More specifically, the connection is between ἀλήθεια and the λόγος that, every time and in different ways, performs this ἀληθεύειν or this operation that consists in disclosing entities in their being, in removing the world from concealedness and coveredness. Let me stress that this operation of uncovering or revealing takes place primarily in speech (*Sprechen*) and in language (*Sprache*), in what the Greeks designated precisely as λόγος. In place, then, from the very start, is the essential connection between truth and language, a connection that Heidegger will never cease to rethink and to revisit, particularly on the basis of a renewed interpretation of the artwork and of poetry. For Aristotle, however, speech is not the sheer articulation of sounds: it is a hermeneutic operation, an utterance that signifies, an utterance through which a world is disclosed. As such, human λόγος is ἑρμηνεία as well as φωνή. As a result, all the modes of ἀληθεύειν that Aristotle identifies, and that Heidegger analyzes, are rooted in this original uncovering designated as λόγος or language. It is only insofar as man is endowed with language that there can be all the other modes of truth. What are these other modes?

In Book VI of the *Nicomachean Ethics,* Aristotle programmatically enumerates five modes of ἀληθεύειν. In Heidegger's own "hermeneutic" translation, or rather, in our own translation of Heidegger's idiosyncratic translation, the passage reads as follows:

> Hence there are five ways human existence [*Dasein:* ψυχή] discloses [ἀληθεύει] beings in affirmation [καταφάναι] and denial [ἀποφάναι]. And these are: know-how [*Sich-Auskennen:* τέχνη] (in taking care [*Besorgen*], handling [*Hantieren*], producing [*Herstellen*]), science [*Wissenschaft:* ἐπιστήμη], circumspection (insight) [*Umsicht-Einsicht:* φρόνησις], understanding [*Verstehen:* σοφία], perceptual discernment [*Vernehmendes Vermeinen:* νοῦς].[6]

Of course, this translation presupposes the entire operation of phenomenological interpretation that serves to illuminate the Aristotelian text
from out of its ontological-factical ground. In other words, the translation itself is a translation of the Greek back into the most concrete experience of human existence, back into the concreteness of life itself.

These five modes of truth are in turn distributed according to a basic
distinction Aristotle had introduced at 1139a6. This is a distinction
within the sphere of λόγος itself, which, we recall, rules over all the
modes of truth, but for νοῦς, which is in a sense para- or metahuman,
in other words, divine. The distinction is that between the λόγον ἔχον
ἐπιστημονικόν and the λόγον ἔχον λογιστικόν. Whereas the first type
of λόγος is reserved to those beings that are necessarily and always, and
thus serves to designate the type of speech that corresponds to the
knowledge of the ἀρχαί or principles, the second type of λόγος rules
over the sphere of deliberation, in which the things under consideration
can be also otherwise and also not be at all. Whereas ἐπιστήμη and
σοφία belong in the first category, τέχνη and φρόνησις belong in the
second. Now, in each category there is one instance of truth that is "truer"
or more disclosive than the other: these are σοφία and φρόνησις. With
respect to their degree of disclosive power, there is therefore an analogy
between the higher modes of truth (σοφία and φρόνησις) and the lower
modes of truth (ἐπιστήμη and τέχνη). Why art (as τέχνη) is considered an inferior, that is, only partially disclosive possibility, and what
the consequences of this are for Heidegger's own thought is what we
need now to address.

Having simply situated art within the general context of the
ἀληθεύειν of λόγος, let me focus on two essential connections within Aristotle's analysis, and contrast them with some of the decisive traits
that characterize philosophy and circumspection.

The object of τέχνη, that is, the being to which this activity is directed,
is what Aristotle calls the ποιητόν, or the being that is to be produced
and hence does not yet exist. Τέχνη is essentially concerned not with
what actually and already is, but with what is only *potentially* and as a
governing principle, as an εἶδος. The thing with which this activity is
concerned comes into being only through the activity of the artist or
the artisan. This is in contrast with σοφία, for example, which is concerned exclusively with that which exists always and necessarily, and
never becomes, and on the basis of which everything that is in becoming becomes. Thus, σοφία is concerned with the highest principles and,
most of all, with the highest of all principles, which Aristotle describes
as thought thinking itself, or as the prime mover. Σοφία is philosophy
precisely insofar as it uncovers beings in their principle by way of
thought, makes them visible from out of their being. In thus revealing
beings in their being, philosophy is most concerned with truth itself and

is the highest activity, the highest possibility and comportment for man. And insofar as the θεωρεῖν or the seeing of σοφία is directed towards the uncovering of everything that is on the basis of the highest principle or ἀρχή—which, for Heidegger, is being itself—it is *first* philosophy. In light of Heidegger's own interpretation of Aristotle's text, and with the necessary caution, we could say that the project of fundamental ontology is Heidegger's own attempt at reviving and articulating a πρώτη φιλοσοφία, yet one that would precisely not result in a metaphysics, or in an onto-theology, one that would precisely not translate being back into a being.

The ἀρχή or the source of τέχνη resides not in the thing that is being produced (as is the case, for example, in natural things), but in the producer himself, and more specifically in the εἶδος produced or revealed in the soul by way of προαίρεσις, this process that makes present through anticipation. In the case of τέχνη, and in contrast with φρόνησις, the finished work itself (the ἔργον), the result of the activity in which the activity is gathered resides precisely παρά, in other words, beside and outside the activity of the producer. The artwork, the artifact, is essentially a *parergon*. To the extent that it is completed, and this means to the extent that is has reached its end (τέλος), in which it is gathered as work, it is precisely an object no longer of production, but of use. In other words, τέχνη is an activity such that its very τέλος— the production of the work—signifies its own end as an activity. The work, which would not have been possible without τέχνη, ultimately exhausts it, setting itself free from its grip. As such, Heidegger claims, τέχνη is a deficient or inauthentic mode of ἀληθεύειν. Such a claim begs the question as to what would constitute a genuine mode of revealing. Would it be a mode in which the end of the revealing would not lie outside the revealing itself, a mode in which the outcome of the activity would not lie beside the activity itself, and not reveal anything outside itself, outside its own self-revealing? This mode of revealing is precisely that of φρόνησις, the ἀρχή as well as the τέλος of which is human existence itself. Indeed, the end of φρόνησις is to establish what is good or best for man, or, as Heidegger puts it, "the right and proper way to be Dasein."[7] Insofar as the very object of φρόνησις is human existence as such and as a whole, there is an absolute coincidence between the revealing and the revealed. The two have the same ontological character.

Where does this preliminary analysis leave us? First of all, a certain connection between art and truth has been established. Yet it is a distant and inferior one, particularly in comparison with the connection between philosophy and truth. In manipulating, in producing and handling things, τέχνη reveals such things only to a certain extent and always presupposes their own uncoveredness, whether in the world or in the idea. Philosophy, on the other hand, addresses the whole of what is with respect to its being and to the horizon from which it comes to be. More than sisters, art and philosophy would, at this stage, seem to be distant cousins. Second, art as such is thought within the general context of a possibility (τέχνη) and an activity (ποίησις), the τέλος of which lies outside the activity. There is, on the one hand, no specific ontological status attached to the artwork, to the work qua work. The work is (only) an artifact. And when, as in the *Metaphysics,* Aristotle mentions the artist, and specifically the poet, it is only, in a gesture reminiscent of Plato's *Republic,* to remind us that "poets lie a great deal."[8] Poets are thus involved in an activity of covering up or over, an activity of concealing. Their discourse reveals, but in such a way that what is spoken of is actually concealed. As such, poetry is more akin to sophistry than to genuine philosophy, insofar as the sophist presents his object as something that it is not, as something other than it is. Like sophistry, poetry would be an art of deception and trickery. In that respect, philosophy would be most opposed to art, for its own discourse is directed at the way in which things show themselves from out of themselves in the way in which they themselves are. As phenomenology, the discourse of philosophy is a letting-be of truth qua truth.

The Work of Art

Given the Aristotelian framework in which Heidegger initially formulated the question of art, how is he able, some mere five years after the lecture course on Plato's *Sophist,* to declare, albeit enigmatically, albeit programmatically, art "the sister of philosophy?"[9] How, in other words, is he able to reverse the order of truth initially established and place art on an equal footing with philosophy, and relegate science, the old ἐπιστήμη, to the role of servant? In doing so, Heidegger does not merely turn away from his early work. Rather, as the early references to art I began by evoking in this chapter indicate, everything happens as if, in turning to art as to the sibling of philosophy, Heidegger remained faithful to his initial intuitions. But these were precisely only that, to wit, intuitions, and conflicted with the conceptual framework within which Heidegger was first led to think the nature of art. The problem thus now consists in identifying the process by which Heidegger was able to free the question of art from its Aristotelian context.

What, then, must have taken place so that art may be in a position to enter in a relation with truth that is as originary and genuine as that of philosophy? What must have taken place so that art may now be in a position to occupy the very center of the Heideggerian problematic? Nothing less than a transformation of the sense and the essence of truth itself. Let me try to be more specific. So long as truth was rooted in Dasein itself, so long as the uncoveredness of things was a function of the ἀληθεύειν of human λόγος, art itself could be considered only as an activity, comparable to other activities, such as the very practical and ordinary activities described in Division One of *Being and Time*.[10] And insofar as it is an activity geared towards the production of a thing that is exterior to it, it is not even as disclosive of the ownmost possibilities of human existence as, say, πρᾶξις. As for the thing produced, once produced, everything happened as if it fell outside the sphere of truth proper. Insofar as the thing marks the end of the activity itself, the yardstick by which truth is measured, it falls outside the sphere of truth. Paradoxically, then, the actual existence of the work marked the end of truth: the coming-into-being of the work was immediately reversed into its non-being. The appearance of the work also meant its disappearance. But if the thing produced marks the end of a certain process, and, indeed, one of ἀληθεύειν, does it not also mark the beginning of something else: of truth itself, not as an activity of Dasein, but as the work's ability to make manifest in and from itself, as a distinct disclosive power? And would this ability not designate the very difference between thing and work, or between equipment and work?

With the work, then, something else would take place. The work would thus mark the end and the beginning of something. As work, it would have this ambivalent or twofold status of a ποιούμενον on the one hand, and of a showing that would show in and from itself, of an autonomous showing, on the other. With the self-showing of the work, truth would actually take place. This movement from product to work, as well as the transformation of truth that accompanies this movement, is precisely and rigorously enacted in all three versions of "The Origin of the Work of Art."[11] In fact, the most dramatic and sudden formulation of this shift is perhaps and paradoxically enacted in the "first" version of the text, where Heidegger insists on the *necessary* nature of the link between truth and art:

> The work, that is to say, art, is *necessary* [my emphasis] in the happening of truth. The most concealed ground of the essence of the artwork, its ownmost origin, is the essence of truth itself. Where truth must happen, that is, where there must be history, then there must be a work, that is, there must be art as the foundation [*Stiftung*] of beyng.[12]

Now, this double displacement of the problematic of art simultaneously consumes a double break with traditional aesthetics: with the problematic of ποίησις on the one hand, and with that of μίμησις on the other hand. It is this double move I now wish to trace, albeit schematically. But before I do this, I wish to introduce yet a further question, a question to which I shall return towards the end of this second development, yet a question that is as decisive as the double twisting free I have just mentioned. Decisive not only because of the role it plays in the overall economy of the problematic of art, but decisive because of its highly problematic character. Eventually, it is by pursuing this question that we shall be in a position to raise anew the question of the relation between art and philosophy, or, to put it programmatically at this stage, between poetry and thought. This question is that of language, or λόγος.

Let me now turn to the first move, that is, the move from the ποιούμενον, or the product, to the artwork. I have already alluded to the peculiar ontological status of the work, which marks the end of a process or an activity, that of production, and the beginning of something else, altogether disconnected from that initial activity. Heidegger is most explicit about this twofold status of the work. In the Freiburg version of "The Origin of the Work of Art," he writes:

> The singular artwork is always also the production of an artist, yet this being-produced of the work does not constitute its work-character [*Werksein*].

So, although we cannot deny that the artwork is actually produced by an artist, what characterizes the artwork qua *work*, the *being* of the work (as opposed to its sheer *existence*), is entirely disconnected from the activity that governed the coming into existence of the work. In both versions of the lecture, Heidegger goes even as far as to suggest that "the artist remains inconsequential as compared with the work, almost like a passageway that destroys itself in the creative process for the work to emerge."[13] Thus, everything happens as if the birth of the work as work meant the death of the artist, as if the very being of the work was simultaneously the sacrifice of the artist. The artist is, of course, the cause or, Aristotle would say, at least one of the causes of the artwork. But the specificity of the artwork is to point beyond its thingly, produced nature, to something that from the very start exceeds the language of causality, something that allows us to see the work as a work of *art*. This something is the origin, the *Ursprung*, which Heidegger is careful to distinguish from the cause. If the artist is indeed the cause and only the cause of the artwork, the work also has an origin, one that does not lie with the artist. But where does it lie? And how does origin differ from cause? Origin differs from cause in that while it does point to the thing in the sense of its existence, or of its coming-into-existence, it also points to the thing from the perspective of its being and its essence, that is, from the perspective of that which allows it to be or unfold in its essence, that which allows it to *work* and to continue to work as the work it is. Thus, the origin of the artwork is to be found not outside the work, but in the very way in which the work works, in the work-character of the work (*Werksein des Werkes*).

What takes place in this first move, then, amounts to a decisive break with the previous (Aristotelian), essentially poietic conception of art. Art is no longer primarily envisaged as the outcome or the result of a productive process governed by the producer's ability to mold matter after an εἶδος, a "look" that is also an "end." Rather, it is now envisaged from the work itself, from what Heidegger designates as the unfolding proper to the work, its work-character: from the work's work, from what the work is able to put to work and bring to work into the work. And this work that belongs to the work is precisely the origin of the work. In the face of the artwork, the question is now: "What does it do, what sort of work does it do?" But what is it that the work brings to work into the work? This question brings me to the second move and to the twisting free it introduces, namely, the move to another sense of truth, and the twisting free from μίμησις.

So far, we have been able to establish that what distinguishes the art-work from a mere artifact is that something actually takes place in the work itself. Something takes *place*, something happens, and the work is nothing outside this *taking* place or this happening. Thus, the work is not just a thing; it is also an *event*. An event of what? Of truth. But what is truth? Is it the ἀληθεύειν of human λόγος, this very discursive oper-ation of truth we began by examining in the Aristotelian text, and that Heidegger himself began by endorsing? If this were the case, we would be thrown back into a problematic of τέχνη and ποίησις, back into a specific mode of the operation of disclosure or truth that coincides with the being of this being Heidegger calls Dasein, and away from the work itself, from its own being or essential unfolding. In order for the work to be envisaged qua work, and not as the end-product of a process of pro-duction understood in terms of truth, the work needs to develop its own relation to truth, it must itself be a site for the happening of truth. Only to that extent, only to the extent that it can function as the very space in which truth takes place, can it be seen as an event. And it is only as such an event that the work is indeed a work of *art*, and not merely a thing. The decisive move, then, consists in raising the question of truth with a view to the work qua work.

In what, then, does this new sense of truth consist? And what is the essence of the artwork, such that it can display a happening of truth? Truth has now become the play, or rather, in Heidegger's own words, the "strife" (*Streit*) between its two constitutive opposed tendencies, between clearing (*Lichtung*) and concealing (*Verbergung*), between that which of itself is drawn towards the Open, the Visible, light, and that which is drawn towards concealment, withdrawal and shelter, the Invisible. Truth, Heidegger tells us, is indeed a process: not a thing, not a fact, but the eternal struggle between clearing and concealing, the primitive scene of an irreducible *chiaroscuro*. It is this very scene which the ancient Greeks captured with the word ἀλήθεια, before truth came to be associated with a human capacity, with judgment and reason. This primitive scene stages the encounter between World, as the drive towards the Open, towards the manifest and the phenomenal, and Earth, as the drive towards sheltering and concealing, as the other side of the phenomenal. And from this en-counter, from this strifely assemblage, actual historical configurations are born, and what we generally call the world opens up:

> World and earth are essentially different from one another and yet are never separated. The world grounds itself on the earth, and earth juts through world. But the relation between world and earth does not wither away into the empty unity of opposites unconcerned with one another. The world, in resting upon the earth, strives to surmount it. As self-opening it cannot endure anything closed. The earth, however, as sheltering and concealing, tends always to draw the world into itself and keep it there.[14]

Now, the artwork provides a place for this primordial strife. It does not represent it in any way. Rather, it itself happens *as,* and is born *of,* this strife. It is a mode—and only one mode, albeit a remarkable one—in which the essential strife of truth finds a place, takes place. It is a happening of truth. As such, the artwork brings the essential strife to work: it sets it to work into the work, quite literally brings it to *work.* The artwork is the work of truth: it is a work of truth as well as truth's own setting-to-work into the work. This happening of truth is perhaps best expressed in the following passage from the Freiburg version of the lecture:

> *Im Werk ist ein Geschehen der Wahrheit ins Werk gesetzt. Und diese Ins-Werk-Setzung der Wahrheit ist das Wesen der Kunst. Die Kunst ist demnach eine Weise, wie Wahrheit geschieht, die Eröffnung des Da im Werk.*

> In the work, a happening of truth is set to work. And this setting-to-work of truth into the work is the essence of art. Art is therefore a mode in which truth happens; it is the opening up of the There in the work.[15]

In the work, then, it is the very "Da" that is freed up—not the actual, physical contours of the work, its presence here and now, but the scene of presence itself, the "there is" in excess of everything that actually is, including the artwork itself. "There" is here to be understood as the unfolding of truth itself in its primordial strife, the very be*ing* of truth: Da-sein. In this context, the artwork, while coinciding with the event once reserved to designate the being of the existent being (the human Dasein), does not so much ex-sist or stand out into the Open as it in-sists, or lets the Open itself stand in the work. It is a mode in which truth comes to stand, an in-stance of truth.

But how, exactly, does truth happen in the artwork? How does the artwork set truth to work in the work? The work, Heidegger tells us, "is" or unfolds to the extent that, "installing [*aufstellend*] the world and bringing-forth [*herstellend*] the earth," it releases their essential strife, accomplishes it.[16] It is therefore the specific double operation of "setting up" (*Aufstellen*) a world and "setting forth" (*Herstellen*) the earth that characterizes the work. It is through this twofold operation that the work brings truth to stand in the work. Allow me to follow Heidegger's complex and subtle analysis as economically as possible.

The setting up of world is not to be understood here in the ordinary (German and English) sense of placing, as when a work is placed in a collection or at an exhibition. The setting up that is in question here is rather an erecting (*erstellen*), a bringing to stand (*errichten*), as in the case of a building (a church, a temple) or even a poem, a tragedy, for example, that one would present (*darstellen*) at a festival. In all such cases, the work itself sets up, opens up something that is not reducible to the purely material aspect of the work: the building, the work commemorates, dedicates, consecrates, or simply presents. It gives something to see. Yet what it gives to see is precisely what would otherwise remain invisible, what is never seen as such: the world. We dwell in the world, the world is all around us, yet precisely to that extent the world is never present to us as such. In the work, the world itself comes to be gathered, and our experience of it is precisely the experience of this gathering, as when, faced with an ancient Greek temple, we cannot help notice the way in which the Greek world, a world made of mortals and gods, unfolding between sky and earth, between the political community and wild nature, comes together in the temple. In the temple, the world is allowed to world, it is brought to presence without being represented. Room is made, a space is freed for the unfolding of the world, and for its peculiar spaciousness which we, as beings-in-the-world, inhabit.

And yet, while allowing the world to unfold and to deploy its own spatiality, while providing a place for the Open, the work also provides a place for that which resists being drawn into the Open, for that which, by its very nature, withdraws in the very drawing forth of the world. In a strange and surprising way, the work is said to set forth precisely that which of itself sets itself back, withdraws from the setting up of world. This aspect of the work is what is often referred to as the material, and which is perhaps best described here, borrowing the term from John Sallis, as the "elemental."[17] For the work is indeed made of something: stone, steel, words, color, etc. But, contrary to what happens in the production of equipment, in which the material is used up, disappearing into the very function of the product, into its serviceability and usability, the artwork is such as to allow the very material of which it is made, and into which it sets itself back, to come forth and shine as such. Matter, far from receding into usefulness, is brought forth as if for the first time, for it is brought forth precisely as the horizon or the origin whence worldly things and the world itself unfold. To be sure, the sculptor uses stone just as the mason uses it, but he does not use it up. Similarly, the painter uses paint, but in such a way that color is not merely used up in the process. On the contrary: in the artwork, stone, colors are made to shine forth, and this shining forth is the very shining of earth itself. In and through the work, our belonging to earth is at once remembered and affirmed. But this belonging to earth is precisely the belonging to that which, from within the world, resists the logic of world, namely, the logic of disclosure and accessibility, of availability and appropriation. Whenever we turn to earth in an attempt to grasp it, as if it were a part of the world, it withdraws as earth. Such is the paradox of earth, that it can be broken open only by being lost. The work of art alone retains earth as the impenetrable, unbreakable. Let us take the example of the stone, on which the temple rests, and of which it is made. If we attempt to penetrate it by breaking it open,

> it still does not display in its fragments anything internal or disclosed. The stone has instantly withdrawn again into the same dull pressure and bulk of its fragments.[18]

Similarly, the colors of a canvas shine. That is all they do. If we approach them with a view to analyzing them, their physical being as it were, measuring their wavelengths, they are instantly gone. Colors, like all earthy materials, show themselves and shine amidst the visible, only to the extent that they remain undisclosed. "Earth thus shatters every attempt to penetrate into it."[19]

With the transformation of the essence of truth comes also a decisive break with the interpretation of art as μίμησις. This should no longer come as a surprise. Indeed, from what we have seen thus far, art can no longer be seen as an imitation of truth, and the work as an image of truth. The work is indeed perhaps an image, but precisely in the sense of a shining, and not of a copy. Truth is not a model, something given in advance and outside the work, but what takes place in the work, whose work-character consists in making room for truth, in clearing a space for the unfolding of truth. And if the work is beautiful, it is not because it resembles truth, not because it reproduces a model faithfully, but because in and through it truth itself shines forth. In art, we have a putting-itself to work of truth into the work, a bringing of truth itself into the work. In this process, truth as such happens. This, in turn, means that under no circumstance can truth be distinguished from the very way in which it puts itself to work into the work. Under no circumstance can the work itself be envisaged outside of the strife that takes place within it, as if for the first time. Every artwork is an original.

Let me now turn to the third and last move I began by introducing at the outset of this second part. This move, broached towards the end of "The Origin of the Work of Art," is quite peculiar in that it brings us back to our point of departure, back to the original connection established between truth and language. It is on the basis of this transformed connection that we shall be in a position to raise anew the question of the relation between art and philosophy.

In order to try to mark the move in question, it is necessary to take a step back. We recall that all the modes of ἀληθεύειν identified in the lectures on Plato's *Sophist*, with the exception of νοῦς, were characterized as modes of human λόγος or language, which Heidegger even translated as speech (*Sprechen*). Now, the question is one of knowing whether, with the shift in the essence of truth, from an ἀληθεύειν based in human λόγος to a play of clearing and concealing that belongs to the very unfolding of being, and with the emergence of the artwork as a site and a happening of truth thus redefined, does the original λόγος, which ruled over the happening of truth, simply vanish? Or is the problematic of the artwork such as to reinstall language ever more forcefully, ever more decisively in the operation of truth, albeit at the cost of a transformation of the sense and the essence of language itself? And is this not the sense Heidegger already perceived and experienced, albeit diffusely, albeit incompletely when, in his earlier work, before he ever turned explicitly to art as to a site or an event of truth, he called upon it when attempting to describe the way in which things come to shine from themselves, independently of any theoretical act? This, then, would be the third major transformation, the third move that we would need to address in the context of the question regarding the nature of the link between art and philosophy for Heidegger.

It might at first be surprising to even think of reintroducing language at this stage. For if the artwork is no longer the work of the artist, but of truth, how could there still be an essential connection between the work and language? After all, is language not essentially a dimension of the human ψυχή? What does the artwork, a painting, for example, have to do with language? Nothing at all, apparently. Unless language, when considered from its essence, turned out not to be a dimension of the human ψυχή, at least not primarily. Unless the essence of language turned out to be the very language of essence, that is, the language of the historical and destinal unfolding of truth itself.

The connection of essence between art and language is introduced towards the very end of the Frankfurt version of the lecture and towards the middle of the earlier Freiburg version.[20] In both cases, it is introduced abruptly, leaving us very few clues as to how to interpret this connection. All art, Heidegger writes, is in essence *Dichtung*. Let us resist, for the time being, the temptation to translate this word; let us resist translating it with the word "poetry." To be sure, this is a translation that Heidegger himself makes, within the German idiom itself, when he declares that "the linguistic work, poetry in the narrower sense, has a privileged position in the domain of the arts." But this translation is only derivative, and occurs as a second step, once the broader and more primordial sense of *Dichtung* has been, if not clearly articulated, at least indicated. In the sentence immediately preceding the one I have just quoted from the Frankfurt version, Heidegger writes that "truth, as the clearing and concealing of beings, happens insofar as it is *gedichtet*." The two earlier versions somewhat qualify the use of this past participle by associating it with another participle:

Aus dem schon Vorhandenen wird die Wahrheit niemals abgelesen. Vielmehr geschieht die Offenheit des Seienden, indem sie entworfen wird: gedichtet.

Never will truth be gathered from what is given in advance and present-at-hand. Rather, the openness of beings happens insofar as it sketched: *gedichtet*.[21]

In any given artwork, then, truth occurs insofar as it is *gedichtet,* and it is to that extent that it is *Dichtung.* How are we to translate *gedichtet?* "Composed" could be a solution, so long as we understand that in being thus composed, truth finds its position and its posture, its *Setzung:* the work sketches or configures that which is merely thrown into the open. In addition, we would need to hear in composition a sense of gathering and bringing together, of assembling truth in its twofold, strifely essence. *Dichtung,* a word that would designate the operation proper to all types of artworks, says something of the process of composition or configuration thus understood. *Dichten* designates the work-character of the artwork, and not the creative process. It is impersonal, and points in the direction of an event that exceeds the mere boundaries of human creation. It does not presuppose the artist. Once again: the cause of the work must be distinguished from its origin. Art is an impersonal field in which truth happens. Art is the voice of truth.

And yet, Heidegger insists, what is most *dichtend* in that sense, what most has the ability to bring things into the Open as if for the first time, what is most able to open up the world and bring us close to everything in it is language. Not, of course, the language that we use and use up in communication, but the language that, like the colors of the canvas, testifies to our belonging and our openness to the earth and the elemental. Such is the nature of poetic language, that, suspending the purely economical, practical aspect of language, it allows the essence of language to shine forth as the very place where we are born to the world, as the very site where world and earth are allowed to unfold in their strife. Poetry allows language to unfold according to its essence, this very essence that returns us to the disclosedness of the world. Language is the originary artwork, insofar as it is there that, for the first time, as our ownmost possibility, we are born to the very birth of the world itself, exposed to the very exposedness of the Open—not just to things in the world, then, not just to the world as such, but to the earth whence the world grows and opens up. The human being is thus not just a being-in-the-world, surrounded by stuff, immersed in a network of needs and communication, as Heidegger claimed at first. It is also, and primarily, of earth—of the wind and of the sky, of forests and stones, of water and air, even if, perhaps, this origin is becoming increasingly distant, foreign to contemporary man. Even if, increasingly, earth withdraws in the face of world. Thus, language has undergone a radical transformation. It no longer designates speech as the ability to articulate sounds producing meaning. Rather, it now designates this primordial and infinitely repeatable openness to beings in their disclosedness. And in that respect, everything happens as if Heidegger was finally in a position to be true to his initial intuition regarding the nature of poetry, as if he could finally return to the *truth* of the passage from Sophocles' *Antigone* he quoted some twenty-five years before.[22] In language, it is in the end not so much the voice of Dasein as the murmur of being that speaks. As Heidegger puts it in the "Letter on Humanism": "Language is the clearing-concealing advent [*Ankunft*] of being itself."[23] But the realization of this paradoxical truth required Heidegger to overcome all traces of the anthropological interpretation of language to which he remained attached in his early work, and specifically in his reading of Aristotle.

Thinking and Poetizing: A Relation of Neighborhood

To finish, I wish to simply allude to the way in which the later Heidegger characterizes the nature of the relation between art and philosophy. This relation, Heidegger says, is no longer of sisterhood, as was the case in the 1929–30 lecture course, but of neighborhood. And what allows Heidegger to characterize it in this way is precisely his transformed conception of language as I have tried to trace it. It is on the basis of a reformulated conception of the essence of language that Heidegger is able to think anew the relation between art and philosophy. But in thinking art and philosophy from out of the essence of language, art comes to be thought as poetry (*Dichten*), and philosophy as thinking (*Denken*). And to speak of the relation between the two in terms of neighborhood is, of course, not an innocent and innocuous gesture, but one in which proximity and distance, nearness and farness, in short, the very nature of space itself come to be rethought radically.

Language, we recall Heidegger saying, "is the clearing-concealing advent of being itself." What does this mean? It means that being is constantly coming to language, perpetually underway to language. In a sense, then, being is what is always given, what is closest. In that respect, Heidegger is simply reiterating a point made in his earlier work, when he claimed that the being of Dasein is what is "ontically" closest to Dasein itself.[24] And yet, precisely insofar as being is given form the start, precisely insofar as it is ontically closest, it is *ontologically* farthest. This is a closeness of which, for the most part, we are oblivious, since we *are* it, a givenness and a gift we do not acknowledge as such, and which we can take up only in a gesture of appropriation, or reappropriation, of the most proper. Thus, the truth of being that occurs in language, even though it is always there, with us, coextensive with our very being, becomes what is most foreign and unfamiliar, what is least worthy of questioning and thought. And the familiar, the relation that we establish with the world and with others through language, and the very familiar relation we develop towards language, as this "thing" that is there for us to be used and used up, is in turn what turns us away from our essence, which consists in nothing other than being turned towards the event of being that speaks in and through language. And so, turning back to this essence will involve a turn back towards the essence of language itself, a transformation of our very comportment towards language. It will require that we turn "back to where we are already properly [*eigentlich*] abiding [*aufhalten*]."[25] So language is *where* we are: it is the site at which we are, the site at which we begin to be; at the same time, it is this "there" that we are or exist. If the "abiding turn" (*die verweilende Rückkehr*), the turn back to where we already are, and in the return to which this "where" becomes a place of dwelling, is the most demanding and most difficult, it is precisely insofar as it is not a turn to something radically other, to another place, but to our own-most self. Only thinking at its deepest, and poetry at its highest, Heidegger claims, can carry out such a conversion. Why? Simply because they alone are able to operate on language in this way, to submit language to this most demanding and violent transformation, in which it is returned to its own place and essence. In such a transformation, the world, twisting free of its immediate familiarity, is opened anew, opened to this excess within it, which reveals itself as the very place of our dwelling, that is, as the very place whose spaciousness is born of the essence of truth. In genuine thinking and poetizing, it is the very essence of language that is allowed to shine forth:

Thinking and poetry never just use language to express themselves with its help; rather, thinking and poetry are in themselves the originary, the essential and therefore the final speech that language speaks through the mouth of man.[26]

Yet the essence of language is nothing other than the language of essence, that is, the ability to disclose the very event of disclosedness itself, truth. In thus experiencing and bringing forward the essence of language, poetry and thought open themselves to the openness of world in its strife with earth, and dwell among things as if for the first time. There, every word becomes an event, or an offspring born of the event of being. Language itself becomes the epiphany of being. Now, this experience of language, this *Erfahrung* of its essence, has nothing to do with either a lived experience (*Erlebnis*) of it, that is, a subjective experience or encounter, or an experimentation on language, with the development of an experimental language. The "concepts" of the thinker, the "images" of the poet are not driven by a desire for innovation and a need to experiment. Rather, thinking and poetizing occur only where and when language is left to speak the advent of being, only when saying becomes a listening and a *Sichsagenlassen*. In poetry and in thought it is the word itself that is made to speak, for the word alone—which is neither a concept, nor a philosopheme, neither an image nor a metaphor—speaks the thing:

The word first lets a thing [*ein Ding*] be as thing. The word makes the thing into a thing—it determines [*bedingt*: literally, "bethings"] the thing.[27]

There is, therefore, a relation of absolute proximity between poetry and thought—a proximity to the source whence language arises. Because this relation is based on a shared proximity to the source, it also involves a certain distance. Such is the reason why it is a relation of neighborhood. The *Nachbar*, Heidegger reminds us in "Building Dwelling Thinking," is the *Nachgebur*, the *Nachgebauer*, that is, he or she who dwells (from the old German *buan*) nearby (*nach* comes from *nah*, near, close). Yet neighbors do not become such simply as a result of a process whereby they draw near to each other, thus establishing a nearness, a neighborhood. Rather, as Heidegger puts it, "the nearness that draws them near is itself the event [*die Nähe, die nähert, is selbst das Ereignis*] by which poetry and thinking are directed into the proper [*das Eigene*] of their essence."[28] Naturally, this event is not just any event, but the event or the unfolding of being itself, and its advent to language, in which man first penetrates the sphere of what is most proper to him, that is, the sphere of his essence. The Greeks, Heidegger tells us, those Greek thinkers and poets prior to the birth of metaphysics in the Pla-

tonic and Aristotelian texts, possessed a single word to name the reciprocal belonging and the coming-together of the event of being and the
event of language, of being and saying, a word which, furthermore,
also served to designate being and saying individually, as if each always
and already included the other. This early and single word, which
Heidegger translates as *Ereignis,* was λόγος.

Here we are, then, back to λόγος — even though, of course, the sense
of λόγος here at work is such as to enact the step back from its Aristotelian, and canonical, interpretation, back into its essence, as the word
designating the originary connection between being and saying. Without wanting, in the light of this essential link, to stigmatize, hastily and
carelessly, Heidegger's thought as a version of logocentrism (a logocentrism which, in any case, would not be a phonocentrism, unless the
voice of being were itself to be understood as modeled after the human
φωνή, a claim that would be met with the most serious reservations
from the Heideggerian perspective), we can still pause and wonder
about the following, bearing in mind the problematic of art, and of the
visual arts in particular: by consistently reinscribing art within the
broader context of language, and of language's originary connection
with the event of being, does Heidegger not seal off the space that most
properly belongs to the visual arts, and to painting in particular? Does
he not rob us of the possibility of thinking that space as such? Does he
not construct art in such a way that it will have almost immediately
slipped back into language, back into its supposed ground and origin?
But are the visual arts, and painting above all, not such as to resist such
a move? Does art not open up the realm of the visible as such, of light
and color, of shining, and does it not, as such, constitute an invitation to
tarry along with it, to dwell for a while in the sphere of pure visibility?
In short: can't we begin to see art as precisely *not* language? Must we
not acknowledge a certain autonomy of art, a certain resistance on its
part to philosophical discourse, whose tendency it is, coming out of language, always to return to language, and to return everything to it,
instead of pausing and lingering before art's almost excessive visibility?
Perhaps, then, we ought to listen to the artwork's invitation to linger
before its space of visibility, this space which, no longer a thing and not
yet a word, extends and unfolds between thing and word, always at the
risk of being folded back onto thing and word.

6

The Place of Architecture

Architecture is the will of the epoch translated into space.
—Ludwig Mies van der Rohe, "Baukunst und Zeitwille"

The problem of the house is a problem of the epoch.
—Le Corbusier, *Towards a New Architecture*

The present epoch will perhaps be above all
the epoch of space.
—Michel Foucault, "Of Other Spaces"

Seen from a Heideggerian perspective, the question of architecture will remain subordinated to the following—more fundamental and decisive —questions: What does it mean to dwell? How does man dwell? Whence this aspiration to dwell or sojourn and not merely this need for shelter? Whence this longing in excess of vital necessity? And the question, for Heidegger, will have always been of knowing whether man dwells simply amid beings, or whether the measure, as well as the possibility, of his dwelling is a function of his openness to that which, in excess of beings, allows them to stand and unfold as those beings which they are. Dwelling, Heidegger will insist throughout, is indicative of and made necessary by the openness to this excess that marks the human in its essence, and not by, say, the building itself, or the economy that it harbors. Never can a building, no matter how well it is built, "how well planned, easy to keep, attractively cheap, open to air, light and sun,"[1] assure us that *dwelling* takes place therein. For dwelling in the Heideggerian sense presupposes the openness to—and the experience of—that which throws us beyond the familiarity of things into the uncanny of the Open as such, where we find ourselves primarily not-at-home. Dwelling in the most fundamental sense begins with *Unheimischkeit*. A distinction therefore needs to be made between dwelling and residing. Residence presupposes a certain economy, whether of needs and shelter (from the cold, the heat, the rain, the sun, wildlife, others, etc.), or symbolic, and even encompasses the aesthetic, ornamental dimension of architecture. But dwelling belongs to a different order altogether. It belongs in the order of being as such. To be, Heidegger will suggest, is to dwell. We humans inhabit the world as dwellers. And so architecture will appear as a technical solution to a problem or a question which itself is nothing technical, but ontological. And historical. For the ontological is such as to have always explicated itself in a number of ways, such as to have always already begun to unfold in history, science, economics, politics, etc. The ontological is never encountered in its purity, and in isolation from the field within which it explicates itself.

From Building to Dwelling

Any attempt at understanding the question of building and architecture from a Heideggerian perspective must begin with a *genesis* of the question. For Heidegger does not so much begin with that question as he encounters it along the way. The question of architecture emerges from the very depths of Heidegger's thought, in the form of a meditation on dwelling and building, but his thought is not first and foremost concerned with architecture. To claim that Heidegger's is a "philosophy of architecture" would amount, to say the least, to a vast exaggeration. So how does this question emerge?

In order to address this question, we need to turn to Heidegger's early formulation of the question of dwelling and of space within the project of fundamental ontology. In *Being and Time,* Heidegger goes as far as to equate dwelling with the very essence of man, and this means with the very way in which man *is,* or with the "how" of his being. But if Heidegger is able to qualify the essence of the human in terms of dwelling, it is because he understands the human not on the basis of a pre-given concept of animality, and thus as something like the "rational" animal, nor on the basis of the Cartesian determination of the human in terms of a thinking substance (*res cogitans*) that stands opposite substances extended in space (*res extensa*), but, in a radically novel way, as the existent being (*Dasein*), that is, as the being whose stance is not one of im-manence, but of trans-cendence, not of permanence, but of transience. It is only to the extent that the essence of the human—and by this we need to understand the mode of its being—is existence itself, and nothing else, that the human can be said to dwell amid things. And the human dwells meta-physically, that is, in such a way that, in its very being, it encounters not just things, or beings, but the very horizon from out of which these things are: the event of presence itself, being as such. There is, if you will, something in excess of beings themselves in Dasein's mode of being, and this is the Being (itself not a being) or the "there is" that sustains and precedes the manifestation of all beings.

Now, the "dwelling" dimension of existence is explicitly brought forward and contained in the further qualification of Dasein as "being-in-the-world." But if the world constitutes the totality of things or beings, whether real or imaginary, that are encountered, do not all beings have the structure of Dasein? Are they not all "in" the world? They are indeed all encountered in the world; they emerge from within the world, and it is there that they find their place. And yet, Heidegger insists, they are not in any way "in" the world in the way in which Dasein itself is in the world. There lies the difference between the purely immanent sense of "in," characteristic of all things other than existence, and the "in" of existence itself, which is transcendent. The difference between the two senses of being "in" is precisely that between a relation of inclusion or enclosure and a relation of dwelling. For Dasein's way of being *in* the world is radically or qualitatively different from the way in which water is *in* the glass or the tree is *in* the forest. The world to which Dasein relates by in-habiting it is precisely not an empty container, pre-given and pre-constituted, awaiting to be filled up with things and events. Unlike the glass with respect to the water within it, the world is not this neutral and indifferent enclosure within which existence would find itself. Nor is the world of Dasein the natural environment of animal life. Rather, ex-sistence, as this standing-outside, or as this being which, already thrown into the world amid things and their being, always pro-jects itself into a myriad of possibilities and projects, is nothing outside or in excess of this world. Dasein *is* its world. And this must be understood transitively: Dasein exists its world; its being is precisely its worlding. Between Dasein and the world, then, there is a relation that is not so much one of indifference as of concern or care (*Sorge*): in the very way in which Dasein is, or exists its own existence, its own being is at issue for it. Existence *is* in such a way that, in its very being, the world as such and as a whole is at issue for it. To be in something in such a way that one inhabits it or feels "at home" in it thus presupposes this relation of familiarity born of an impossibility not to be concerned with or to care for that within which one finds oneself. Such is the reason why Heidegger insists that we understand the "in" of Dasein's "being-in" on the basis of the Old German verb *innan*, to inhabit, to dwell—a sense still present in the English "inn." The verbal dimension is here of decisive importance, and must be constantly born in mind: Dasein is itself this verb, this ability to be in the world, amid things and others, in such a way that it *dwells* in their midst. To be "human" is to dwell existingly. Thus, the question of dwelling and of the home, of building and of architecture, can be raised only for a being whose ontological specificity is to be in-the-world. And if the human can be in the world in such a way that this world appears as its home, if the human dwells in the world in such a way that dwelling itself becomes an issue for it, one materialized in actual buildings and in architecture, it is in a way that is altogether different from the way in which the South American rufous-breasted castle builder is said to have its home in its nest, or the chambered nautilus in its shell. What is at issue in the question regarding the home is something quite distinct from considerations regarding the natural habitat or environment of living or extinct species. This is tantamount to saying that the category of world is heterogeneous to that of environment, nature, and territory. That such categories also apply to the human, and play a significant role in its history, is beyond doubt. That architecture itself cannot simply ignore them is also clear. And yet the question of architecture, the problematic or questioning in architecture, is itself not derived from such categories. For architecture becomes a question only when and where dwelling is possible. And dwelling—and by this we mean a way of being (in the world) such that this mode of being can itself become a question—is possible only on the basis of an ontological structure, marked by a relation of nearness or proximity of Dasein to its own being.

In thus dwelling amid things, in relating to things in the world in such a way that one is from the start there *with* them, *near* and *alongside* them, and not op-posed to them, in what amounts to a derivative and abstract position that presupposes the identification of the human with a power of representation, a new sense of space also emerges. For the distinction between the relation of insideness that characterizes the water's relation to the glass, and the relation of *innan* or dwelling that characterizes Dasein's relation to its world, is spatial. More specifically, it is a distinction between two senses of space: whereas the former draws on a sense of space commonly accepted, as the physical enclosure within which things are contained or found, or as the set of coordinates according to which a material body or a dynamic system can be located, the latter corresponds to a more originary phenomenon and coincides with an ontological understanding of space. If it is more originary in Heidegger's eyes, it is because the "objective" sense of space—and there is no denying that the physical-mathematical space is objective—presupposes the objectification of a phenomenon which is primarily of the order of an event. And it is precisely in the move from—or in the space between— an understanding of the primitive phenomenon of space as spacing or space-giving to its representation as a three-dimensional axis according to which phenomena can be associated with measurable points and trajectories that the question of dwelling, and subsequently of architecture, is played out. For Heidegger, any attempt at addressing the question of building and dwelling on the basis of a preconception of space as enclosure, as delimiting a physical perimeter that marks a difference between inside and outside, as traditionally considered to be marking the very beginning of architecture, is bound to fail. For such an approach will have always and from the start conflated a sense of space specific to existence with *objective* space; it will have failed to acknowledge that the architectural space, while subjected to the laws of physics and objective

And so, in the end, we orient ourselves in this world on the basis of those pre-established regions, those buildings and those places, those landscapes which we in-habit, and which provide us with our sense of space, our sense of belonging to a place, familiar or unfamiliar (when we travel, for example, and find ourselves "out of place," amid streets, buildings, and landscapes which our bodies are not accustomed to, and for which we lack a proper context), close or distant (which can happen even when and where we are actually and physically there, in those places that are unfamiliar, and which we encounter perhaps for the first time).

Yet the spatiality of innerworldly, useful things, while pointing in the direction of the spatiality of Dasein itself, does not circumscribe its specificity. For Dasein is, as we have already seen, essentially not an inner-worldy thing, and this despite the fact that it is "in" the world. The senses of "in" in the case of innerworldy things and in the case of Dasein's being-in-the-world differ fundamentally. The two significant aspects of Dasein's spatiality are, according to Heidegger, *Ent-fernung*, which can be translated as de-severance, and *Ausrichtung*, directionality. *Entfernung* is not taken here in its usual sense of "distance," but, playing on the privative prefix "ent-," as what abolishes or cancels distance and remoteness, as what brings things close or nearby. As Heidegger himself emphasizes,[7] it should be understood not as a thing or a noun, but actively and transitively—in keeping with the way in which Da-sein itself is understood:

> De-severing amounts to making the farness, and this means the remoteness of something, vanish; it amounts to a bringing close or a nearing. [*Entfernen besagt ein Verschwinden machen der Ferne, d. h. der Entfernheit von etwas, Näherung.*][8]

Thus, things are encountered from out of the essentially de-severant comportment of existence, and from out of this comportment alone can things appear as "far" or "close," "here" or "there." How far or close they are is a function not of some objective distance or quantity, and is not "measured" in such objective terms, but is always the result of how we relate to them, and from what horizon: "The objective distances of things present-at-hand do not coincide with the remoteness and closeness of what is ready-to-hand within-the-world."[9] When, in order to go to some place yonder, we say, for example, that it is "a good walk," "a stone's throw," or even "half an hour," we intend not an exact measure, a quantitative stretch of time, but a "duration," a qualitative dimension that is imbued with the life and comportment of existence itself. For the most part, this comportment is practical and useful, and thus Dasein's relation to things is driven by a desire to have them nearby, to bring them closer. The result is an increasing shortening of distances, a world in which things are primarily things of use, and are becoming increasingly readily available:

> *In Dasein there lies an essential tendency towards closeness.* All the ways in which we speed things up, as we are more or less compelled to do today, push us on towards the conquest of remoteness. With the 'radio', for example, Dasein has accomplished a de-severance of the 'world'—a de-severance which, in terms of its meaning for Dasein, cannot yet be visualized— through a removal and destruction of its everyday environment [*Umwelt*].[10]

Later on, when Heidegger's thought will have taken on a decisively historical turn, it will become a question of taking the full measure of this phenomenon, of precisely "visualizing" the meaning of this abolition of all distances in and through technological "advances." When the central question will have become that of technology, Heidegger will wonder whether the extent to which this physical closeness to things, this ability to dwell technologically amid them, does not also mark an increasing inability to dwell in their midst, that is, to tarry alongside the world, not as the world of readily available things (*Zeuge, Bestände*), but as those things in which the world as such and as a whole is gathered, and the truth within which they emerge revealed. Never has distance been less of a problem: the network of tele-techno-communication within which we live brings us the world at the tip of our fingers; information has never been more readily available, resources of all sorts more immediately mobilized and moved around. And yet, Heidegger will ask, does this allow us to dwell more easily on earth? Can we really in-habit a world, the sole horizon of which has become techno-scientific and capitalistic? But, in the context of fundamental ontology, Heidegger remains content with describing the ontological-existential structure underlying this longing for closeness and proximity to things. Things find their place on the basis of Dasein's place amid them. If Dasein occupies a place, it is not in objective space-time. Rather, if and when existence is envisaged as occupying a place within such a framework, then it is no longer as Da-sein, and this means as the being whose being is at issue for it, but as something objectively present, or *vorhanden-sein*. The being of this being has been modified, from being the Open space or the place (the "Da") within which things find their place, and a world organizes itself on the basis of this proto-place, to a re-presented thing, an object-thing among object-things.

The second character that serves to define the spatiality of existence is that of *directionality*. Existence is always oriented towards things in a particular way, always engaged in this transitive activity of "nearing" or "bringing close" [*Näherung*], even if and when those things appear as out of reach, too far, unattainable. In other words, existence is always directed at something, intrinsically directional: right, left, up, down, above, beneath, behind, in front are all according to some thing encountered there, and it is that very thing, in its relation to an embodied existence as proto-place, that provides Dasein with its sense of direction. These directions, which Dasein is said to always take along with it, are inscribed within its very body, as this lived body which it is. In an illuminating and unusual passage, which in some respect echoes Husserl's reflections regarding the constitution of bodily beings (*Leiblichkeit*) and pre-figures Merleau-Ponty's phenomenology of the lived body, and of the flesh, Heidegger alludes to the way in which dwelling amid things, and finding one's way in the world, presupposes the intrinsically "bodily nature" of Dasein, at the same time postponing (indefinitely) a detailed examination of this question:

> Dasein's spatialization in its 'flesh' [*Leiblichkeit*] is also marked out in accordance with these directions. This 'flesh' hides a whole problematic of its own, though we shall not treat it here.[11]

The body is itself the site of habits and of a constant exchange with familiar surroundings. It is it that "remembers" places and orients itself accordingly. The body, as it evolves within specific surroundings, from which it cannot be abstracted, becomes familiar with them and is itself constituted though a process of sedimentation, each region and local situation leaving its mark in the body, which by now has become the unconscious of existence, its ontological memory. And throughout, it approaches the world with the depth and the thickness of these accumulated strata, the world thus becoming the continuation of its own body, its own body becoming world. This is the way in which we in-habit the world: as ecstatic bodies, as a fleshy fabric woven with the very threads of the world itself. Drawing the conclusions of the lived body's centrality in dwelling for architecture, Casey writes:

> Even if it is (just barely) imaginable that space exists without the contribution of lived bodies, it is not imaginable that a dwelling place could exist independently of corporeal contributions. We deal with dwelling places only by the grace of our bodies, which are the ongoing vehicles of architectural implacement. A bodiless architecture is as unthinkable as a mindless philosophy.[12]

Ultimately, the spatiality of those things ready-to-hand we encounter circumspectively is a function of the spatiality of Dasein itself. In other words, "only because Dasein is spatial in the way of de-severance and directionality can what is ready-to-hand within-the-world be encountered in its spatiality."[13] This is tantamount to saying that in letting things be encountered within the world, we give them space. Dasein is spatial to the extent that it is space-giving [*Raum-geben*] or room-making [*Einräumen*]. In other words, Dasein frees or clears a space for things to emerge, and frees the space or the place that is proper to such things. The "Da" of Da-sein is precisely to be understood as this clearing or this making room for things, and in such a way that those things are freed for their own spatiality. The primordial phenomenon of space, which we began by distinguishing from the physical-mathematical space of representation, is this active and transitive spacing, this ecstatic clearing whence the world worlds. Space, when properly understood, "*is not in the subject*" [Kant], "*nor is the world in space*" [Newton]. It can become the homogeneous space of nature only through a transformation of its essence, that is to say, only when the phenomenon of space, in essence active and transitive, and co-extensive with existence itself, is abstracted from its existential-ontological soil and re-presented as something objectively present. In and through this process, which defines the techno-scientific attitude that characterizes modernity,

> the world loses its specific aroundness; the environment becomes the world of Nature. The 'world,' as a totality of equipment ready-to-hand, becomes *spatialized* [*verräumlicht*] to a context of extended things which are just present-at-hand and no more. The homogeneous space of Nature shows itself only when the beings we encounter are discovered in such a way that the worldly character of the ready-to-hand gets specifically deprived of its worldhood.[14]

Only then can space be equated, as in Descartes, with extension, and only then can it be envisaged as this screen on the surface of which, or this container within which, natural phenomena take place, as in Newtonian space. Against such conceptions, or rather prior to them, Heidegger attempts to retrieve an originary space that coincides with the very doing of existence, with existence as spacing and clearing: as truth.

And so, if the question of dwelling, and subsequently of building, is to make any sense for Heidegger, it will be on the basis of a conception of space that brings us back to the originary existential-ontological phenomenon of space as *spacing*, to existence as the very site or proto-place of presence, and to dwelling in the world not as things amid a neutral and indifferent container, but as beings who, in their very being or existence, always encounter their own being or essence as something that matters to them. Does architecture provide a place for such beings? Which architecture? If the modern conception of space, inherited from Descartes and Newton, indeed corresponds to Heidegger's description, does it prevail in modern and contemporary architecture, in such a way that existence would no longer be in a position to dwell authentically, and this means on the basis of its ecstatic essence? Does architecture free a space for existence, or does it force it to become a thing, in a world where there is space (and time) for things only?

Dwelling in the Age of Technology

Now, if the problem to which architecture responds and which it addresses is ontological—if dwelling, as a question, concerns a specific being whose essence consists in that it has its being to be, the ontological is never given as such, in its pure problematic nature. Rather, the ontological or the problematic is always and already explicated historically, and this means culturally, symbolically, socio-economically, scientifically, and artistically. And this in such a way that in raising any question, in articulating any problem that is ontological in essence, one also needs to inquire about the historical horizon within which it takes place. The problem is never only ontological, for the ontological itself has always already begun to articulate itself in contexts and configurations that are also economical, social, political. And so, with respect to dwelling, and to architecture, the question arises as to the kind of dwelling that is granted to us today. How do we dwell on earth *today?* Where does the difference between the ancient Greek, the Medieval, and the contemporary dwelling lie? Is it, after all, a coincidence that Heidegger, in his seemingly neutral analysis of the being of the existent being, focused on the way in which this being is always practically and equipmentally involved with the world? Is such a world, the world of the ready-to-hand, not the historical trait of our time, and a manifestation of a historical process in which the ontological structure laid out in the analysis will have always already begun to explicate itself or unfold, and by this I mean the techno-scientific and late capitalistic era? Is modern man not the *homo technicus* and *economicus,* and no longer—at least primarily—the *ens creatum* of the Christian world, or the ζῷον λόγον ἔχον of the Greek world? This is not to say that the ontological presupposes the historical, or the socioeconomic, and that it is therefore only an ideological "effect" of a more fundamental material (or spiritual: *geistliche*) process. It is, once again, to recognize that the ontological, or the event of being itself, is always incarnate, specific, and singular, always doubled or unfolded in a concrete historical configuration. And this is precisely what Heidegger came to recognize in the 1930s.

It is only when Heidegger's thought became concerned with the question regarding the possibility of a historical dwelling in the age of what he called "machination" (*Machenschaft*) in the 1930s, and "technology" (*Technik*) subsequently, that a number of analyses to do with building and with architecture began to emerge, with an urgency and a decisiveness not felt before. But the emergence of this question itself presupposes a transformation within the fundamental question, the question regarding being. Specifically, it presupposes that the question regarding being be no longer simply and solely envisaged in terms of its existential-ontological meaning, but of its truth. This means that the question no longer be formulated in terms of the ecstatic-temporal horizon on the basis of which beings manifest themselves and find their place within the world, but on the basis, or from out of the truth or the clearing, of being itself. Such a truth, no longer simply associated with the existent being, is nonetheless still envisaged as the clearing or the space — the "Da" — of being (*Sein*). Truth, as the place or the configuration within which the event of presence as such is gathered in presence, is no longer the sole prerogative of existence.

At stake, then, in this reworking of the problematic is a twofold transformation in the sense of truth. First, and as we have begun to identify, truth takes on a historical dimension: the clearing or the site — the "place" — within which things find their particular place, and man his own place in relation to such things, to the world and to nature, is recognized as a historical and destinal process to do with the very way in which being unfolds. And the specificity of this unfolding lies in its withdrawal or its erasure as it inscribes itself: the historical inscription of the truth of being is at the same time the erasure of its essence: the event of being effaces itself in the face of those beings to which it grants presence and place in the first instance. In other words, being has a structural tendency to turn itself away from beings — and man — as it frees the space within which beings come to presence. While presupposing the *event* of presence, beings come to coincide with presence only, thus erasing the very past they presuppose, and which remains in excess of anything merely present (for the simple reason that it is nothing *actually* present, but only the *virtual* condition of presence of anything present). And man himself is left with beings only, to which his questioning and care comes to be directed exclusively. And so, in a way, being is the nearest, yet because the nearest effaces itself before the presence of things, it remains for the most part hidden and farthest from man, who concerns himself with beings only. This originary phenomenon Heidegger calls "the abandonment of being" (*die Seinsverlassenheit*). And out of this abandonment grows what Heidegger, already in *Being and Time,* calls "the forgottenness of being" (*die Seinsvergessenheit*), or "falling" (*Verfallen*):

> Because man as the one who ek-sists comes to stand in this relation that being destines for itself, in that he ecstatically sustains it, that is, in care takes it upon himself, he at first fails to recognize the nearest and attaches himself to the next nearest. He even thinks that this is the nearest. But nearer than the nearest, than beings, and at the same time for ordinary thinking farther than the farthest is nearness itself: the truth of being.

Forgetting the truth of being in favor of the pressing throng of beings unthought in their essence is what "falling" [*Verfallen*] means in *Being and Time*.[15]

This forgottenness of being, and this means of the event of being as the clearing of the Open within which things manifest themselves, reaches its peak in contemporary techno-science, for which there are things only, and for which the world is only to the extent that it can be re-presented. Although announced and prepared since the very dawn of Western history, this erasure of the essence of being in beings has taken on a decisive turn in contemporary science and technology: man has become the central point of reference and the instrument of domination of the earth as a whole; beings are there for man and for the will to power with which it has identified itself, as things ready to be used, manipulated, transformed, produced, and consumed. And this, to the point where one can wonder whether there is still any possibility of *dwelling* amid things: not as the worker-consumer for whom things are always there, readily available, not as the technologized and capitalized subject for whom the world begins and ends with an aggregate of things as *Bestand* or constant presence, but as the finite, mortal being whose being consists in standing out into the truth of being, open to Openness itself, to the light that provides things with their visibility. When the Dasein understands itself on the basis of its essence, then the "Da" is understood as the "house" of being: as the "space" or the "place" where truth, as the event of disclosedness, is preserved—sheltered and gathered. The "Da" of the Da-sein points in the direction of the question or the problem concerning its mode of presence to being, as one of dwelling. For in this "Da" being finds refuge and shelter. In this recourse to the vocabulary of the home, the house and the shelter, we should not see an image or a metaphor, then, but the need to situate the possibility of a dwelling beyond a mere animal economy, on the one hand, and beyond a metaphysics of representation, and of its techno-scientific taking-hold of beings as a whole, on the other hand. But Heidegger sees such a possibility as increasingly threatened, and goes as far as to identify the process of *Seinsverlassenheit* with a historical homelessness [*Heimatlosigkeit*], the homelessness of modern man:

Homelessness so understood consists in the abandonment of beings by being [*die Seinsverlassenheit des Seienden*]. It is the sign of the forgottenness of being [*Seinsvergessenheit*]. Because of it the truth of being remains unthought. The forgottenness of being makes itself known indirectly through the fact that man always observes and handles only beings.[16]

What was already acknowledged in *Being and Time,* and which called for a destructuring of the history of metaphysics, namely, the patent forgottenness of the event of being, is now envisaged as the quasi-inevitable consequence of a yet more originary event, the abandonment of being. Such an event is now seen as the history-making event, as the event with which history as such coincides. This means, paradoxically, that the event of being—history—is nothing other than the progressive erasure of being as event. With the phenomenon of *Seinsverlassenheit* comes an inevitable homelessness, if not an outright estrangement or alienation (*Entfremdung*): an alienation from one's essence, from the truth of being. Paradoxically, then, it is at the very moment when man seems to be at home everywhere in the world, when distances have been abolished and information has become immediately and readily available, when we live the epoch of absolute presence and instantaneity, that Heidegger sees the greatest danger of alienation and the increasing difficulty to dwell in proximity with the closest, namely, the truth of being. For the sphere of presence has become so overwhelming, and so saturated with things and facts, "space" has been identified with presence and "time" with instantaneity, that the "truth" of presence itself, the event that underlies it and is effaced by it, is less and less in a position to be encountered in the technological age. We live in the epoch or the era in which things manifest themselves as there for us, to be re-presented and re-produced. Their givenness is considered a given; there is no longer a space for questioning them in their origin or givenness. In that respect, ours is the age of evidence and obviousness, the age of the total lack of questioning. What matters is getting on with our business. The age of control, of information and information technology, of problems and solutions is to be radically distinguished from the possibility of questioning in the most fundamental sense. This is the reason why, for Heidegger, and independently of any optimism or pessimism, the possibility of genuine dwelling in the age of technology has become very thin indeed, and is always envisaged in counter-technological terms:

> Modern technology and, with it, the scientific industrialization of the world, in their unstoppable course, are destined to erase all possibilities of sojourns [*Aufenthalten*].[17]

I shall return to this question regarding building in the technological age. At this stage, let me simply emphasize the fact that the question of dwelling, of what it means to dwell and be at home, is now entirely subordinated to the *seynsgeschichtliche* or onto-historical background against which it unfolds. We cannot even begin to address the question of architecture before we understand the historical-destinal context within which this question arises.

The second transformation in the concept of truth amounts to its broadening and extension to things other than existence itself. Whereas

Being and Time identified truth with the temporally ecstatic existing of existence, and to the exemplary phenomenon of resolute disclosedness, in and through which Dasein was ex-posed to its exposedness, and disclosed to its own disclosedness or truth, Heidegger now identifies other sites of truth, and this means other events of clearing or spacing in which not just things in their presence, but the very event of presence that sustains such things is able to shine. For besides those types of things identified in *Being and Time* (existence, simple presence, readily available things), Heidegger now recognizes beings whose being cannot be subsumed under any such type previously identified. Particularly, and in an exemplary way, Heidegger extends such a shining power to the work of art and of language, but also, yet in a way that remains less thematized (to the point that Heidegger abandons it later on), to the instituting of the *polis* or the State.[18] Buildings, too, and architecture, are now seen as happenings of truth, as sites or places in which something in excess of the mere physical space encountered takes place—and this is the very possibility of genuine dwelling, as dwelling not just amid things, but amid the event or the coming into presence of things from out of a non-thingly horizon. As such, they too clear a space, make room for something (the event or truth of being). Architecture spaces place. Its recourse to geometrical space is always subordinated to the possibility of some event in excess of pure physical space, in excess of the merely human, too, but in which the human finds its proper place: its home. One can be at home away from one's home: feeling-at-home is not a function of being in one's home, or in a home, but of being situated at the crossroads between being and beings, in this interstitial space, where, in a way, we always already are, but in such a way that this space never comes to presence as such. In art, in architecture, this interstitial space is as it were materialized: truth is doubled or repeated, and this means staged, put to work in the work—revealed. Such would be the beauty of architecture: to render tangible, to inscribe in three-dimensional space something "placial" and interstitial: the invisible and intangible space of the difference between being and beings. More than the beauty of just architecture, this would amount to the event of beauty as such:

> Truth is the unconcealment of beings as beings. Truth is the truth of being. Beauty does not occur alongside and apart from this truth. When truth sets itself into the work, it shines forth [or appears: *erscheint sie*]. The shining forth [*das Erscheinen*]—as this being [here to be understood actively and transitively] of truth in the work and as work—is beauty. Thus the beautiful belongs in the self-happening [*das Sichereignen*] of truth.[19]

By opening space to place, by organizing, planning, and articulating—in short: sculpting—space, volumes, and light, architecture creates a work of truth. Beauty does not follow from form, even though it is bound up with form. For form is born of the event of truth, to which it testifies. The force of the artwork, or the work of architecture, resides in its ability to bring truth to shine in and through it, in its power to bring truth to stand in the work. The essence of art, Heidegger famously writes, consists in "the truth of beings setting itself to work into the work" [*das Sich-ins-Werk-Setzen der Wahrheit*].[20]

How does it achieve such a feat? Through a specific operation of gathering (*Versammlung*). The happening or the taking *place* of truth in the work or the building, and this means the very specific way in which the work "spaces" place or "makes room" for things is through *gathering*. This is the word that comes to be associated most closely with the operation of space, and thus with what it means to dwell. By contrast, we recall how, in *Being and Time*, and in his attempt to articulate the fundamental meaning of being, Heidegger conceived of the spacing proper to Dasein as ecstatic and dispersive (as *Zerstreuung*), horizonal and horizontal—as temporal. Dasein makes room through thrownness and pro-jection. Dasein clears through transcendence. Such is his dwelling. In the 1930s, however, Heidegger comes to rethink space itself, albeit still in terms of "place" (*Ort*), and not as objective-mathematical space.[21] More specifically, and less straightforwardly, it is the very possibility of place, in contradistinction from the space of techno-science, which is now at issue: can space, in the age of techno-science, be conceived otherwise than mathematically and objectively? Is there still room for another space? And does the artwork, the architectural work, free such a space? In a short text from 1969 entitled "Art and Space," and dedicated to the Basque sculptor Eduardo Chillida, Heidegger speaks of the work's relation to space in the following terms:

> Does sculpture amount to a seizure of space, to its domination? Does it match therewith the techno-scientific conquest of space?

As art, sculpture is admittedly a confrontation with the space of art. Art and scientific technology regard and work upon space towards diverse ends in diverse ways.

> But space—does it remain the same? Is space itself not that space which received its first determination from Galileo and Newton? Space—is it that homogeneous expanse, not distinguished at any of its possible places, equivalent toward each direction, but not perceptible with the senses?
>
> Space—is it that which, since that time, challenges modern man increasingly and ever more obstinately to its utter domination?
>
> . . .
>
> Yet can the physically-technologically projected space, however it may be determined henceforth, be held as the sole genuine space? In comparison

with it, are all other articulated spaces, the space of art, the space of every-day practice and commerce, only subjectively conditioned prefigurations and modifications of one objective cosmic space?[22]

In a world threatened by the complete takeover of techno-capitalism, whose reach knows no limit, and that has reconfigured space according to its own demands and logic of total, unrestricted accessibility, Heidegger still sees pockets of placial resistance, of counter-techno-spatial activities. These are not so much sites of hyperactivity and will to power as of passivity, of letting-be (*Gelassenheit*). The originary phenomenon of space is still thought on the basis of an event, of a spacing (*Räumen*). Such an event is to be understood in the following way:

> To clear out [*roden*], to free from wilderness [*die Wildnis freimachen*]. Spacing brings forth the free [*das Freie*], the Open for man's settling and dwelling.[23]

Yet the major distinction with Heidegger's earlier formulation of space as place is that the word that is now associated with the operation of spacing and of clearing (*Einräumen*) is that of gathering (*Versammlung*). One cannot but note the insistence with which, in his examples of buildings, as in works of art, Heidegger focuses on this distinctive trait. In fact, this operation coincides with the event of the work or the building itself:

> Place always opens up a region, in which it *gathers* [my emphasis] the things in their belonging-together.
> *Gathering* [my emphasis] comes to play in the place in the sense of the sheltering that frees things for their region.[24]

In the same text, a few pages farther down, Heidegger suggests that a rehabilitation of place in the age of technology also presupposes that "the emptiness of space" no longer be seen as a mere "deficiency," as a "failure to fill up a cavity or a gap [*Zwischenraum*]." For emptiness is not nothing, nor even a deficiency, but an event, a *Leeren* or an "emptying" to be interpreted as a *Lesen* "in the originary sense of the *Versammeln*, which reigns in place."[25] Such as in a room, or a jug, for example. And what Heidegger says of the potter might as well be said of the architect, for whom the building "holds" not as a result of the right combination of matter and form, but in and through the "void" it harbors:

> He only shapes the clay. No—he shapes the void. For it, in it, and out of it, he forms the clay into the form. From start to finish the potter takes hold of the impalpable void and brings it forth as the container in the shape of a containing vessel. The jug's void determines all the handling in the process of making the vessel. The vessel's thingness does not lie at all in the material of which it consists, but in the void that holds.[26]

. . .

How does the jug's void hold? It holds by taking what is poured in. It holds by keeping and retaining what it took in. The void holds in a twofold manner: taking and keeping. . . . The taking of what was poured in and the keeping of what was poured belong together. But their unity is determined by the outpouring for which the jug is fitted as a jug. . . . To pour from the jug is to give. The holding of the vessel occurs in the giving of the outpouring. Holding needs the void as that which holds. The nature of the holding void is *gathered* in the giving. . . . We call the *gathering* of the twofold holding.[27]

It is not just the sculpture, presumably a sculpture by Chillida, or an artifact, such as a jug, but all the works of art and all the buildings discussed by Heidegger, which consist in a gathering, beginning with the famous non-representational example of the so-called "temple at Paestum," presumably that of Hera II, also known as the temple of Poseidon.[28]

Is there still, today, a single place in the sense intimated in Greek architecture? Where does gathering take place today? Dwelling, Heidegger goes on to say in "Building Dwelling Thinking," is born of this need to find our place on earth. And this place, this place to which buildings open ourselves and which they serve to open up, is precisely "on the earth" and "under the sky," "before the divinities" and "before our own mortality." Our sense of place, of where we belong, is intimately bound up with this fourfold horizon: with our sense of finitude, first and foremost, out of which grows our sense of awe and wonder in the face of nature, which, as mortals, we receive and shelter; with our sense of having a roof above, the sky, and a floor below, the earth, both intimating a depth and a life of their own: the material, motherly earth, which supports and nourishes, which rises up into plant and animal, spreads out into rock and water; the sky, which includes the vaulting path of the sun, the course of the changing moon, the wandering glitter of the stars, the year's seasons, the clemency and inclemency of the weather . . . Earth and sky mark these dimensions according to which we situate ourselves and these axes according to which we orient ourselves. Sky and earth, mortality and divinities provide us with our very first sense of place. Mortals dwell, Heidegger claims, in that they "save" and "shelter" the earth. This means: to set it free into its own presencing, as opposed to mastering it and subjugating it. Mortals dwell in that they "receive the sky as sky," "leave to the sun and the moon their journey, to the stars their course" and "do not turn night into day nor day into a harassed unrest." Mortals dwell in that "they await the divinities as divinities." Buildings, insofar as they allow us to dwell, gather this fourfold horizon into a sort of intimacy and a tense harmony, as we have already begun to see in the case of Greek architecture.[29]

But if such a description corresponds indeed to a certain world, a world which, like the world of ancient Greece, or of Christianity—to limit ourselves to epochs of Western history—was still governed by its relation to the elemental, a world, therefore, whose architecture gathered the elemental together by being itself elemental, has our time not moved away from such an elemental dwelling, and irreversibly so? In reading Heidegger's description of the fourfold horizon within which dwelling takes place, where does this feeling of absolute distance, and possibly of nostalgia, come from, if not from the sense of a literally archaic, and at times highly seductive, invitation to a voyage which we feel we can no longer embark on?[30] If the fourfold is the sole measure of a dwelling on earth, are we not irremediably and irreversibly destined to err, and never to find another place for ourselves? For in this technological age, where night is indeed turned into day, when divinities are no longer awaited, when the earth is indeed controlled and subjugated, where the relation to the sky in large cities, where most of us live these days, is, to say the least, not essential and somewhat irrelevant, the Heideggerian model of dwelling, independently of its desirable or undesirable aspect, seems irreconcilable with the demands of technological, industrialized, urban life.[31] We can no longer pretend that the sky is the only horizon, and the horizon at which the flight or the return of the gods is played out, when science ventures into the depths of the cosmos, expanding the celestial horizon to a vertiginous and awesome infinity. Nor can we pretend that, in the face of an explosive demography in developing countries, the earth will provide generously. Abundance and famine, subjugation and destitution reign on earth, simultaneously, and in such a way that, in a globalized economy, one can no longer compartmentalize the earth, and forget the destitution of others. Only mortality, this irreducible and primordial horizon, that very horizon which, in *Being and Time*, Heidegger so compellingly revealed as the unsurpassable and defining possibility, remains. And there, one may wish to agree with Heidegger. It is a horizon with which technological life wants to have nothing to do, a buried horizon. The temple, the church, one's home, even, reserved a place for death. Death once had its place in life, and space (and time) was made for it. But we no longer have time, nor make room, for death. There are now so-called "homes" especially made for dying, far from everything and everyone, far from life, but where, in a way, one is deprived of the possibility of dying. Death has become an embarrassment and a nuisance, and mourning a matter to be done with quickly, and privately.

If place and, with it, the possibility of dwelling, of being-at-home, is entirely dependent on its ability to gather within itself the extreme horizons within which the essence of the human unfolds, and if our sense of space today is no longer primarily governed by place thus understood, then does it not mean that dwelling has become altogether impossible? That ours is a state of fundamental homelessness, of a structural impossibility to be at home in the world, even and precisely at the very moment when the world as such has become this absolutely familiar thing, taken for granted and unquestionable beyond its mere availability and presence? And would this not explain the fact that, in thinking the possibility of dwelling as the decisive question underlying building and the *Wohnungsfrage*, Heidegger turns to constructions such as the house in the black forest, the old bridge over the Neckar in Heidelberg, the temple at Paestum, the cathedral at Bamberg, which all speak of a world which is no longer, even though the buildings themselves remain in place, yet without their sense of place. Not once does Heidegger turn to contemporary, urban architecture, to the way in which the question of dwelling and inhabiting is addressed, say, through the buildings and writings of Le Corbusier, Gropius, Behrens, Wright, or Mies van der Rohe, to name only a few architects whose work has so decisively marked construction in the twentieth century. Of course, on one level, such buildings (at least some of them) can be seen from a Heideggerian perspective as merely confirming this impossibility of dwelling in the technological age.[32] For have not all references to the earth, to the sky, and to the mortality of the human and its relation to the holy and the divine simply disappeared? Are they not characterized by their inability to gather, and to some extent by their indifference to an elemental surrounding which they have entirely mastered? Has the home itself not been reduced to a mere "machine for living in," as Le Corbusier so famously declared? Does building itself not attempt to free itself of earth, as in Le Corbusier's Villa Savoye in Poissy, 1928–31, and to celebrate what it considers an emancipation from nature and the elemental through techno-science? Henceforth, the engineer will allow the modern architect to triumph over the earth-bound character of traditional architecture, and Van Doesburg's "Towards a Plastic Architecture," for example, demands of architecture "a floating aspect (in so far as this is possible from a constructional standpoint—this is the problem for the engineer!) which operates, as it were, in opposition to natural gravity."[33] In a homogeneous, physical space, places themselves must be interchangeable, open to various functions, and adaptable.[34] The place of worship is no longer distinguishable from the technological space of the thermodynamic machine.[35] If the epoch is indeed that of technology, and this means of this "frame" (*Gestell*) that governs the manner in which things and nature as a whole are present to us today, then, modernist architecture argued, buildings themselves, and our relation to space as such, must reflect and organize spatially this technological seizure of the world, this "will of the epoch" that Heidegger characterized as "will to will." In the words of Mies van der Rohe:

> Architecture is the will of the epoch translated into space. . . . It must be
> understood that all architecture is bound up with its own time, that it can

only be manifested in living tasks and in the medium of its epoch. In no age has it been otherwise.[36]

This architecture of the will to will is also clearly and programmatically expressed in the following statement by the authors of the ABC manifesto:

> *The machine* is neither the coming paradise in which technology will fulfill all our wishes—nor the appropriating hell in which all human development is destroyed—*The machine* is nothing more than the inexorable dictator of the possibilities and tasks common to all our lives. It dictates how we are to think and what we have to understand.[37]

This is a definition of the machine-age to which Heidegger subscribes. Technology is all encompassing and absolutely demanding. It is a process that envelops human beings as well, who increasingly appear as no more than natural reserve to be organized, stored, mobilized, and managed for optimal productivity. Along with technology comes homogeneity and growing uniformity, particularly in urban environments. Cities look more and more alike. We understand why Heidegger stayed in the provinces.[38] This is where he belonged, and so much of his thought originates there. Heidegger opposed the authentic dwelling to the technological residing; he opposed place in the genuine sense (as the space in which the fourfold unfolds) to the grid space of technology, a space of representation and mathematical projection (one thinks here of the grid so typical of most American cities). How radically opposed to architectural modernism is Heidegger's description of the peasant house in the Black Forest:

> Here the self-sufficiency of the power to let earth and sky, divinities and mortals enter *in simple oneness* into things ordered the house. It placed the farm on the wind-sheltered mountain slope looking south, among the meadows close to the spring. It gave it the wide overhanging shingle roof whose proper slope bears up under the burden of snow, and which, reaching deep down, shields the chambers against the storms of the long winter nights. It did not forget the altar corner behind the community table; it made room in its chamber for the hallowed places of childbed and the "tree of the dead"—for that is what they call a coffin there: the *Totenbaum*—and in this way it designed for the different generations under one roof the character of their journey through time. A craft which, itself sprung from dwelling, still uses its tools and frames as things, built by the farmhouse.[39]

In the light of such examples, should we conclude that contemporary architecture, and by this we mean architecture in the age of technology, signifies nothing other than the setting to work into the work of truth as the reign of man's supremacy and unlimited power over beings as a whole, and thus the radical impossibility of dwelling? For can there still be dwelling on earth, when earth has withdrawn altogether, leaving man as the sole measure of a world saturated with things in their readily available presence and representedness? Does contemporary architecture only seal the technological, machinic fate of an inhabiting reduced to the macro-economic demands of late capitalism, or does it, in some instances, open up a space beyond that economy, yet not simply returning construction to the sense of place developed by Heidegger?

Hestial and Hermetic Architecture

Bearing this question in mind, I would like to take a little detour and allude to a topographical and, indeed, a cosmo-political configuration that decisively shaped ancient Greek culture and that, I believe, still governs, only perhaps indirectly, our contemporary world. This configuration revolves around two dimensions, axes, or poles, with which a divinity is in each case associated. The divinities are Hestia and Hermes, and the distinction that can be derived from them is that between a hestial and a hermetic mode of dwelling, and subsequently between hestial and hermetic architecture. This distinction is taken up, rather remarkably, and its ramifications explored by Edward Casey in *Getting Back into Place*. In a chapter entitled "Two Ways to Dwell," Casey draws on an article by Paola Pignatelli[40] in order to generalize the distinction between hestial and hermetic architecture.[41] Now, Hestia is a divinity that is not unknown to Heidegger, who, in his 1942 lecture course on Hölderlin's "Der Ister," devoted (for the second time) a long analysis to the chorus from Sophocles' *Antigone,* the last strophe of which refers to ἑστία, the hearth and the abode of the human, the place that is proper to it. But at no stage does Heidegger refer to Hestia's relation to Hermes. Nor does Heidegger relate specifically what he says about the ἑστία to architecture. This, I believe, is no coincidence, as Heidegger's model of dwelling will turn out to be hestial more than hermetic and, in fact, hestial to the point that, in an age, such as ours, decisively and predominantly marked by the hermetic, an irreducible tension will inevitably emerge between Heidegger's dwelling aspiration and the reality of our time. At the same time, I would like to suggest that Heidegger's distinction between world and earth, and the strife in which it is engaged, does more than simply echo the ancient dyad Hermes-Hestia: it actually reinscribes it, doubles it, and sets it against the onto-historical background of technology. Thus, the economy of dwelling involves the specific configuration of world and earth, Hermes and Hestia, and one to which contemporary architecture finds itself forced to respond.

Daughter of Rhea (the earth) and Kronos (time), Hestia is the goddess of the hearth and has her place at the center of the home, which she defines by her very presence. She rules over family life and domestic economy. Altars to Hestia were built in every private home in Greece as well as in front of the prytaneion (the town hall) of capital cities. Honored by a sacred fire, she was invoked at the beginning and the end of feasts and sacrifices. And to invoke Hestia was to invoke a presence dwelling within the home. Credited with having been the first deity to construct a house, she was a somewhat lonely and retiring being. In Greek houses, the hearth was located at the center of the house, and it was here that Hestia presided. She was also a central presence at temples (e.g., at Delphi and, much later, at the temple of the Vestal Virgins in the Roman Forum). Both the hearth and the temples were circular in structure, a shape that exemplifies self-enclosure and promotes attention to the center, bringing everything and everyone within, in-gathering. Any built place that aims at encouraging hestial dwelling will therefore tend to be at once centered and self-enclosed, and preferably circular. Greek domestic architecture echoes this counsel:

> [Hestia's] circular altar, placed in the center of an utterly introverted house . . .
> is the symbol of the visceral relationship between home and earth (Rhea) and
> between family lineage and the continuity of time (Kronos). Actually, the
> Greek house is crossed by a vertical axis that, through the hearth, binds
> together the depths of earth with the summit of the heavens.[42]

And so, very much in the way described by Heidegger himself, whose conception of dwelling is not only profoundly Greek, but also hestial, the home unfolds between earth and sky, which it brings together into a single place. It is not surprising, therefore, that, in one instance where it is a matter of understanding what dwelling means, Heidegger recounts the famous anecdote regarding Heraclitus receiving his friends in the intimacy of his kitchen, by the fire.[43]

But we should not assume that Hestia ruled solely over the home understood as the οἶκος or the *domus*, over the restricted domestic economy. She also rules over the larger, political economy, as the ἐστία κοινή, the common hearth and center, materialized in the *agora*. This is because, for the Greeks, the πόλις was also, and possibly more so than the domestic home, considered as providing one with a genuine sense of place: the homeland, the *Heimat*, as exemplified in those Greek tragedies where one is faced with the horrific spectacle of banishment,[44] was perceived as the most precious of goods and the most cherished of gifts. The sense of having a place and feeling at home was therefore not a function of the very bourgeois ideal of the actual, physical home, of the comfort of one's interior. The reign of Hestia did not coincide with that of the private only, to which the public would be opposed. Being-at-home was as much, if not more, a public and political matter than a private, domestic one.

This brings me to the second aspect of this dwelling economy: Hermes. He is the god of motion and communication, who moves essentially in the public sphere — a "political" god par excellence, the tutelary deity of the assemblies situated in the open space of the *agora*. Associated with heaps of stones that mark crossroads and territorial boundaries in ancient Greece — his name connotes "heap" or "cairn" of stones — Hermes is also the god of roads and of wayfarers. As a god of intersections, he is responsible for the disposition of entire regions of public space. If the hestial mainly *gathers in* (and lets out by escape or indirection), the hermetic *moves out* resolutely. The hermetic represents the far-out view, a view from a moving position, in which the slow motions of the caretaker and homemaker give way to the impatient rapidity of the thief, the trespasser, and the traveler. Under the sign of Hermes, the con-centric becomes ec-centric. But, once again, it is crucial to bear in mind that Hermes and Hestia were not so much opposed to one another, as two modes of dwelling, as they complemented one another and required one another. Thus, wandering, departing, voyaging, which was an integral part of Greek culture, always presupposed the *polis*, and one's private home, as the hearth to which one belonged and was destined to return:

> Hermes . . . stands outside the house to conduct the traveler away from the shelter of Hestia's fire. The traveler returns guided by Hermes to the more central and ever-abiding origins of self, family, and nation.[45]

And there lies the crucial difference between the odyssey, the voyage, dwelling as wandering, no matter how endless, and banishment, or errancy: it is the abyssal difference between homecoming and erring, between having a homeland and homelessness. This is the difference between Odysseus and Medea, or Aeneas and the Flying Dutchman. The question, with respect to our contemporary situation, is to know the extent to which the global economy — an economy beyond the general economy of the *polis*, for no longer tied to the *polis* or the nation-state, an economy, in other words, which has transformed our very being, and set itself almost entirely free from the "place" in which it was traditionally anchored, reconfiguring also the private space itself as no longer private, but as entirely traversed by this essentially fluid and plastic force: capitalism — that is sweeping us away is not simply a state of homelessness depriving us of any sense of place, deterritorializing the nation and the homeland, and thus, indirectly and reactively, triggering all the nationalisms and regionalisms that are proliferating today, including Heidegger's own. When a global economy threatens to homogenize and bring together people by way of the lowest common denominator (the ability to consume) and level all differences, when it reveals itself as a force of de-localization stronger than the locus provided by the nation-state, should we be surprised to see identities reconstitute and reterritorialize themselves on race, ethnicity, or religion? Is there not, in such a context, an erring and a lack of place far more threatening and colossal than anything hitherto experienced, a sort of perpetual banishment fed and kept alive by the economic machine? Are we not, in short, living the absolute hermetization of the world in techno-capitalism? Has earth itself, Hestia, not withdrawn altogether?[46] In the strife between world and earth, between Hermes and Hestia, it would seem that world has overshadowed earth. The "self-disclosing openness of the broad paths [weiten Bahnen]" of world have eclipsed earth as what is "continually self-secluding and to that extent sheltering and concealing."[47] Earth, as the dimension of the elemental that is not so much used up as it is used in the work in such a way that it comes to shine forth only then, is forced back onto the world, which is now the mere techno-economic space for which everything is a potential resource. The sheer horizontality of our contemporary sense of space, the eminently fluid nature of our tele-techno-communications, of our information system, our goods, capital, and work force—and the extent to which this fluidification and adaptability is at the heart of the triumph of capitalism is not to be underestimated—has, so it seems, irremediably put place out of place, forcing earth to retreat back into itself, forcing it into oblivion.[48] The world, Heidegger alerted us in "The Origin of the Work of Art," is pure openness, pure disclosure, and as such cannot endure anything closed; as a result, it is always striving to surmount earth, to impose its own clearing over the concealing of earth.[49] Techno-capitalism is essentially worldly, and in the strife opposing it to earth—the strife constitutive of the essence and the history of truth itself—world has surmounted earth, thus severing itself from its other, allowing it to slip back into concealment, into oblivion. And must we not also recognize that, in this age of homelessness, where we are at home everywhere, the possibility of genuine dwelling would presuppose bringing earth back into world, and this means bringing Hestia back into its strife with Hermes?

Coming back to architecture, and to the way in which it can address these questions at a molecular level, we see how, whereas hestial architecture tends to be curvilinear and concentric, turned inward towards a center, and vertical, turned upward towards the sky, thus gathering together earth and sky, hermetic architecture tends to be ec-centric and rectilinear, turned outward towards the horizon—straight and horizontal:

[Hermes] represents the centerless dynamic space, oriented toward many directions which, in the absence of a center, can only congregate into parallel lines, perhaps set into grid-like patterns (linear cities, urban quadrillages).[50]

Where the mosque at Córdoba, Palladio's Villa Rotonda, or Bramante's St. Peter's basilica in Rome can be seen as good examples of a hestial architecture, the Forum of the Pantheon in Rome or the Piazza San Marco in Venice can be seen as examples of hermetic architecture. That the former are examples of actual buildings, and the latter of squares involving urban planning, is no coincidence. This distinction corresponds to a traditional configuration of a public space, open to the exchange of speech (and perhaps goods) and the movement of bodies, and a more private, perhaps religious forum, which requires in-gathering and in-timacy. But each side must be viewed within the more general topographical system within which it is inscribed, as essentially open to this other economy from which it nonetheless distinguishes itself. The question, of course, is to know the extent to which such examples still hold for contemporary life, and this means for a life that is traversed, at all times and in virtually every context, by the hermetic, by the absolutely fluidified techno-capitalistic machine. Contemporary architecture, when addressing the question regarding the mode of dwelling that is specific to our age, has for the most part answered by opening the building, and particularly or most particularly the home, to the general hermetization of modern man: the circular center or house has been straightened, its ancient, vertical link with the divine nature of the skies, translated laterally, the walls, demarcating the inside from the outside, have been opened to the outside (Johnson's glass house); in short, the contemporary building is no longer governed by a demand to gather, for gathering is no longer the decisive mode of dwelling, the paradigm after which dwelling is defined and evaluated. In some instances, as exemplified in deconstructive architecture, buildings are themselves without anything resembling a center, and stage this radical de-centeredness of contemporary man. Buildings become host to the hostlessness or the hermetization of dwelling.

But this does not mean that as such the hestial dimension is no longer there, that its need is no longer felt, that one does not long for it. Even in the full swing of our technological age, who does not think of "home" and of "being at home" as, if not a shelter from the machinic, at least a place where the question of place is itself in question, where dwelling itself is at issue, as the issue concerning our proper place? For everywhere we look, we see people choosing to live in nineteenth-century bourgeois interiors rather than in Johnson's or Le Corbusier's houses. Now, such a bourgeois reaction does not have simply to do with a need for privacy—although this very bourgeois ideal is now deeply entrenched. It has to do, also, with a conception of the home, and with the feeling of being at home—whether in the comfort of one's own house, or someone else's, or on the street or in the countryside—as shelter from the macro-economy within which we are thrown and used, as micro-places that counterbalance the techno-scientific and capitalistic horizon within which we live. Am I right to think that today, and, I imagine, to the architect's dismay, the "home" is lived not as symbiotic with the outside, not as this space that is open to the outside, that lets it infringe on its inside, thus blurring the distinction between inside and outside, quite differently from the way in which this dialectic would have been negotiated in the Greek or the Roman city (in the Pantheon in Rome, for example), or in the Medieval and Renaissance city (as exemplified by the Piazza San Marco in Venice, or Palladio's Villa Rotonda), but above all negatively and reactively, as shelter from an outside identified with one's technologized and capitalized self. But even the bourgeois home is now entirely penetrated by the outside: television, the radio, the internet provides a constant flow of information and a constantly renewed ability to generate new needs and desires through advertising. The macro-economic machine must be fed and injected with the need to consume at all times.

The question is to know whether one can dwell purely horizontally, without earth, purely rhizomatically; every process of deterritorialization needs to reterritorialize itself at some point; there is no "pure" nomadism. This is a mode of dwelling, perhaps best exemplified by Odysseus's journey, which we encounter also in later narratives, such as in Cervantes' *Don Quixote,* Melville's *Moby Dick,* or in more recent so-called road novels and films, such as *Thelma and Louise.* For even where the journey seems to depart radically from the homecoming of Odysseus, there is still the vessel, on which the hestial is reterritorialized: the ship, the car, the train. There is still the need to re-locate, to gather in: the car, the cabin, the horse, even become the moving hearth, a character in the end as important as, say, the house in Henry James's *The Spoils of Poynton,* or Orson Welles's *Citizen Kane.*

But we can wonder whether there have not been modern responses to this dissemination, this hermetization, responses that would attempt to strike a balance between the hestial and the hermetic, the closed and the open, the private and the public (in the private as well as in the public), the vertical and the horizontal, earth and world.[51] It is, after all, the dialectic of the vertical and the horizontal, of gathering and dissemination, of earth and world, which finds a new configuration, and an elegant solution, in Frank Lloyd Wright's architecture, perhaps nowhere more visible than in the Edgar Kaufmann residence, Fallingwater.[52] There, as in a Mondrian, but in a far more elemental way, the horizontal, worldly lines mix elegantly with the vertical lines, which bring earth (and water) together with sky and ether, composing a harmonious whole that is neither closed off to the openness of world, nor simply swept away by it, but that gathers it around the central vertical axes, thus giving it stature and vastness. Similarly, in the

Robie House in Chicago[53] (as in all the other Prairie houses), where the horizontal lines prevail, internally as well as externally, thus giving a sense of a line of flight floating on the horizon, a wandering line, as it were, what could easily amount to a sense of placelessness is counterbalanced by the discrete yet decisive presence of a free-standing fireplace in the middle of the house, standing like an altar dedicated to Hestia. And so, despite its lack of verticality, despite the fact that the house has more the appearance of a vessel at sea than of a house born of the earth and rooted therein, the house remains anchored in the earth, and gathers together earth and sky. It is not adrift in the world, placeless, but, gathered around the fireplace, it frees the space within which to dwell. Speaking of "the typical American house" of around 1890, Wright asks,

> What was the matter with the typical American house? Well, just for an honest beginning, it lied about everything. It had no sense of unity at all nor any such sense of space as should belong to a free people. It was stuck in thoughtless fashion. It had no more sense of earth than a "modernistic" house. And it was stuck up on wherever it happened to be.[54]

Commenting on that very passage, and echoing my own interpretation, Norberg-Schulz writes:

> In his houses, Frank Lloyd Wright wanted simultaneously to express belonging to the earth and "freedom" in space. Thus he composed the building of planes of "infinite" extension parallel to the ground, but introduced a vertical core as well as low hipped roofs to give it anchorage.[55]

If the whole of being is interpreted or envisaged as readily available "stuff" and object, as *Bestand* and *Gegenstand,* then we dwell in a certain way; if beings are envisaged from out of the truth of being qua truth, then we dwell in yet a different way. Our dwelling depends on how we stand in the world and on earth, it depends on our stance, on where we stand with respect to the world. But this stance is the mode of our dwelling. Constructions are the image of how we stand in the world, of our relation to the earth; they bespeak our stance and harbor it. They are an expression of how we make room for things, of our relation to space: they themselves organize or articulate a space, but their spatiality is already given to them. They are spaces that always inscribe themselves within a pre-given spacedness. Space—at least the space of dwelling—is not objective and universal; nor is it subjective (the space of the architect, for example). For to speak of objectivity and subjectivity in this context presupposes that a decision has taken place, the decision to distribute space along the lines of object and subject—and this decision is not a matter for "us." For who are we? This question is played out precisely in the way in which we spatialize and are spatialized, that is, distributed not within space, but spatially. Do we inhabit our world as subjects? Are we subjects in contemporary constructions? Are constructions objects, objects that we fill with objects? These questions cannot be taken for granted. What is the difference between a Greek temple and a museum, the Guggenheim Museum in Bilbao, for example? It is, we say, a difference of time, a difference in epoch, or a historical difference. But do we know what we mean when we say this? This historical difference is spatialized. It is a spatial difference. Not because the temple and the museum are two different spaces, but because they are sustained or shot through with two different ways of making space or room, two different ways—*onto-historical* ways—of dwelling amid things, and therefore two radically different experiences of space. Technological dwelling has provided the human with a unique and hitherto unknown state of historical homelessness. If and where contemporary architecture, beyond its modernist moment, which embraced the machinic and the technological in perhaps too naïve and too messianic a way, recognizes the danger identified by Heidegger, it needs to reopen a space, between gathering and dissemination, between earth and world, at once bringing them together and holding them apart. Only in this between, in this inter-stitial space, can we properly *dwell*. Only thus will architecture give space to space itself, free and construct a space for human existence.

Running parallel to, or rather, perhaps, intersecting with the techno-capitalist economy of production and consumption, could we not envisage another, more restricted economy, and, with it, a different space? Could we not envisage places of resistance that would suspend and interrupt this fluidity, tangents, tears, or slits that would reconfigure our relation to the world?[56] Could we not envisage spaces that would be burstings of earth, eruptive events that would dislocate the dominant organization of space, and which, in taking place *in place of*, as well as *within* that space, would leave a tear within the social fabric? There is still space, there must be space for architectural resistance. This does not mean the coming about of a reactive and reactionary space. This space of resistance must become architecture's own. This is a space to come, a space, or rather a manifold of spaces, still to be invented. Architectural space must not be fascinated—enraptured, Heidegger would say, for reasons that have to do with the essentially enrapturing logic of techno-capitalism—by the absolute fluidity of space, by its smooth, rhizomatic contemporary essence. Rhizomatics alone can also be a form of alienation.

The space of architecture today is at the limit of two spaces: smooth and striated; it is situated at the limit of world and earth, of the rhizome and the root. This is the space it must weave: it must become something like a membrane, a lip, a fold. This is where our spatial contemporaneity is played out: between the potential alienation of absolute deterritorialization, and the still more alienating culture of identity politics. This is the space of difference, the inter-stice. This is where we must learn to be at home, together.

Afterword
Translating Essentially

It has often been argued that modern German was constituted principally through one specific translation, that of the Bible by Luther. As a result, translation occupies a privileged cultural role in Germany: cultural identity is very much a function of the essential relation between various idioms. This relation refers back to what Walter Benjamin sees as the essence of language.[1] Equally important, in relation to the birth of philosophical German, is the role of Kant: in the same way in which Luther wrests the Bible from Saint Jerome's Latin, Kant wrests metaphysics from scholastic Latin. The *Critique of Pure Reason* can even be seen as a workshop for the preliminary elaboration of a genuinely philosophical German idiom.[2] I cannot trace here the general movement within philosophy that attributes a decisive cultural role to translation for the constitution of *Bildung* or culture.[3] From Schlegel, Schleiermacher, and Hölderlin to Nietzsche, Rosenzweig, and Benjamin, virtually the whole of the history of German philosophy and literary theory is concerned with this problem of translation in relation to questions of history, culture, and national identity, and with the very possibility of thought itself. Rather, I would like to situate the specificity of Heidegger's conception of translation and the role it plays in his thought. Ultimately, I want to use this conception in order to look back on a specific move to which the various chapters of this book will have testified, back on what will turn out to be a sustained operation of translation governing the very movement of Heidegger's thought. Ultimately, it is the very connection between the possibility of thought itself and translation that will turn out to be decisive.

169

By all "objective" criteria, Heidegger was a poor translator. And were his own translations of, say, a passage from one of Pindar's Olympic odes,[4] or the famous first choral ode from Sophocles' *Antigone*,[5] to be shown to a tutor in ancient Greek, one can only imagine the latter's utter bewilderment and despair before such eccentricities and inelegant renderings of what no doubt counts as some of the most beautiful poetry ever written. Likewise, Heidegger's now famous translations of Aristotle, or of the pre-Socratics are, to most philosophers, hardly recognizable, and evidently the sign of a highly original but entirely misled mind. Never, perhaps, were more incorrect and unorthodox translations ever produced.

"Incorrect," perhaps, Heidegger would have replied, drawing on one of his most forceful distinctions, but "true" nonetheless. "And what, exactly, Herr Heidegger, allows you to make such a distinction? How does such a distinction justify the degree of violence to which your own translations are subjected? Besides, if, when faced with the necessity to translate, we simply set aside those very criteria of objectivity whereby the truth or untruth, sense or non-sense of utterances are measured, are we not left with the realm of the subjective, the arbitrary, and the fanciful? You may do as you please, Herr Heidegger, but you cannot expect us to consider your so-called translations as genuine translations. Translation, like all rational operations, must be subjected to criteria and rules of scientificity. And if there is indeed a perhaps irreducible share of interpretation in all translations, no doubt a function of the intrinsic ambiguity of natural language, this should not stop us from attempting to produce the most faithful and objective rendering of the meaning of any given text."

While identifiable in its origin, and commonly held, this objection misses the nature of Heidegger's engagement with idioms other than his own, with his own idiom, with language in general, as well as with the question and the practice of translation. And this is because it misses the nature of the relation binding this activity to Heidegger's own conception of truth, which, while neither objective nor scientific, is certainly not subjective and fanciful. Heidegger's distinction between "correctness" (*Richtigkeit*) and "truth" (*Wahrheit*) is not an opposition between objective truth and subjective opinion, or even between absolute and relative truth, but between two *historical* conceptions of truth—more still: between two moments in the history of truth. In other words, where we, today, equate the essence of truth with correctness, Heidegger introduces a decisive distinction. Whereas we see these two concepts as coextensive, Heidegger sees them as historically disjunctive and heterogeneous, refusing to equate the essence and origin of truth with what turns out to be only a derivative interpretation of that essence. But how can truth have a history? Is not truth precisely that which is *not* subject to change, that which remains unaffected by the vicissitudes of history? Over against this a-temporal or trans-historical conception of truth, Heidegger goes as far as to suggest that history is itself *of* truth, belonging to truth, that is, and this in such a way as to implicate a movement of translation belonging to truth itself, to what he calls the essence of truth. History, in other words, must be seen as the inner transformation and the translation of the sense of truth itself:

> This transformation is distinctive in that it remains concealed but nevertheless determines everything in advance. The transformation of the essence of truth and being is the genuine event in and of history.[6]

But in order for such a thesis to be formulated, Heidegger must displace the very sense and origin of truth itself, from "correctness" to "unconcealment," from an intrinsically metaphysical conception of truth, in and through which metaphysics constitutes itself as such, to a pre-metaphysical (where the "pre" must be understood in logical as much as, if not more than, in chronological terms) conception of truth as designating the light in which all things come to shine, as marking the clearing or the overall configuration in which all beings find their place.

Let me be a bit more specific regarding the difference between these two senses and conceptions of truth and the way in which the former unfolds from the latter. It is on the basis of this difference alone, and of its inner transformation, that Heidegger's own translating practice can come to light. So long as we do not open his translations to this decisive distinction, we shall continue to miss the singularity of his approach to translation. In the lecture course on Parmenides from 1942-43, Heidegger sets out to produce a genealogy of the modern concept of truth, which, he believes, does not provide us with an access to the conception and the fundamental experience of truth expressed in the words of the goddess "Truth" or ἀλήθεια.[7] The reason for this is that the modern concept of truth, characterized in terms of a correspondence between homogeneous and convertible terms, is itself born of a transformation in the sense and the essence of a more primordial and archaic conception of truth as unconcealment, which constitutes the very soil on which Parmenides' *Poem*—and the entire historical being surrounding it—grows. This is a transformation which, in Heidegger's analysis, takes place in ancient Rome, when the primordial and originary λήθη or concealment, on the basis of which the archaic truth or ἀλήθεια unfolds as the very event or coming into presence of presence itself, is progressively interpreted as derivative, and equated with the *opposite* of truth. In the process, it has become falsity (*falsum*), and the very negation of truth. Truth and untruth come to be polarized, and a certain value, if not an entire axiology, comes to be associated with this opposition. Untruth is no longer experienced as the counter-essence and counter-effectuation of truth, as the very horizon whence it itself unfolds, but as what usurps the place of truth, as its very negation. Detached from its origin and essence, truth falls in the space of representation and is associated with the correspondence between an intention and the intended, between mind and thing. Truth, in short, falls in the hands of *ratio* and rationality:

> In the early Middle Ages, following the path set by the Romans, ἀλήθεια, presented as ὁμοίοσις, became *adaequatio. Veritas est adaequatio intellectus ad rem.* The entire thinking of the Occident from Plato to Nietzsche thinks in terms of this delimitation of the essence of truth as correctness [*Richtigkeit*]. This delimitation of the essence of truth is *the metaphysical concept of truth;* more precisely, metaphysics receives its essence from the essence of truth thus determined.[8]

I do not wish, here, in the context of an Afterword that seeks to look back upon an itinerary that took us across many Heideggerian *topoi,* to engage in a critical analysis of Heidegger's relation to the concept of truth, and to the role ascribed to ancient Rome in the transformation of that concept. Others, successfully, I believe, have developed such an analysis.[9] Rather, I wish to focus on the way in which Heidegger's conception of the essence and history of truth opens up the question of translation, and this in such a way that it coils back upon the essence of thought itself. And what better point of entry into that question than looking at the way in which the essence or the history of truth unfolds according to a series of dis-locations and re-locations, to a process of translation? And this, in such a way that, when it becomes a question of translating truth back into its essence, back into its forgotten horizon of originary concealment, we cannot simply convert it into those very terms that characterize our modern conception and experience of truth, thus forcing the very operation of translation into a hitherto unsuspected direction, binding us to a process of expropriation and alienation in the most positive sense of the term, to the possibility of experiencing the difference that lies at the origin of our own historical identity. Following this privileged example of the translation of truth back into its own, and of an epochal configuration back into an other, we shall see how translation, in the genuine and decisive sense, remains bound to this other concept of truth, and this in such a way as to coincide ultimately with the essence of thought itself.

Let us, for the moment, in an effort to follow Heidegger's own translation, remain with the word ἀλήθεια. We translate it with the word "truth." In so doing, we have not said anything yet. Everything remains to be said about that word, about what it means. And yet, it seems we have only stated the obvious, what everybody already "knows." And yet, in a way, we have already said too much: everything is already played out in this translation. This is precisely because literally everything has played itself out in this translation — "everything," in this context, being precisely the process by which an epochal configuration of being translates itself into another, the process by which a specific economy of presence comes to be replaced by another. In the word "truth," which I take to be a translation of ἀλήθεια, and rightly so, although for reasons quite different from the ones I believe, "something" speaks for me, in my place and despite myself, and this in such a way that, it would seem, nothing could be added: ἀλήθεια "means" truth. And so, if, when I translate ἀλήθεια by "truth," nothing decisive takes place, it is because the decisive event has already taken place, behind my back as it were: precisely the event whereby ἀλήθεια became *veritas,* and *veritas adaequatio* and *rectitudo,* drawing in its wake a decisively different relation of the human to the world, to others and to history, drawing history itself towards veracity and exactness, calculation and measurement, subjectivity and representation, science and technology.

Refusing to be drawn in this way, refusing to equate the Greek, and specifically Parmenidean, ἀλήθεια with our modern concept of truth before even having had a chance to raise the question concerning the kind of event that takes place in such a translation, attempting to resist this almost inevitable urge, Heidegger suggests we "translate" ἀλήθεια, literally, by "unconcealedness" (*Unverbogenheit*). Yet, in doing so, it seems that little has been achieved:

> What the Greeks name ἀλήθεια we ordinarily "translate" with the word "truth." If we translate the Greek word "literally," however, then it says "unconcealedness" [*Unverbogenheit*]. It seems as if the "literal translation" consisted simply in patterning our word to correspond with the Greek word. While this is the beginning of literal translation, it is also in fact its end. The work of translation does not exhaust itself in such reproduction [*Nachbildung*] of "words," which then often sound artificial and ugly. If we merely replace [*ersetzen*] the Greek ἀλήθεια with our "unconcealedness," we are not yet actually translating [*übersetzen*]. That occurs only when the translating word "unconcealedness" carries us over [*uns* übersetzt] into the domain of experience and the mode of experience out of which the Greeks or, in the case at hand, the primordial thinker Parmenides says the word ἀλήθεια.[10]

It would seem, then, that in adopting a so-called more literal translation, we would get closer to the original meaning. In translating ἀλήθεια with, say, "unconcealedness," and not simply "truth," we would approach the true meaning of the word. But, in fact, our having adopted such a translation, nothing has yet taken place. We have indeed exchanged one idiom for another; we have indeed replaced one word (truth) with another (unconcealment). We have found a word in our idiom that corresponds with a word in another idiom, and proceeded to convert one into the other, as if the possibility of such a conversion went without saying, as if the two idioms were straightforwardly convertible. But how can we rely so patently and heavily on correspondence as the proper criterion for translation, and on a conception of translation as so unproblematically transversal and reversible, when it is the very nature or essence of truth that is here at issue? When, in opening ourselves to the word ἀλήθεια, it is precisely a question of wondering whether our metaphysical interpretation of the essence of truth as correspondence between concept and thing actually holds for the Greek, and specifically Parmenidean experience of truth? Similarly, at issue in our attempt to translate the Greek ἀλήθεια is precisely the issue concerning the continuity or discontinuity, the relation of imitation or caesura between the ancient experience of truth, and so of the world and nature as a whole, and our modern experience. For the issue concerning the passage from original to copy or derivative is, of course, at the very heart of the common conception of translation, which speaks of the original and the need to remain faithful to it in the translation by producing a good image of it. But such a conception is itself metaphysically determined, insofar as it is first and foremost a theory of truth, one which, to make things more complicated, has its roots in Plato's text, as Heidegger himself has attempted to show.[11] It is the theory whereby the truth of an image is measured according to its ability to correspond with or to resemble an original. And this, then, in such a way that one could not simply talk about a "Greek," as opposed to a "medieval" or "modern," conception of truth, as if the decisive line separating the pre-metaphysical from the metaphysical were simply chronological, coinciding with pre-defined lines of articulation of epochs in history, when it is precisely the conception of truth that is to serve as such a decisive and incisive criterion, as the truly historical or epochal pivot around which history turns. We begin to see, then, the extent to which our common conception of translation, and the criteria by which we judge a good translation, are a function of a more hidden, subterranean conception of truth, the nature of which is precisely at issue in Heidegger's attempt to "translate" the Greek ἀλήθεια, as it appears, for example, in Parmenides' *Poem*. The difficulty with this type of translation has to do with one's inability to rely on the pre-given criteria and demands of translation, with the need to invent or redefine the hermeneutic practice on the basis of which the origin or the truth of truth itself will be uncovered. We begin to see, then, the extent to which, in translating ἀλήθεια with "truth," or even "unconcealedness," nothing has actually yet begun to take place. Why? Because in doing so we have not even begun to *transpose*—displace, exile, or uproot—ourselves into the fundamental experience of truth for the Greeks, we have not even touched on the ontological soil on which this experience grew. We have not begun to leave the familiar shores of our own experience of truth in order to venture in the unclear waters of another. In other words, we translate; we proceed to exchange, according to a familiar economy of reversibility and interchangeability, but we fail to *understand,* and this means to experience. We do not yet provide ourselves with the tools to open ourselves to the radical unfamiliarity of that experience: far from opening our own language to the fundamental experience underlying that of another, we bring it back and reduce it to our own, thus indeed betraying it.[12]

But the remarkable thing is that, in order for this experience to come to light, the detour through an idiom other than Greek—in this instance German—is required. In other words, this experience can be brought about only through translation, only by opening up the German (or English, French, etc.) idiom that defines the site of our historical being today to the Greek idiom, yet in such a way that this repetition constitutes a moment of invention. In other words, it has become a question of knowing, not how we can find an "equivalent" of ἀλήθεια in German—for there is none readily available—but how German can be taught to think Greek, how, in other words still, the German idiom can open itself to the very essence of truth, despite and beyond it being the heir to the essential transformation of truth that took place in Roman antiquity and the early Middle Ages. With this issue, we touch on the very difficulty that we, as readers of Heidegger, all have in reading his texts, in following the torsions and twists to which he submits his own language. This is to say nothing, of course, of the added difficulty of having to translate such torsions and twists in yet another language, in English, for example. While perhaps less trying and decisive than the first translation, the latter nonetheless also requires a moment of invention. For what is then demanded of the English language is something equally transformative.

In the end, it is always language itself that must be able to speak. It is always a question of letting language itself speak. And it is this letting-speak which, paradoxically, seems to harbor an irreducible violence, one which, inadequately perhaps, we refer to as "interpretation." It is only at the cost of this translation inherent to the original idiom, at the cost of this ability to let language speak beyond what it says, to let it repeat itself or stutter, that there can be a genuine translation from one idiom to the next. But this language can be made to speak only through translation, only by being made to stutter. Only through the detour of the German idiom was Heidegger able to make the Greek speak Greek. What was required, in order for the Greek language to speak from within its fundamental domain of experience, a domain which itself and as such had never come to language, was nothing less than its repetition in another idiom. How exactly does this work in Heidegger's text? Let me take the specific example of the two "contraries" or, better said perhaps, the two counter-essences (*Gegenwesen*) of ἀληθές already operative in ancient Greek, discussed by Heidegger near the beginning of the *Parmenides,* and which Escoubas has stigmatized as "the second stage" in the mutation of the essence of truth.[13] These are ληθές (λαθόν) and τὸ ψεῦδος. There occurs, then, within the Greek language itself an operation of displacement or dislocation, what Heidegger calls an *Umschreibung* or a "rewording," and this in such a way that the place of truth itself comes to be modified: τὸ ψεῦδος comes to replace ληθές as the contrary of ἀληθές. And this is precisely the first moment in the transformation of the nature of the relation between untruth and truth, a transformation whereby untruth, initially experienced as the counter-essence of truth, and by that we need to understand its counter-effectuation, in a movement that retains truth and untruth as belonging essentially to one another, comes to be seen as its contrary, thereby opening the way to its subsequent interpretation as what contradicts truth. In this transformation, where τὸ ψεῦδος comes to be thought in place of ἀληθές, a double operation takes place. First, ψεῦδος loses a dimension contained in ληθές (the dimension of forgetting), but at the same time retains the dimension of the hiding and the dissimulating. Second, ψεῦδος introduces another dimension, that of showing and shining (*scheinen*) by way of dissimulating: the ψεῦδος shows something in dissimulating something else. Now, the important point here is that as a result of this displacement of the "contrary" of ἀληθές—from ληθές (λαθόν) to ψεῦδος—the prefix ἀ- of ἀληθές loses its negative-privative connotation, so that the German translation of ἀληθές can no longer remain satisfied with the initial translation of *unverbogene* and must now introduce *entborgene* instead. The *ent-* indicates not so much a privation as a spacing. We now have a displacement that is readable in the German language; through the operation of translation, we can now actually see a displacement where the Greek language gave a deceiving impression of continuity. Were it not for this doubling or this repetition of the Greek in and through the German, the transformation—indeed, the onto-historical translation—that takes place within the Greek as such would remain invisible.

The purpose of genuine, originary translation, then, is to carry us across and over, into a domain of experience that is wholly other, into a land that is not our own. Only insofar as we can transpose ourselves into the Greek experience is there translation in the proper sense of the term. But, as we have witnessed, such a transposition can take place only in and through translation. We cannot do away with this detour, with the need to allow our own idiom to speak, say, Greek. This transposition does not simply consist of a lateral movement into another idiom. Rather, it presupposes that this other idiom be allowed to speak in an idiom other than its own, that it be itself submitted to the possibility of its repetition in a moment that is not there to begin with, either in the "original" or the idiom in which this original is translated. This is the logic to which, before Heidegger, Hölderlin himself had responded in his translations of Sophocles' *Oedipus Tyrannous* and *Antigone*, as well as of some of Pindar's odes.[14] And beyond this act of actual translation, it is Hölderlin's entire relation to the Greeks and his attempt to write a modern tragedy based on the figure of Empedocles that can be seen as responding to the same logic. And if the latter project "failed," if it remained unfinished, it is because Hölderlin himself came to grasp the epochal rift separating us Moderns from the Ancients, and thus the historical impossibility of such a project. By that, we need to understand that if there was indeed a passage, a historical translation from a Greek experience of truth, an ancient relation to nature as φύσις, and this in such a way that history itself came to take a different turn, thus orienting itself in a different direction, such a historical translation cannot itself be annulled. It is literally irreversible, and this in such a way that we cannot translate ourselves back into the world of the Ancients. As such, far from marking a failure, the incompleteness of Hölderlin's project testifies to a fundamental experience of the very nature of Western history, a fundamental experience of the very essence of truth itself.

On the basis of these preliminary yet decisive remarks concerning the translation of ἀλήθεια, we can reflect further on the nature and task of translation itself. For, as we began by suggesting, our conception of translation is entirely dependent upon an implicit concept and a fundamental experience of truth. And the modern, common conception of translation is one that is based on a conception of truth as correspondence and correctness. In order to illustrate this point, let me turn to another example of translation to be found in Heidegger's text.

Turning for the second time, in a second set of analyses, to the opening lines of the first choral ode from Sophocles' *Antigone*, Heidegger suggests that we translate τὰ δεινά, a plural, by τὸ δεινόν, a singular, and that τὸ δεινόν be understood as *das Unheimliche*, the uncanny.[15] The opening two lines (333–34),

Πολλὰ τὰ δεινὰ κοὐδὲν ἀνθρώπου δεινότερου πέλει:

thus read in Heidegger's translation:

> *Vielfältig das Unheimliche, nichts doch*
> *über den Menschen hinaus Unheimlicheres ragend sich regt.*

Manifold is the uncanny, yet nothing
more uncanny looms beyond Man.

Having thus translated Πολλὰ τὰ δεινὰ with "manifold the uncanny," Heidegger pauses and reflects on the nature of his translation and on translation as such. This translation, he admits outright, is itself initially alien or uncanny, for it contains a certain violence. It is, from a philological perspective, quite "wrong." A more "correct" or orthodox translation, such as, in English, David Grene's, would read as follows:

> Many are the wonders, none
> is more wonderful than what is man.[16]

This is very close to Dudley Fitts and Robert Fitzgerald's earlier translation, which reads:

> Numberless are the wonders, but none
> more wonderful than man.[17]

These two translations seem to be largely justified in light of Liddell and Scott's *Greek-English Lexicon*, which, under δεινός, ή, όν, lists "wondrous," "marvelous," but also "strange," which would take us closer to Heidegger's own translation. But the significant point, here, is that Heidegger is not disputing the unorthodox nature of his own translation, which suggests that his Greek was at least good enough to recognize just that. What we cannot help asking about, then, is the fundamental motivation behind the violence wreaked by Heidegger on Sophocles' text. He begins by calling into question the criteria by which the "correctness" of translations is ordinarily measured. The dictionary, it is thought, is the ultimate authority or reference to which we turn when attempting to translate. Yet, Heidegger insists, "we too readily forget that the information in a dictionary must always be based upon a preceding interpretation of linguistic contexts from which particular words and word usages are taken."[18] In other words, in consulting dictionaries, or, as the German language has it, "wordbooks" (*Wörterbücher*), while we do indeed have access to words and their meaning, we do not to the more general context, and by that we need to understand the onto-historical ground and experience within which they first appear, and from out of which their very meaning is extracted. As a result, Heidegger adds, if it is indeed the case that "in most cases a dictionary provides the correct information about the meaning of a word," this correctness "does not yet guarantee us any insight into the truth of what the word means and can mean, so long as we are asking about the essential realm [*Wesensbereich*] named in the word."[19] And so, here, once again, we see Heidegger mobilizing the distinction between correctness and truth, where the truth of the word would refer not so much to the word itself as to the essential realm, the horizon or what we often refer to as the "context" from within which it appears and unfolds.

Naturally, when it is simply a question of exchanging an idiom into another idiom, in what amounts to an economy whose exchange rate and regulations have been set in advance, when, in other words, language is envisaged from its purely communicative, practical dimension, then the dictionary is the tool to which we turn, as the standard by which the validity of the exchange will be measured. When envisaged solely as a vehicle of information and calculation, language operates at a level entirely accountable in the terms defined by the dictionary and anticipated in it. Furthermore, the operation of translation involves a sense of space, and thus of displacement and replacement, that is fairly unproblematic, insofar as the two planes or idioms involved are continuous and homogeneous. The two idioms exist side by side, they are simply coextensive, and this in such a way that the passage from one to the other, while no doubt raising technical difficulties, is not threatened in its very possibility. Guaranteed in its possibility, the passage is such as not to require another sense of truth to be mobilized. It is justified by its reliance on the metaphysics of correspondence and correctness to which it testifies. This is the very metaphysics that presides over the vast majority of translations, translations that we, as researchers, for the most part endorse: we seek to establish equivalencies and correspondences, we aim for the word and the sentence that is closest to what we take the original to mean. We operate in a reversible and continuous world.

Yet, with the issue of translation as it appears in Heidegger, it is a question of wondering whether language does not also operate on another level: one that is not simply reversible and continuous, but irreversible and discontinuous, not merely horizontal and flat, but vertical and deep. What is the depth and verticality at issue here? Precisely that of truth and essence, where truth and essence refer to the historical unfolding of a language, to the onto-historical horizon from which a given language unfolds. And this is what dictionaries, even philological and historical dictionaries, cannot access or provide. The depth is that of the history of an idiom, what Heidegger calls its "historical spirit." Like geological formations, languages are surfaces that live off a past that is not so much behind as beneath and that act as the very soil from which they speak. Those idioms are not so much coextensive as superimposed: they do communicate, but not as this spatial continuum. Their spatiality is disjunctive and interspersed with gaps and drops. Between them, there are no straightforward or easy passages, no ready-made transitions and pre-established equivalencies. For the ground or the history that sustains them is not immediately translatable into another, especially where and when one such ground is in fact the transformed ground of an idiom that it is to translate back. Translation also takes place, therefore, and in a way that is infinitely more fundamental, where it is precisely concerned with bringing out the very depths whence a language unfolds, as well as in a way that is essentially historical, insofar as something like a historical event, if not the event of history itself, actually takes place in such a translation, in the movement from the *spirit* of one language to that of another. The question, then, with which translation is now concerned, is the following: how do we move from the spirit of a language, and an epoch, to that of another? How do we move from one depth to another? How do we go about transposing ourselves in such a way, once we have recognized that there is no tool that is readily available, pre-formatted for such a journey, once we have recognized that the realm of pre-given equivalents is no longer available? There is no straightforward answer to that question. Every situation, every idiom will command its own response.

Heidegger's relation to translation, his very own practice as a translator, is inseparable from his conception of truth, and from the basic distinction between the intrinsically metaphysical conception of truth as *adaequatio* and correctness that governs our ordinary conception and practice of translation, and a more fundamental conception of truth as unconcealment, in the space of which Heidegger wants to situate his own translating practice. It is through the latter, and through the latter alone, that a given object or matter is made to speak from itself, that is, allowed to speak in such a way as to disclose its own essence. This means that the sense of what is given, whether a text or any other phenomenon, can never be given in advance, and on the basis of a standard after which it would be measured. Opening oneself to the thing in question, opening oneself to its essence or its truth-character, always entails that we not bring it back to what is already familiar, reduce it to what we already know, in a gesture which, from the very start, condemns its singularity. Rather, it presupposes that we open ourselves to that which, in and through the text, speaks from its own site, to that singular space whence the text itself emerges — in short, to the origin or the essence of the text. And so, Heidegger would go on to suggest, while incorrect, his translations are perhaps "truer" than the most correct of all translations. And while seemingly unorthodox, they are perhaps best defined as anorthodox, escaping the imperatives of the doxa, of its demand for common sense, that is so fundamentally bound up with the preconception of truth as *adaequatio* and *rectitudo*. For my translations are a matter for thinking, Heidegger would presumably say, not opinion, and the question of what thought is, of where it belongs, is itself intimately bound up with the question of truth.

Yet even before addressing the issue of translation from one historical language to another, should we not recognize a prior level of translation, one that would be immanent to every historical language?

Should we not, in other words, begin with our own language, by recognizing, in what would amount to an appropriation of what is given to us from the start, that our own idiom, in its literal superficiality, needs to be translated back into its own essence, back into its own historical-destinal depth, and thus understood for the first time, made our own? It is only from out of such an operation that a genuine relation to other languages becomes possible, as languages that speak from their own singular geo-historical depth. Every act of interpretation, in the fundamental sense in which to understand means to relate to the truth or the essence of a text, is thus an act of translation, insofar as what is being read is subjected to a trans-position and a dis-placement back into the sphere of its essence. And so, Heidegger admits, the "interpretation of Hölderlin's hymns is a translating within our German language," in the same way in which an interpretation of Kant's *Critique of Pure Reason* or Hegel's *Phenomenology of Spirit* is also a translation.[20] In order to understand the nature of translation as ordinarily conceived, in a restricted sense, we must understand the nature of reading and understanding as involving interpretation in a broader sense. To the restricted economy of trans-linguistic translation, we need to add the general economy of intra-linguistic translation.

Having recognized the intrinsically delicate nature of any translation involving two idioms separated by an onto-historical rift or turn, as well as the perhaps lesser problematic nature of a translation involving two idioms within the same onto-historical or epochal horizon, we would be greatly mistaken in assuming that such a horizon—or, to use a different image, the very ontological soil of our most decisive experiences—is itself given from the start, immediately accessible. We would be greatly mistaken, in other words, in believing that access to the essence of our own idiom does not itself require an operation of translation, a certain originary dis- and re-location through which that idiom would precisely become our own. But is this not the point at which the operation of translation coincides with that of thought? Is there not a sense, and indeed a fundamental one, in which the essence of thought itself involves translation, not between two idioms, or even between two epochal configurations, but within one and the same idiom? And is it not precisely this movement which, no matter which field or topic it is applied to, we are made to experience, and which this book attempted to retrace? In what have we repeatedly seen Heidegger to be involved, if not an operation of essential translation, an operation whereby a given site or topic—a *topos*—was brought back into the sphere of its own essence, at once dis-placed and re-placed, carried across the space of its own unfolding? What did we ourselves experience as readers if not the uncanny nature of such a journey across, if not our own displacement, we who, for the most part, come across

such spaces as already constituted, as given in their plentiful manifestness? What did we undergo, if not the transformation of essence itself
so intimately bound up with the very operation of thought? It is
thought itself that is translational, essentially: it moves across the space
in and as which a thing unfolds, it swims upstream as it were, back
towards its source, back into the open expanse or the clearing in which
it first shines—back into its truth. Throughout, the question leading our
investigations will have been that of essence. Not so much, as one might
first expect, in the guise of a question bearing on the quiddity of any
domain, but as the question concerning the unfolding or the coming
into being, the "how" or the style that is specific to the domain in question. And this, then, in such a way that the essence of any given *topos* is
not so much given, there, precisely as this factually existing thing, but
as the eventful horizon whence it unfolds in presence, a horizon that is
always a matter for thought, whose task it is to extract the truth-hori-
zon that most properly belongs to all beings. Thought is engaged in this
endless operation of dis-location and re-location, in and through which
it experiences the dystopic power of the essence of truth, yet in and
through which the human and its world, its actions and words, beings
as such and as a whole are brought back into the site of their essence,
back into the onto-historical horizon whence they unfold. There is
something metonymic about the question of translation: while being
one site of truth among others, it also serves to reflect on the movement and the essence of thought as such. But thought itself, as translational, is also, quite literally, metaphorical, insofar as it consists in
carrying a domain across and over into its forgotten and erased essence.
The movement of thought, what Heidegger calls its essence, is the
thought of movement itself, or of essence, of the very way in which
things come to stand and shine within presence, come to be those very
things they are. There comes a point, then, when translation coincides
with the operation of thought itself. For the movement of thought consists in appropriating what is most proper to us, in bringing to the word
and into language that which, of itself, withdraws, recedes in the background of everything that presents itself. The very soil of our experience, on the basis of which we relate to others, to animate and
inanimate things, in short, to the world, while in a way still given in the
world, is never given as such. It is the very nature and task of thought
to bring worldly problems back into their pre-worldly horizon. It is the
very function of thought to bring innerworldy phenomena back into
their truth. And Heidegger's own language, at times so unfamiliar, is
itself a function of this demand that we transpose ourselves in the
realm of essence, where we, as those beings who belong to truth, truly
belong.

Consequently,

> the more difficult task is always the translation of one's own language into
> its ownmost word. That is why, e.g., the translation of the word of a Ger-
> man thinker into the German language is especially difficult—because
> there reigns here the tenacious prejudice to the effect that we who speak
> German would understand the German word without further ado, since it
> belongs, after all, to our own language, whereas, on the contrary, to trans-
> late a Greek word we must in the first place learn that foreign tongue.[21]

The illusion, therefore, consists in believing that, in speaking or writing
a language, we have immediate access to its truth, when it is perhaps
the exact opposite that is actually happening: our constant use of and
familiarity with our own language gets in the way of a genuine relation
to its truth, and by that we mean the fundamental tone and experience
on the basis of which it unfolds. What we are most cut off from, in our
everyday relation to language, is precisely its essence, the ground or soil
from which we speak. Often we take this ground to be our own lived
experiences, our own selves. But we, and language with us, speaks
from greater depths, and from a horizon that exceeds that of the lived
experience: we must not mistake the truth of fundamental experiences
(*Grunderfahrungen*), which are onto-historical or onto-destinal in nature,
for mere lived experiences (*Erlebnisse*), which are psychological and anthro-
pomorphic:

> In every dialogue and every soliloquy an essential translation holds sway.
> We do not here have in mind primarily the operation of substituting one
> turn of phrase for another in the same language or the use of "paraphrase."
> Such a change in the choice of words is a consequence deriving from the
> fact that what is to be said has already been transported for us into another
> truth and clarity—or perhaps question-worthiness [*Fragwürdigkeit*]. This
> transporting can occur without a change in the linguistic expression. The
> poetry of a poet or the treatise of a thinker stands within its own unique
> proper word. It compels us to see this word again and again as if we were
> hearing it for the first time. These newborn words transpose us in every
> case to a new shore. So-called translation [*Über*setzen] and paraphrase are
> always subsequent and follow upon the transporting [Über*setzen*] of our
> whole being into the realm of a transformed truth. Only if we are already
> appropriated [*übereignet sind*] by this transporting are we in the care of the
> word. Only on the basis of a respect for language grounded in this way can
> we assume the generally lighter and more limited task of translating a for-
> eign word into our own language.[22]

With this intra-linguistic level of translation, we reach the very origin and most fundamental sense in which this term needs to be considered. For this is the level at which things, brought back into the realm

of essence and truth, begin to speak to us as if for the first time, the literally phenomenological level at which things can manifest themselves in and from themselves. In and through this translation, things are returned to themselves, that is, to their own power of manifestation. Everything happens as if things, up until then, and through the way in which we refer to them ordinarily, call upon them and use them, had kept themselves away from us. Thinking is translating as a learning again, as an ability to transpose itself, and the whole of the sphere of human experience, back into the disclosive power of language itself, as essentially belonging to truth, and in which things come to shine for the first time, as shinings of truth itself.

Notes

Introduction

1. WhD, 3/6. While a certainly acceptable translation of the German "was heißt denken?" the English "what is called thinking?" fails to capture the various senses of the German, specifically those addressing thinking in its meaning ("what does it mean to think?") and its calling ("what calls for thinking, and calls it forth?"). The latter sense of the question will turn out to be decisive here.

2. WhD, 4/7.

3. WhD, 4/7.

4. WhD, 5/9.

5. WhD, 7/11.

6. WhD, 12/30.

1. *Homo Heideggerians*

1. See E. Husserl's marginal annotations to his copy of Heidegger's *Being and Time*, originally published in *Jahrbuch für Philosophie und Phänomenologische Forschung* (Halle and Saale: Niemeyer Verlag, 1927), vol. VII, and *Kant and the Problem of Metaphysics* (Bonn: Cohen Verlag, 1929), as well as the lecture entitled "Phenomenology and Anthropology" (*Husserliana* XXVII, *Aufsätze und Vorträge* [1922-37], ed. T. Nenon and H. R. Sepp), delivered on three occasions in June 1931.

2. So, in raising the question of man as the question concerning his essence, Heidegger simply refuses to think man on the basis of some history, some

narrative that would account for his birth, for his emergence from out of the realm of animality, or *ex nihilo*. Thus, Heidegger refuses to think the origin of man in terms of a mere branching off, of a differentiation of a unique, singular process called "life." If man as such, or man according to his essence, is alive—and indeed he is—it is in quite a different sense: already the Greeks, and Aristotle among others, made a distinction within the human between the life of needs and necessities (ζῷον) and the life that can become an object of pursuit, debate, and argument (βίος). Similarly, and after Husserl, one must distinguish here between the body that lives according to such necessities, the body that survives (*Körper*), and the body that lives onto-phenomenologically, the existing body (*Leib*). If man lives, it is not simply as an organism; nor is it, for that matter, as an organism with something specific and non-organic in addition to the organic, a soul, for example, or an intellect. The metaphysical representation of man as ζῷον λόγον ἔχον is essentially complicit with the biological representation of man. Thus, Heidegger wishes to wrest the question of man from the grip of representation by bypassing the classical determination of man with respect to its animality, or with respect to the problematic of organic life, on the one hand, and with respect to the problematic of the supersensible, on the other hand, which locates the origin of man in the representation of a higher being. For further details concerning the issue of life, and Heidegger's problematic attempt to distinguish the life of Dasein from that of animality, see GA 29/30, Part Two, and particularly §45.

3. Wm, 157/248.

4. Wm, 203/283–84.

5. See SZ, 54/80, where Heidegger refers the preposition "in" of Dasein's being-in-the-world to the old German verb *innan*, to dwell.

6. Wm, 200/281.

7. GA 24, 393/277–78.

8. And today there are, as we know, an almost infinite number of types of historiography: history of ideas, of mentalities, of civilizations, history of life (evolution), of the universe, of history itself, etc.

9. Wm, 155/247.

10. See Wm, 191–92/274.

11. Wm, 155–56/247.

12. SZ, 133/171.

13. SZ, 220/263.

14. SZ, 226/269.

15. See SZ, §§15–18.

16. See GA 19, Introductory Part.

17. SZ, 69/98.

18. SZ, 67/95.

19. GA 19, §7.

20. In that respect, Division One of *Being and Time* is in agreement with Husserl's analyses of the lived body or the flesh (*Leib*) in *Ideas . . . II*. There the

body is described as the instrument or the immediate expression of the ego, not as an "I think," but as an "I can." Thus, subjectivity is rearticulated along the lines of power or potentiality, in other words, along the lines of a certain power to *be*, more than a mere power to *think*. Thinking would thus need to be seen as a specific power, as indicative of what the lived body can do, in what would amount to an overcoming of the Cartesian dualism between mind and body, *res cogitans* and *res extensa*. See Edmund Husserl, *Ideen zur einer reinen Phänomenologie und phänomenologischen Philosophie. Zweites Buch: Phänomenologische Untersuchungen zur Konstitution*, ed. Marly Biemel (The Hague: Martinus Nijhoff, 1952) (Husserliana IV), §§35–42.

21. Wm, 30/26; my emphasis in the last sentence.

22. GA 19, §8 and §22.

23. SZ, 307–8/355.

24. SZ, 236/280.

25. SZ, 243/287; my emphasis.

26. SZ, 325/373.

27. GA 19, 51/36.

28. SZ, 251–52/295.

29. SZ, 254/298.

30. SZ, 261/305.

31. SZ, 310/358.

32. SZ, 262–63/307.

33. Insofar as the repetition involved here brings existence to a greater level of intensity, it is not a mere reiteration, but the very beginning of ethics. Repetition as an ethical, that is, life-enhancing, concept must therefore be distinguished from a purely mimetic and ontologically redundant concept of repetition, which reiterates the same. A more sustained discussion of the issue of repetition is carried out in Chapter 2 ("The Politics of Repetition") of this book.

34. SZ, 264/309. The possibility of such an ethical turn is explicitly addressed in the context of the somewhat undeveloped and therefore incomplete discussion of "metontology," which took place in the years 1928–30. In GA 26, and following the problematic of fundamental ontology, Heidegger argues in favor of a special problematic concerned with the whole of being (*das Seiende im Ganzen*). This problematic, referred to as metontology, in the sense of an overturning (*Umschlag*, μεταβολή) of fundamental ontological questions back into existentiell questions, coincides with "the domain of the metaphysics of existence." And there, "the question of an ethics may properly be raised for the first time" (GA 26, 199/157).

35. Heidegger describes the mode of discourse that is at work in anticipation as "the call of conscience" (§56), in which Dasein is summoned (*aufgerufen*) to itself, that is, to its ownmost *Seinkönnen*, precisely by remaining silent, by not telling anything, by not disclosing any content, any information regarding the world: "in the content of the call, one can indeed point to nothing which the voice 'positively' recommends and imposes" (SZ, 294/340). It is a call, then, which is literally empty, speechless, bereft of language, the very

silence of which is precisely such as to bring Dasein face to face with itself; it is a call that resonates from within, but also from afar, that is, from ahead of and beyond everyday existence, from that very limit or end whence existence is disclosed. It is interesting to note here that the authentic mode of speech, in which the singular existence calls Dasein back from its lostness in the One and into the truth of existence takes on the form of silence; the alien voice that bespeaks silence is the mode of discourse that coincides with Dasein being wrested from its ordinary and familiar relation with the world, normally expressed in "idle talk." Also, this is the point at which Heidegger locates the possibility of praxis in the genuine sense of the term, resisting anything like a prescriptive ethics in favor of an existential one, in which the true object of action, that which needs to be enacted, is existence as such, that is, as disclosedness, or truth. That which needs to be enacted or liberated is the power or the capacity that is proper to Dasein; this is the point at which Heidegger's treatment of the call of conscience comes close to Spinoza's ethics: it is, after all, a matter of persevering in one's Being, of freeing one's power to be. Man is first and foremost a power of disclosedness, a power of letting things be within the Open, a capacity to open itself to the Open as such, to comport itself to truth as such. It is an ethics of the self, which does not mean a "selfish" ethics, but an ethics for which a true concept of action can be derived only from a genuine understanding of what it means to be for man (of the essence of man as existence), and from an appropriation of the proper thus understood. It is a matter of self-appropriation. De facto, it is not just a description, but also an affirmation and a celebration of the essential finitude of human existence as condition of possibility of existence as the site or the place where truth happens. Heidegger says it all quite explicitly in the following passage:

> We miss a positive content in that which is called, because we expect to be told something currently useful about assured possibilities of 'taking action' [*Handeln*] which are available and calculable. This expectation has its basis within the horizon of that way of interpreting which belongs to common-sense concern—a way of interpreting which forces Dasein's existence to be subsumed under the idea of a business procedure that can be regulated. Such expectations (and in part these tacitly underlie even the demand for a *material* ethic of value as contrasted with one that is 'merely' formal) are of course disappointed by the conscience. The call of conscience fails to give any such 'practical' injunctions, *solely because* it summons Dasein to existence, to its ownmost capacity-to-be-its-Self. With the maxims which one might be led to expect—maxims which could be reckoned upon unequivocally—the conscience would deny to existence nothing less than the very *possibility of taking action*. But because the conscience manifestly cannot be 'positive' in this manner, neither does it function 'just negatively' in this manner. The call discloses nothing which could be either positive or negative as something with which we *can concern ourselves;* for what it has in view is a Being which is ontologically quite different—namely, *existence*. On the other hand, when the call is rightly understood, it gives us that which in the existential sense is the

'most positive' of all—namely, the ownmost possibility which Dasein can present to itself, as a calling-back that calls Dasein forth [*als vorrufender Rückruf*] in its capacity-to-be-its-Self every time. To hear the call properly means bringing oneself into a factical taking-action. (SZ, 294/341)

36. SZ, 264/308; my emphasis.

37. SZ, 266/311.

38. No matter how one decides to translate this term (resolution, resolve, resoluteness, decision, etc.), the intimate connection with the term of which it is an essential modification, to wit, *Erschlossenheit,* is lost. Yet this connection is what matters most here. *Enthschlossenheit* designates first and foremost a mode of disclosure, or a mode of truth: specifically, the mode whereby existence discloses itself to itself as disclosedness. It is thus a mode of disclosure in which the whole and the essence of existence is at issue, and not just this or that aspect or concern that belongs to existence.

39. SZ, 298/344–45.

40. GA 29/30, 247/165.

41. This is where, despite Heidegger's acknowledgment of his debt to Kierkegaard's concept of the moment, his conception of the *Augenblick* becomes irreconcilable with Kierkegaard's. See SZ, 338 note/497.

42. SZ, 328/376.

43. SZ, 338/387–88.

44. GA 29/30, 224/149.

45. GA 29/30, 224/148.

46. GA 29/30, 247/165.

47. GA 29/30, 248/166.

48. GA 29/30, 248/166.

49. SZ, 300–301/347–48.

50. SZ, 146/186.

51. GA 19, 163–64/112–13.

52. GA 29/30, 10/7.

53. GA 29/30, 5/4.

54. SU, 11–12.

55. See GA 19, §25.

56. GA 19, 175/120.

57. GA 19, 175/120.

58. Wm, 145/239.

59. GA 19, 178/122–23. When, in 1946, at the demand of Jean Beaufret, Heidegger takes up again the question of ethics, his interpretation of the Greek concept of ἦθος remains unchanged: "If the name 'ethics,' in keeping with the basic meaning of the word ἦθος, should now say that ethics ponders the abode of the human being, then that thinking which the truth of being as the primordial element of the human being, as one who eksists, is in itself originary ethics" (Wm, 187/271).

60. For the latter, see "Letter on Humanism," in Wm, 185ff./351ff.
61. Wm, 187/271.
62. GA 29/30, 28–29/19.
63. GA 29/30, 31/21.
64. GA 29/30, 33/22.
65. Plato, *Republic*, 476 c f., 520 c, 533 c.
66. GA 29/30, 34/23.
67. GA 29/30, 35/23.

2. The Politics of Repetition

1. These issues are the focus of work in progress.
2. SZ, 385–86/436–38; GA 26, 265–67/205–7; GA 24, 407/287.
3. GA 26, 266/206.
4. SZ, 385/437.
5. Ten years after the publication of *Being and Time*, Heidegger will recapture his statements in the following way: "The properly temporal is the stirring, exciting, but at the same time conserving and preserving extension and stretch from the future into the past and from the latter into the former. In this extension, man as historical is in each case a 'spread.' The present is always later than the future; it is the last. It springs from the struggle of the future with the past" (GA 45, 42/40).
6. SZ, 386/438.
7. GA 26, 197/155.
8. GA 26, 197/155.
9. GA 20, 187/138.
10. GA 20, 188/138.
11. SZ, 22/24.
12. See Heidegger, *Beiträge zur Philosophie (Vom Ereignis)*, GA 65, especially Part Two ("Der Anklang"); *Nietzsche*, GA 6.2, "Der europäische Nihilismus."
13. I have tried to tackle this delicate and complex issue in my *Heidegger and the Political: Dystopias* (London: Routledge, 1998).
14. GA 45, 40–41/38.
15. GA 45, 41/39.

3. Boredom

1. GA 26, 196–202/154–59.
2. In addition to the works already mentioned, see "Was ist Metaphysik?" (Wm, 103–21/82–96), "On the Essence of Ground" (Wm, 123–73/97–135), and *The Fundamental Concepts of Metaphysics* (GA 29/30).
3. GA 3, 232/158.

4. The following works and articles should nonetheless be mentioned: David Farrell Krell, *Daimon Life: Heidegger and Life-Philosophy* (Bloomington: Indiana University Press, 1992), Part I, Chapter 3; Parvis Emad, "Boredom as Limit and Disposition," *Heidegger Studies* 1 (1985): 63–78; R. J. A. van Dijk, "Grundbegriffe der Metaphysik: zur formalanzeigenden Struktur der philosophischen Begriffe bei Heidegger," *Heidegger Studies* 7 (1991): 89–109; William McNeill, "Metaphysics, Ontology, Metontology," *Heidegger Studies* 8 (1992): 63–79.

5. SZ, 186/231.

6. SZ, 187–88/232–33.

7. GA 29/30, 7/5.

8. I have tried to say a few things regarding these connections in Chapter 4 ("The Free Use of the National") of my *Heidegger and the Political: Dystopias* (London: Routledge, 1998).

9. SZ, 344/394.

10. GA 29/30, §44.

11. GA 45, §§36–38.

12. GA 29/30, 236/157.

13. One can only remain perplexed before Heidegger's choice of historical references (Ludwig Klages, Oswald Spengler, Max Scheler, Leopold Ziegler), which he captures, all too easily perhaps, under the name "philosophy of culture": Why these? Why only four? Why only German? True, if Heidegger considers this *Kulturphilosophie*, it is only to dismiss it instantly, precisely as that type of philosophy which is unable to distinguish between *Zeitgeist* and *Grundstimmung*. Yet it is precisely this "philosophy" that provides him with his clue, and ultimately with his diagnosis, concerning the *Stimmung* of the time.

14. GA 29/30, 122/75.

15. GA 29/30, 115/77.

16. GA 29/30, 207/137.

17. GA 28/30, 216/144.

18. GA 29/30, 531/366.

19. It is a question, in other words, of knowing how the time of boredom, which drags (such is the meaning of boredom as "long-while" or *Lange-weile*), to the point of leaving us in a quasi coma, manages to invert or reverse itself in its opposite, in what amounts to an extreme contraction of time and an intensification of life as such.

20. GA 29/30, 218/145.

21. GA 29/30, 224/149.

22. GA 29/30, 243/162–63.

23. GA 29/30, 245/164.

24. GA 29/30, 244/163.

25. The reader may wish to contrast this increasingly politically oriented analysis with the ethics of potentiality exposed in Chapter 1 ("*Homo Heideggerians*").

26. GA 29/30, 245/164.
27. GA 29/30, 254/171.
28. GA 29/30, 255/172.
29. GA 29/30, 255/172.
30. GA 29/30, 254/171.

4. Science, "Servant of Philosophy"?

1. GA 29/30, 7.

2. On a previous page, Heidegger rejects with vehemence the idea that philosophy would need to model itself after the sciences: "perhaps even to judge philosophy according to the idea of science is the most fateful debasement of its innermost essence" (GA 29/30, 4). The somewhat polemical tone of these formulations, perhaps due to the boldness of youth, is toned down, if not altogether dismissed, some twenty years later, when Heidegger, in another lecture course, speaks of philosophy's relation to science with the following words: "it would be both tactless and tasteless to take a stand against science upon the very rostrum that serves scientific education. Tact alone ought to prevent all polemics here. . . . Any kind of polemics fails from the outset to assume the attitude of thinking" (WhD, 49/13).

3. This dialogue is one which, following Hölderlin's poetic project, expressed in the verse of a sketch for an unfinished poem, according to which "we are a dialogue" (*ein Gespräch wir sind*), Heidegger restricted to art and thought, to language in the most essential sense. See "Hölderlin und das Wesen der Dichtung" (EHD, 36–38).

4. WhD, 49/14.

5. "Vom Wesen der Wahrheit" (Wm, 191–99/148–54).

6. For further developments on the question of the human, see above, Chapter 1 (*"Homo Heideggerians"*).

7. Hw, 69.

8. Hw, 70.

9. Hw, 73.

10. Hw, 72.

11. Hw, 74.

12. Hw, 82.

13. Hw, 100.

14. It is not only Nietzsche who, in that regard, constitutes an emblematic figure of modernity, but also a certain Kantian heritage, most visibly expressed in Schopenhauer's conception of the "world" as will and representation. See Schopenhauer, *Die Welt als Wille und Vorstellung*, and the opening sentence of the book, according to which "The world is my representation."

15. For a further discussion of the difference between "originary thinking" and metaphysical thought, see the Introduction to this book, "The Provenance of Thought."

16. WhD, 16–17/41–42; translation modified.

17. WhD, 142/234; translation modified.

18. *Beiträge zur Philosophie*, GA 65.

19. GA 65, 111/78.

20. GA 65, 111/78.

21. GA 65, 111/78.

22. GA 65, 141/98.

23. DF, 8.

24. EHD, 36–38.

25. To be fair to the Cartesian project itself, one would need to recognize the extent to which the ambiguity of contemporary science I am attempting to reveal here was already operative in that very modern project. A careful reading of the *Discourse on Method*, Part I, would reveal the extent to which, while laying the ground for the transformation of the very sense of nature, such that it would become domesticated and turned towards the human as towards its very end, the Cartesian metaphysical project also identifies mathematics as an object of awe and wonder due to their formal perfection, the ultimate destination of which could not be anything as trivial as the mechanical arts, but rather the indication of a deeper mystery and wonder, that of the hidden order of nature itself.

26. I am thinking here of a few passages from "What Is Metaphysics?" and "The Self-assertion of the German University," in which Heidegger, in speaking of science, and of science as what unites the university as an institution, includes in a single gesture philosophy and all the natural and human sciences, as grounded in a certain comportment of awe and wonder before the very presence of the world and of nature: "Our existence — in the community of researchers, teachers and students — is determined by science. What happens to us, essentially, in the grounds of our existence, when science becomes our passion?" (Wm, 103/82). As Heidegger emphasizes throughout his Rectoral address, the conception of science, to which all sciences are indebted, is the Greek *theoria*, which is defined first and foremost as a certain comportment to beings as a whole, as an ability to stand questioningly amid nature. Science is at bottom metaphysical, as this ecstatic stance or posture.

27. SZ, 49–50/75; my emphasis.

28. GA 29/30, 313/214.

29. GA 29/30, 275/187.

30. GA 29/30, 278–79/189.

31. On this part of the course, see above, Chapter 3 ("Boredom: Between Existence and History").

32. GA 29/30, 282/191.

33. GA 29/30, 280/190.

34. GA 29/30, 282/191.

35. GA 29/30, 277–78/188.

36. GA 29/30, 378–79/260.

37. See Hans Driesch, *Die Lokalisation morphogenetischer Vorgänge. Ein Beweis vital. Geschehens* (Leipzig, 1899). Other embryologists, such as Boveri (whom Heidegger also refers to in the lecture course of 1929-30 [386/261]), the Hertwig brothers, or Loeb, could also be mentioned in the context of Heidegger's discussion. See François Jacob, *La Logique du vivant* (Paris: Gallimard "tel," 1970), p. 232. This holistic approach was already favored by Lamarck, who insisted that what needed to be considered in a being was not each and every one of its parts in isolation, but the totality, "the composition of every organization in its totality, that is, in its generality" (*Histoire naturelle des animaux sans vertèbres* [Paris, 1815-22], vol. 1, pp. 130-31; cited in Jacob, *La Logique du vivant*, p. 99).

38. GA 29/30, 380/261.

39. See Jacob, *La Logique du vivant*, pp. 14-15.

40. GA 29/30, 318/217.

41. See N. Wiener, *Cybernetics or Control and Communication in the Animal and the Machine* (Cambridge, Mass.: MIT Press, 1948).

42. See Jacob, *La Logique du vivant*, pp. 104-14. This is how Jacob describes the problem up until the middle of the nineteenth century: "All the efforts to reproduce the mechanisms [*les jeux*] of nature through the art of the chemist had failed. . . . Unable to associate carbon with hydrogen, chemistry thought the obstacle separating the organic from the mineral to be insurmountable. The vital force alone was able to counteract the forces acting on matter" (*La Logique du vivant*, pp. 248-49).

43. Founder of the Institute of Umwelt Research in Hamburg University in 1926, and author of a book entitled *Umwelt und Innenwelten der Tiere* (2nd, expanded and improved edition, Berlin, 1921), which Heidegger draws from in his own discussion of animal life. Other works by Uexküll available in English include *Theoretical Biology*, trans. D. L. MacKinnon (London: Kegan Paul, 1926); "A Stroll through the World of Animals and Men: A Picture Book of Invisible Worlds," *Semiotica* 89, no. 4 (n.d.): 319-91. For a rather different interpretation of Uexküll's work, see Gilles Deleuze and Félix Guattari, *Mille Plateaux* (Paris: Minuit, 1980), p. 113 ff. For a comparison of Heidegger's and Deleuze and Guattari's interpretations, see Keith Ansell Pearson, *Viroid Life* (London: Routledge, 1997), pp. 118-22, and *Germinal Life: The Difference and Repetition of Deleuze* (London: Routledge, 1999), pp. 185-89.

44. GA 29/30, 321/227.

45. On this whole discussion, see §§52-54.

46. GA 29/30, 342/234-35.

47. GA 29/30, 343/235-36.

48. GA 29/30, 371/255.

49. GA 29/30, 371-72/255.

50. GA 29/30, 360/247.

51. GA 29/30, 361/248.

52. GA 29/30, 349/239.

53. GA 29/30, 377/259.

54. See, for example, Stuart A. Kauffman, *The Origins of Order: Self-organization and Selection in Evolution* (Oxford: Oxford University Press, 1993), and *At Home in the Universe: The Search for Laws of Complexity* (London: Penguin, 1995).

55. GA 29/30, 385/265.

56. GA 29/30, 385–86/265.

57. GA 29/30, 386/265.

58. Ibid.

59. Heidegger refers here to T. Boveri's *Die Organismen als historische Wesen* (Würzburg, 1906).

60. GA 29/30, 386/266.

61. GA 29/30, 388/267.

5. Art, "Sister of Philosophy"?

1. The title of this chapter is, of course, a reference to the title of the previous chapter devoted to Heidegger's relation to science, and entitled "Science, 'Servant of Philosophy'?" The underlying concern, already expressed in that chapter, has to do with the possibility of developing a relation to science that would be as originary and unavoidable as the relation to art. To the extent that the image of sisterhood, drawn on here in order to mark the nature of philosophy's relation to art, is, so far as I know, not to be found anywhere else in Heidegger's *corpus*, I do not wish to explore it in detail. Suffice it to say here that it is almost certainly a reference to Schelling's somewhat humorous appropriation of the Kantian characterization of philosophy's relation to mathematics in the *Doctrine of Method*. The passage from the *Critique of Pure Reason* reads as follows: "From all this it follows that it is not in keeping with the nature of philosophy, especially in the field of pure reason, to take pride in a dogmatic procedure, and to deck itself out with the title and insignia of mathematics, to whose rank it does not belong, though it has every ground to hope for a sisterly union with it" (A 735/B 763). Schelling, in the very last pages of his *System of Transcendental Idealism* (F. W. J. Schelling, *Sämtliche Werke*, ed. Manfred Schröter [Munich: Beck, 1917], vol. II, pp. 624–29), and naturally from within his own problematic, takes up this image and displaces it, and speaks of the "natural affinity" (*Verwandtschaft*) between philosophy and art.

2. Given the date of the lecture course in which Heidegger's reference to philosophy's sisterly union with art is to be found, and the fact that it precedes Heidegger's first explicit and systematic treatment of art and poetry by at least three years, we are made to wonder whether it indeed constitutes as isolated a remark as we might first think, or whether it is indicative of an aspect of Heidegger's thought which, though implicit and undeveloped in the 1920s, is not entirely absent. This, at least, is what comes out of the doctoral thesis of one commentator, who traces a number of more than

occasional and highly suggestive references to art and poetry (Sophocles, Hölderlin, Rilke) in Heidegger's early work, from the 1919 lecture course (GA 56/57, 74) to the last Marburg lecture course (GA 24, 244–47), the Freiburg lecture courses from 1929–30 on *The Fundamental Concepts of Metaphysics* (GA 29/30, 7) and 1930–31 on Hegel's *Phenomenology of Spirit* (GA 32, 212). See Simon Sparks, *Fatalities: Truth and Tragedy in Heidegger and Benjamin*, Ph.D. dissertation, Warwick University, 2000. See also Robert Bernasconi, "Literary Attestation in Philosophy: Heidegger's Footnote on Tostoy's 'The Death of Ivan Ilyich,'" in *Heidegger in Question: The Art of Existing* (Atlantic Highlands, N.J.: Humanities Press, 1993), pp. 76–98. Still, and despite the fact that such references can only nuance and amend what has perhaps too often been interpreted as a sudden, unannounced shift in Heidegger's thought, it remains that, in the early work, art does not figure prominently, that is, is not yet conceptualized as a site in which things are allowed to stand so as to shine in their originary truth. Rather, it is seen, indeed, already decisively, as a mode in which things are made to be "seen" in a way that is markedly and significantly different from, and indeed more "originary" than, the way in which they are envisaged in representational thought, whether by way of philosophical speculation and worldview, or scientific investigation. *Theory,* in the very early work (GA 56, §17), is seen as a process of "de-vitalization" (*Ent-lebnis*), and is contrasted with philosophy, which, as a pre-theoretical science, is concerned to disclose the sphere of lived experience (*Erlebnis*). In this "opposition," art is already situated on the side of originary "life." To the image of a rising sun reduced to a mere natural process by the theoretical understanding of the astronomer, Heidegger, in the lecture course from 1919 (GA 56/57, 74), counterposes the event of the chorus of Theban Elders in Sophocles' *Antigone*, in which "the joyful morning flashes for the first time into view," citing, in Hölderlin's translation:

> O flash of sun, o the most beautiful, that
> On seven doored Thebes
> Has long shone.

3. *Platon: Sophistes*, GA 19.

4. GA 19, 11/8.

5. See Hannah Arendt's testimony in "Martin Heidegger ist achtzig Jahre alt," originally published in *Merkur* 23 (1969), pp. 893–902, and reprinted in *Briefe*, pp. 179–92. See also Walter Biemel, *Heidegger* (Reinbeck bei Hamburg: Rowohlt Taschenbuch Verlag, 1973), Chapter 2, "The Development of Heidegger's Thought," and Hans-Georg Gadamer, "Le Rayonnement de Heidegger," in Michel Haar, ed., *L'Herne: Martin Heidegger* (Paris: Éditions de l'Herne, 1983), pp. 138–44.

6. Aristotle, *Nicomachean Ethics*, 1139b15 ff. Heidegger's translation is in GA 19, 21/15.

7. GA 19, 49/34.

8. Aristotle, *Metaphysics*, I, 2, 983a4.

9. GA 29/30, 5/7. The text consists of a lecture course given at the University of Freiburg in the winter semester of 1929–30. The passage from which the

quotation is extracted reads as follows: "Let us merely recall that art— which includes poetry too—is the sister of philosophy and that all science is perhaps only a servant with respect to philosophy." I address the question regarding the nature of the relation between philosophy and science above in Chapter 4 ("Science, 'Servant of Philosophy'?").

10. See *Sein und Zeit* (Tübingen: Max Niemeyer Verlag, 1953), especially §§15–18.

11. The "definitive" version, published in 1950 in *Holzwege* with the addition of an epilogue, is based on a series of three lectures delivered at the Freie Deutsche Hochstift in Frankfurt in November and December 1936. I shall refer to it as the Frankfurt version. Two earlier versions of the lecture have now been made available. In 1987 an unauthorized edition of the original lecture was published in France (OA). This is the version Heidegger delivered at the Kunstwissenschaftliche Gesellschaft in Freiburg on 13 November 1935. Heidegger repeated it in Zurich in January 1936. I shall refer to it as the Freiburg version. More recently still (1989), the editors of the *Gesamtausgabe* released an undated, but clearly earlier, "first" version under the title "Vom Ursprung des Kunstwerkes. Erste Ausarbeitung" (UK). I shall refer to it as the "first" version.

12. UK, 21.

13. Hw, 25.

14. Hw, 37.

15. OA, 34.

16. OA, 34.

17. See John Sallis, *Force of Imagination* (Bloomington: Indiana University Press, 2000), Chapter 6 ("The Elemental").

18. Hw, 35.

19. Hw, 36.

20. See Hw, 59–65; OA, 38–44. As for the "first" version, it is virtually identical with the Freiburg version; see UK, 17–22.

21. OA, 38; UK, 17. Compare this with the final, more precise version, in which Heidegger writes:

> *Aus dem Vorhandenen und Gewöhnlichen wird die Wahrheit niemals abgelesen. Vielmehr geschieht die Eröffnung des Offenen und die Lichtung des Seienden nur, indem die in der Geworfenheit ankommende Offenheit entworfen wird.*
> *Wahrheit als die Lichtung und Verbergung des Seienden geschieht, indem sie gedichtet wird.*

> Truth will never be gathered from what is present-at-hand and ordinary. Rather, the opening up of the Open and the clearing of beings happens only to the extent that the openness unfolding in thrownness is sketched out or projected.
> Truth, as the clearing and concealing of beings, happens in being *gedichtet*. (Hw, 59)

In this final version, we see Heidegger mobilizing the two early existentials of "thrownness" and "projection," yet at the same time wresting them from any existential interpretation of the truth of being. It is no longer existence that is thrown into a world and projected against a horizon of possibilities. It is truth itself that happens, or takes place, yet in such a way as to require its own projection or sketch, its own configuration in the artwork. Such is the extent to which the artwork is a happening of truth. It projects, sketches, or configures the event of truth itself.

22. See note 2 of this chapter.

23. "Brief über den 'Humanismus,'" in *Wegmarken* (Frankfurt am Main: Vittorio Klostermann, 1967/1976), 158.

24. SZ, 16/37.

25. US, 190/85.

26. WhD, 87.

27. US, 232/151.

28. US, 196/90.

6. The Place of Architecture

1. "Bauen Wohnen Denken," in VA, 139–40; translated as "Building Dwelling Thinking" (BDT, 146).

2. For a thoughtful and insightful interpretation of Hegel's views on architecture, see John Sallis, *Stone* (Bloomington: Indiana University Press, 1994), Chapter 3 ("From Tower to Cathedral").

3. SZ, 103/136.

4. SZ, 103/136–37.

5. Edward Casey, *Getting Back into Place* (Bloomington: Indiana University Press, 1993), p. 129.

6. SZ, 103–4/137.

7. SZ, 105/139.

8. SZ, 105/139.

9. SZ, 106/140.

10. SZ, 105/140.

11. SZ, 108/143.

12. Casey, *Getting Back into Place*, p. 132.

13. SZ, 111/146.

14. SZ, 112/147.

15. "Letter on Humanism" (Wm, 163/253).

16. Wm, 169–70/258.

17. A, 33.

18. "The Origin of the Work of Art" is the text where Heidegger mentions the "founding of the state" and "essential sacrifice" as happenings of truth alongside the artwork; see Hw, 50.

19. Hw, 68.

20. Hw, 25.

21. *Beiträge zur Philosophie. Vom Ereignis* (1936–38) constitutes possibly Heidegger's most sustained and convincing effort to think time and space together, in a single, strifely yet harmonious relation, precisely as the en-counter between dispersion or dissemination (time as intrinsically ecstatic, enrapturing) and gathering (space, or place, as intrinsically withholding, capturing, and enclosing). Heidegger attempts to think time and space together and equally, as calling for one another and as the counter-effectuation of one another. There time is seen as essentially disseminative and dispersive—as "rapture"—and space as intrinsically gathering and withholding—as "alienation" or "captivation"; the two are constantly with-holding one another and balancing one another out, much in the same way in which, in "The Origin of the Work of Art" and other essays, world and earth belong together in their very opposedness or strife. History itself seems to emerge as the epochal configuration of this eternal en-counter between space and time. So much so, that one can wonder whether the age of techno-science, information technology, and post-industrial capitalism cannot be seen precisely in terms of a certain rapport, and indeed a hitherto unexperienced imbalance between the essentially dispersive and disseminative tendency of time and the gathering and withholding power of place. Technology as the age of the horizontal, the straight line, the line of flight. Dwelling as wandering, as departing, as flight.

22. KR, 6–7.

23. KR, 8.

24. KR, 10.

25. KR, 12.

26. "Das Ding" (VA, 161); "The Thing" (T, 169).

27. VA, 164; T, 171–72; my emphasis.

28. There are, in fact, three temples still standing at the archaeological site of Paestum: the first temple dedicated to Hera, also (but wrongly) referred to as the "Basilica," built in the middle of the sixth century B.C.; the second temple dedicated to Hera (Hera II), built in the middle of the fifth century B.C., was until fairly recently thought to be dedicated to the cult of Poseidon; the temple of Athena, finally, erected around 500 B.C. This is how Heidegger describes the temple in question: "It is the temple-work that first fits together and at the same time gathers around itself the unity of those paths and relations in which birth and death, disaster and blessing, victory and disgrace, endurance and decline acquire the shape of destiny for human being" (Hw, 31/OWA, 42). Remarkably, this description is echoed in Le Corbusier's own account of the Greek Doric temple in the Parthenon: "The Greeks on the Acropolis set up temples which are animated by a single thought, drawing around them the desolate landscape and gathering it into the composition" (*Towards a New Architecture*, trans. Frederick Etchells [New York: Dover Publications, 1986], p. 204).

29. This analysis of early Greek architecture should be supplemented, however, by the analysis Heidegger provides of other buildings, especially the old bridge over the Neckar; see BDT, 152–54.

30. This very voyage which Heidegger himself, with some understandable

apprehension, decided to embark on, literally, in 1962, accompanied by his wife Elfride and his close friend Erhart Kästner. In a short text relating his trip to Greece, dedicated to his wife, Heidegger shares his doubt concerning what, perhaps, could have turned out to be a mere projection, if not an outright fantasy, regarding the ancient Greek mode of sojourn. Heidegger expresses his "hesitation" regarding the idea of such a journey, born of a "fear of being disappointed" by a modern, technologized Greece, and increased by "the suspicion, that the thought concerning the land of the flown gods may have been a mere invention" and his "thinking path" (*Denkweg*) an "impasse" (*Irrweg*) (see A, 3).

31. In this regard, I can only agree with Massimo Cacciari, who, reading Heidegger, claims that "non-dwelling is the essential characteristic of life in the metropolis." Contemporary "urban planning," Cacciari suggests, is the effort to organize this "unpoetical dwelling." See M. Cacciari, "Eupalinos or Architecture," in *Architecture Theory since 1968*, ed. K. Michael Hays (Cambridge, Mass.: MIT Press, 2000), p. 400. This article is a review of Manfredo Tafuri and Francesco Dal Co's *Architettura contemporanea* (Milan: Electra Editrice, 1976), which itself engages significantly with Heidegger's thought on dwelling. Cacciari's writings on architecture (including "Eupalinos or Architecture") are collected in *Architecture and Nihilism: On the Philosophy of Modern Architecture*, trans. Stephen Sartarelli (New Haven: Yale University Press, 1993). Cacciari participated in the seminars of the Istituto Universitario di Architettura di Venezia, Departimento di Storia dell'Architettura, directed by Manfredo Tafuri from 1968 to 1996.

32. It is Mies who, after all, in his 1923 text *Building* declared, "We want building to signify truly and only building." "Building," Cacciari comments, and therefore *not* dwelling. The problem of dwelling in the metropolis is simply set aside: only *building* is of concern in the modern metropolis, not the home; see Cacciari, "Eupalinos or Architecture," pp. 403–404.

33. Theo Van Doesburg, "Towards a Plastic Architecture," in *Programs and Manifestoes on 20th-Century Architecture*, ed. Ulrich Conrads, trans. Michael Bullock (Cambridge, Mass.: MIT Press, 1975), p. 79. For a good example of such a construction (seemingly) defying the laws of physics, see Paulsen and Gardner, Shapero Hall of Pharmacy, Wayne State University, Detroit, 1965.

34. See, for instance, Ludwig Mies van der Rohe, Crown Hall, Illinois Institute of Technology, Chicago, 1952–56.

35. See Ludwig Mies van der Rohe, Chapel, Illinois Institute of Technology, Chicago, 1949–52, and Mies van der Rohe, Boiler House, Illinois Institute of Technology, Chicago, 1940.

36. Ludwig Mies van der Rohe, "Baukunst und Zeitwille" (1924), quoted by Leland M. Roth in *Understanding Architecture* (New York: HarperCollins, 1993), p. 459.

37. "ABC Demands the Dictatorship of the Machine," in Conrads, ed., *Programs and Manifestoes*, p. 115.

38. "Warum bleiben wir in der Provinz?" This short text, originally written as a radio allocution broadcasted in Berlin and Freiburg in March 1934, in

which Heidegger explains his reasons for not accepting a Chair at Berlin University offered to him in 1933, is published in volume 13 of the *Gesamtausgabe*, pp. 9-13.

39. VA, 155; BDT, 160.

40. Paola Coppola Pignatelli, "The Dialectics of Urban Architecture: Hestia and Hermes," *Spring* (1985).

41. For an exhaustive and seminal account of the ancient Greek conception of space in relation to religion and politics, see Jean-Pierre Vernant, *Mythe et pensée chez les Grecs* (Paris: Éditions La Découverte, 1994), Chapter 3, "L'Organisation de l'espace," and especially the sections entitled "Hestia-Hermes. Sur l'expression religieuse du mouvement et de l'espace chez les Grecs" and "Espace et organisation politique en Grèce ancienne." For a briefer account of the question, see Jean-Pierre Vernant, "La nouvelle image du monde" in *Les Origines de la pensée grecque* (Paris: PUF, 1962).

42. Pignatelli, "The Dialectics of Urban Architecture," p. 43.

43. See GA 55, 5-13.

44. See, for instance, Euripides' *Medea*, or Sophocles' *Antigone*, both of which represent a tragic conflict between family law and political law.

45. Demetrakopoulos, "Hestia," pp. 59-60; quoted by Casey in *Getting Back into Place*, p. 143.

46. Symptomatic of the process I am trying to describe here, and the anxiety it generates, is the following comment by the Mexican architect Luis Barragán, who, criticizing the overexposed landscape of the contemporary suburb, writes, "Everyday life is becoming much too public. Radio, TV, the telephone all invade privacy. Gardens should therefore be enclosed, not open to public gaze" (in Clive Bamford-Smith, *Builders in the Sun: Five Mexican Architects* [New York: Architectural Book Publishing, 1967], p. 74). And so the garden, so often seen as opening onto the outside, the public, as already inscribing the home as a system open to difference, is here folded back on the home, or on the hestial.

47. Hw, 37.

48. Drawing on Foucault's own work thoughts on contemporary architecture and space (in "Des espaces autres," in *Cercle d'Études Architecturales*, 14 March 1967), Cacciari writes, "The present-day space of the metropolis is made up of the non-hierarchical flow of information connecting disciplines and functions, of discrete, aleatory currents, whose movements are not teleologically comprehensible but only stochastically analyzable" (in "Eupalinos or Architecture," p. 403).

49. Hw, 37.

50. Pignatelli, "The Dialectics of Urban Architecture," p. 46.

51. Examples of such modern responses to a very contemporary problem would include Le Corbusier, Chapelle de Notre Dame du Haut, Ronchamp; Frank Lloyd Wright, Frederick C. Robie House, Chicago, 1908-9; Philip Johnson, Johnson House, New Canaan, Conn., 1945-49; Eero Saarinen, Chapel, Massachusetts Institute of Technology, 1953-55.

52. Frank Lloyd Wright, Edgar Kaufmann residence, Fallingwater, Pennsylva-

nia, 1936–38. See also Kenneth Frampton's commentary on the house in *Modern Architecture: A Critical History*, 3rd ed. (London: Thames & Hudson, 1980/1992), p. 188.

53. Kenneth Frampton also stresses Wright's "obsessive exaltation of the hearth," and quotes G. C. Manson, who traces Wright's concern with "the fireplace and chimney as an expression of shelter and emphasized as the one desired solid substance in an entire of ever-increasing fluidity" back to Japanese architecture, which had a considerable influence on Wright, and to the *tokonoma* in particular, as "the permanent element of Japanese interior"; see Frampton, *Modern Architecture*, pp. 58–59.

54. Frank Lloyd Wright, *The Natural House* (London: Sir Isaac Pitman and Sons, 1971), p. 13.

55. Christian Norberg-Schulz, *Genius Loci: Towards a Phenomenology of Architecture* (London: Academy Editions, 1980), p. 67.

56. In his seminal essay "Towards a Critical Regionalism," Frampton speaks (somewhat provocatively) of the need for a *critical arrière-garde*, or an architecture of "resistance" that embraces neither the myth of progress through technology nor the reactionary impulse to return to the architectural forms of the preindustrial past. See K. Frampton, "Towards a Critical Regionalism: Six Points for an Architecture of Resistance," in Hal Foster, ed., *The Anti-aesthetic: Essays on Postmodern Culture* (Port Townsend, Wash.: Bay Press, 1983). Working in this vein, Frampton argues, are architects such as Mario Botta, Jørn Utzon, Alvaro Siza Vieira, Luis Barragán, and Tando Ando.

Afterword

1. W. Benjamin, "Die Aufgabe des Übersetzers," in *Gesammelte Schriften* (Frankfurt am Main: Suhrkamp, 1980), vol. X, p. 12.

2. See Christian Berner's "presentation" of Friedrich Schleiermacher, in *Des différentes méthodes de traduire* (Paris: Éditions du Seuil, "Points," 1999), p. 21.

3. There is even a sense in which the translation of *Bildung* by culture is justified primarily through the practice of translation. To translate (*überstezen*), F. Schleiermacher argues, is to "transplant into a foreign soil [*im fremden Boden zu verpflanzen*] that which a language produces in the area of the sciences and the arts of discourse, with a view to broadening the sphere of action of such products of the mind" ("Über die verschiedenen Methoden des Übersetzens," in *Sämmtliche Werke* [Berlin: Reimer, 1838], vol. II.2, p. 208; henceforth SSW, followed by volume and page number). Friedrich Schlegel had already used the term "transplantation" in relation to translation: "Every translation [*Übersetzung*] is a *transplantation* [*Verpflanzung*] or *transformation* [*Verwandlung*] or both at once" (*Kritische Friedrich-Schlegel Ausgabe* [Zurich: E. Behler, 1963], vol. XVIII, frag. 87, p. 204). Uprooted, yet pricked out in another linguistic system, the elements of an idiom are reborn and bear new fruits in another idiom.

4. Such as the seventh Olympic ode, in GA 54, 109–10/74.

5. In GA 53, §§10–16.

6. GA 54, 62/42.

7. See GA 54, §3.

8. GA 54, 73/50.

9. I am thinking, here, first and foremost, of Lacoue-Labarthe's work on the logic of mimesis governing so much of German culture, from Hölderlin to Heidegger, and of the privileging of the Greek moment in the question regarding the possibility of a German national identity. See Philippe Lacoue-Labarthe, *L'Imitation des modernes. Typographies II* (Paris: Galilée, 1986).

10. GA 54, 16/11.

11. See "Platons Lehre von der Wahrheit," in Wm.

12. Whether willingly or unwillingly—explicit indications are lacking in this context—Heidegger finds himself in dialogue with Schleiermacher on this hermeneutic ground. Schleiermacher too sees in translation a specific operation of understanding that requires the mediation of interpretation (see SSW II, 215). Yet Heidegger goes one step further than Schleiermacher, specifically in the case of trans-historical translation. It is, of course, the conception of history that is at issue here. For Heidegger, the unfolding of history is itself an operation of translation, such that the operation of translating oneself back into, say, the Greek world becomes a highly complex and problematic task. Yet this is the effort to which Heidegger's entire thought tends, in an attempt to grasp the essence of this unfolding of history. For Schleiermacher, on the other hand, translation remains the act of adapting an other language to my own. His conception of translation remains governed by a logic of appropriation, albeit as impossible, and hospitality (*Gastfreiheit*) ("Ueber Leibnitz unausgeführt gebliebenen Gedanken einer allgemeinen philosophischen Sprache," SSW III, 144; see also SWW II, 207): the other idiom is *invited* to penetrate the sphere of my own. The movement is from outside to inside, from the unfamiliar to the familiar. For Heidegger, it is the other way around: my own language is to become other, foreign to myself; translation is an experience of dis-propriation. This explains the awkwardness of many of Heidegger's actual translations.

13. Eliane Escoubas, "Ontology of Language and Ontology of Translation," in *Reading Heidegger*, ed. John Sallis (Bloomington: Indiana University Press, 1993), pp. 341–47. I am following Escoubas's analysis here. Heidegger's analysis is in GA 54, §2.

14. Friedrich Hölderlin, *Werke und Briefe*, ed. Friedrich Beissner and Jochen Schmidt (Frankfurt am Main: Insel, 1982).

15. The first turn was enacted in 1935 in *Introduction to Metaphysics*, and led to a first translation and analysis of the chorus. The second analysis, which differs in tone and substance, takes place in 1942 in the context of a lecture course devoted to Hölderlin's hymn "The Ister." See GA 53, 73/60.

16. Sophocles, *Antigone*, in David Grene and Richmond Lattimore, eds., *Greek Tragedies* (Chicago: University of Chicago Press, 1991), vol. 1, p. 194.

17. Sophocles, *Antigone,* in Dudley Fitts and Robert Fitzgerald, eds., *The Oedipus Cycle* (New York: Harcourt Brace Jovanovich, 1971), p. 199.

18. GA 53, 74–75/61.

19. GA 53, 75/61–62.

20. GA 53, 75–76/62.

21. GA 54, 18/13.

22. GA 54, 17–18/12–13.

Index

animals: adaptation by, 115–16; Dasein of, 114–16, 141; dwelling and, 141–42; humans and, 104–107, 112–18

anthropology, 13–46; and concept of history, 14–15, 17–18; and Dasein and death, 27–34; and Dasein and resoluteness, 25–26, 34–40; and Dasein's everyday way of being, 21–25; as distinguished from other disciplines, 13, 185n2; and ek-sistence and truth of being, 18–20; and essence of man, 13–19, 185n2; and manipulation/production, 18, 21–25; and philosophical man, 18, 25, 40–46; and prudence/resoluteness, 18. *See also* Dasein

Antigone (Sophocles), 135, 160, 170, 177–78, 195n2

anxiety, 63, 64–66

architecture, 139–68; and abandonment of being, 150, 151–52; and alternative sites of truth, 152–54; architectural resistance, 167–68, 202n56; balancing responses in, 165–68, 201n51, 202n53; beauty and, 153–54; the body and, 147; configurations of public space, 164–67, 201n51, 202n53; configurations of world and earth, 160, 161, 163, 165–67, 201nn46,48; contemporary modernist, 158–60, 165–67, 200n32, 201n51, 202n53; and Dasein's spatiality, 142, 143, 145–48; dwelling, 139–60; dwelling and residing, 139–40;

dwelling as way of being in the world, 140–42; dwelling in the age of technology, 149–60; gathering and, 154, 155–56; global economy and hermetization, 162–63, 201nn46,48; Greek, 156–57, 199nn28,30; hermetic, 160, 162, 163–65; hestial, 160–61, 162, 163–65; "home" and, 161, 164–65; modern urban architecture and non-dwelling, 157–60, 167, 200nn31,32, 201n48; modernism and possibilities of genuine dwelling, 156–60, 166–68, 200n32; nomadic mode of dwelling, 165; ontology and history, 149; and project of fundamental ontology, 140–48; sense of place and fourfold horizon, 156–57; space, new sense of, 142–49, 153; space, the work's relation to, 153–55; space and genuine dwelling, 166–68; space and time, 154–55, 199n21; technology and, 146, 148, 149–60; truth and dwelling, 150–51, 152–54; and two senses of being "in," 141–42, 145

Aristotle, 14, 18, 21, 25, 39–40, 42, 67, 122–26, 170

art, 121–38; as aesthetics, 122; and Aristotelian problematic, 122–26, 129, 135; displacement of problematic and break with traditional aesthetics, 128–34; encounter with philosophy in Heidegger's thought, 121, 126–35, 195n2, 196n9; and five other modes of truth,

Index

About the author

Miguel de Beistegui teaches philosophy at the University of Warwick. He is author of *Heidegger and the Political* and co-editor (with Simon Sparks) of *Philosophy and Tragedy*.